Identity and Difference

Identity and Difference

JOHN LOCKE AND THE INVENTION OF CONSCIOUSNESS

Etienne Balibar

Edited and with an Introduction by Stella Sandford
Translated by Warren Montag

VERSO
London • New York

Liberté • Égalité • Fraternité

RÉPUBLIQUE FRANÇAISE

This book is supported by the Institut français as part of the Burgess programme (www.frenchbooknews.com)

This English-language edition published by Verso 2013
Translation © Warren Montag 2013
First published as *Identité et différence: L'invention de la conscience*
© Éditions du Seuil 1998
Introduction © Stella Sandford 2013

1 3 5 7 9 10 8 6 4 2

Verso
UK: 6 Meard Street, London W1F 0EG
US: 20 Jay Street, Suite 1010, Brooklyn, NY 11201
www.versobooks.com

Verso is the imprint of New Left Books

ISBN-13: 978-1-78168-134-3 (pbk)
ISBN-13: 978-1-78168-135-0 (hbk)

British Library Cataloguing in Publication Data
A catalogue record for this book is available from the British Library

Library of Congress Cataloging-in-Publication Data
A catalog record for this book is available from the Library of Congress

Typeset in Minion Pro by Hewer Text Ltd UK, Edinburgh
Printed in the US by Maple Press

Contents

Preface to the English Edition

When Stella Sandford and Verso proposed an English edition of my work on Locke and the invention of consciousness – essentially a commentary on Book II, Chapter XXVII of *An Essay Concerning Human Understanding* – I was obviously very flattered at the idea that a historical, philosophical and philological text by a French scholar might be made available to, and submitted to the judgment of, Anglophone readers in the land of the author of the *Essay* himself. But I did not entirely anticipate all the difficulties that such an enterprise would entail, nor the degree to which I would have to depend on the indulgence of my new readers.

Part of the difficulty lies in the fact that my work was written nearly twenty years ago, in context of the 1990s, which means that much has been written since on Locke in general, and in particular on the 'theory of knowledge' and the metaphysics of the subject contained in the *Essay*, and finally on his contribution to the 'puzzle' of personal identity – in English and in other languages. I thus will not have taken all of this into account (which is not to say that I was able even then to take into account all that had been written up to that point). This difficulty, however, was in part mitigated by the fact that my friend Stella Sandford agreed to take on the task of writing an original introduction to the work and urged me to complement the introduction with an afterword containing my own new reflections (a suggestion that, as will be seen, I preferred to take up in the form of bringing in a comparison with Spinoza, which had been frequently alluded to but remained essentially missing from the French original edition).

But the rather peculiar genre of the work, determined by the circumstances of its conception and publication, imposes an even greater difficulty. The core of the original French version of this text was the re-publication of Book II, Chapter XXVII of the *Essay Concerning Human Understanding* ('Of Identity and Diversity'), accompanied by two French translations: one from the seventeenth century by Pierre Coste, undertaken under Locke's own supervision, and which served to propagate the author's ideas not only in France but throughout Europe (as demonstrated by Leibniz's reliance on it in the *New Essays in Human Understanding*); and a new translation, with which I did not intend to replace the earlier one, but rather to show the breadth and meaning of the problems of conceptual translation associated with 'the European invention of consciousness' (which I maintain takes place in philosophy primarily in the work of Locke, or at least changes direction on the basis of his *oeuvre*). This labour, which combined philology and philosophy (the first furnishing the materials for an experiment in the comparative semantics of the classical *languages*, while the second was essentially developed on the basis of an analysis of *concepts* understood as constituting the unity characteristic of a philosophical work, rather than 'theories' or 'arguments'), constituted on my part a contribution to the very comprehensive project conceived and edited by Barbara Cassin on the question of the 'untranslatable' in philosophy, and which culminated in the publication of the *Vocabulaire européen des philosophies* in 2004.[1]

My book thus appeared as an assemblage of five parts of unequal length: 1) an introductory essay entitled 'Locke's Treatise on Identity', in which I took as my point of departure the theoretical 'symptom' constituted by Pierre Coste's explanation of the neologisms he was compelled to invent in order to translate Locke's key concepts ('consciousness' and 'self' – to which must also be added 'uneasiness').[2] My aim was to develop a general interpretation of the 'epistemological break' introduced by Locke, as well as of his place in the history of European philosophy; 2) a textual section in which I included first Coste's translation (1700), and then opposite it Locke's original text (revised in accordance with Yolton and Nidditch), and finally my own retranslation; 3) a 'Glossary' of the work's key concepts, intended simultaneously to explore the difficulties of their translation and to expand their definition (by situating them in relation to philosophical debates, both classical and modern, whenever possible); 4) a complementary dossier of texts in a variety of languages (Latin, English and French), taken from Descartes, de la Forge, Malebranche, Cudworth, Régis, Leibniz and Condillac, intended to outline the philosophical debates within which Locke's terms and statements must be situated in order for their strategic significance and function to become clear; and finally, a complementary bibliography. In the present edition, we have retained (in addition to the new texts referred to previously) my introductory essay (unchanged except for the correction of a few errors), and most of the entries in the Glossary (omitting those which may be considered minor, in that they discuss only technical questions of translation). Obviously, we have also omitted Locke's text itself, which English readers have at their disposal, as well as the two French translations (although with some regret, given that they would have been useful in providing the English reader with the experience of 'estrangement' that would permit reader to reflect on the meaning of the concepts in his or her own language – but the work had to be kept at a reasonable length), as well as the dossier of contemporary texts. Stella Sandford has provided a new bibliography.

I have recounted these details so that the reader can understand from the outset the form in which my argumentation developed, as much in the

---

1 Barbara Cassin, ed., *Vocabulaire européen des philosophies*, Paris: Éditions de Seuil, 2004.

2 It should be recalled that the translator's notes were regarded as sufficiently important from a philosophical point of view to be themselves summarized or referred to in most of the scholarly editions of the *Essay*, in particular Nidditch's edition.

introductory essay as in the Glossary. The argumentation is always concerned with the *background* of the philosophical debates, in particular the intrinsic relation between two questions: the invention of consciousness in opposition to conscience,[3] and the 'Lockean criterion of identity'. More generally, my argumentation takes up the question of the idea of the 'person' (the Lockean *name for the subject)*, linked together above all by what I call an 'anti-linguistic turn' or an 'isolation of the mental' (whose relevance to current debates about cognitivism is not simply archaeological). But this always proceeds on the basis, and as a function, of problems of translation (essentially between English and French, although the ancient languages are always present as a background). I am effectively convinced – as was the group that produced the *Vocabulaire européen des philosophies* – not only that the difficulties of translation (and in particular the case of untranslatability, which leads to terminological inventions and to strategies of paraphrase and periphrasis) constitute privileged indicators of the meaning of concepts, but that they form an important part of the conditions of possibility of philosophical thought (as important as logic or rhetoric) in that philosophers *think by means of writing* in a determinate conjuncture, and most often at the intersection of several languages. Obviously, the case of Locke is particularly interesting from this point of view (not to speak of the incalculable extent of the effects of his thought on the whole of Western philosophy up to our own time) because he worked in English, but at the same time in an intimate relation of dialogue and conflict with philosophy in the French language (and notably 'Cartesianism', itself elaborated simultaneously in both Latin and French). I therefore ask the Anglophone reader (but without apologies, since it is the basis of my position, whose interest it is up to him or her to judge) to agree to enter in turn – although from the other side of the 'channel' that both separates and joins us – into a dialogue and a process of translinguistic reflection. It is for this reason that I have left the text as it is (which, in any case, I could not have modified without completely re-writing it), a text in which I discussed the gaps between languages and the means necessary to bridge these gaps in an historical or analytic fashion. Such a position does not, I hope, lead to any relativism, and it certainly is not meant to lead to my proposing 'a French reading of Locke' (or, *horresco referens*, to a reading '*à la française*'). But it might perhaps be useful to see how one can simultaneously radically *historicize* the reading of philosophical texts (and of the debates in which they took shape) and put into practice a reconstruction of systems (of their typical

---

3   In French, unlike English or German, 'conscience' and 'consciousness' (or '*Gewissen*' and '*Bewusstsein*') are signified by a single term, '*conscience*', whose specific meaning the reader must derive from its context [trans. note].

forms of argumentation) in a *structural* – that is, *differential* – fashion, granting all due importance to the 'materiality of writing' and its idioms, which constitutes precisely the privileged link between these two aspects of a rigorous method in the history of philosophy.

Etienne Balibar, 2013

The Incomplete Locke: Balibar, Locke and the Philosophy of the Subject

Stella Sandford

Let us start with the facts. Etienne Balibar's *Identité et différence: L'invention de la conscience* was published in 1998.[1] The book is, essentially, an expansive study of Book II, Chapter XXVII ('Of Identity and Diversity') of John Locke's *Essay Concerning Human Understanding* (1694) – the chapter containing Locke's celebrated theory of personal identity. The form of the book is somewhat unusual. It begins with Balibar's 'Introduction', a long interpretative essay on Locke, followed by the primary text of his study – the original English text of Chapter XXVII – Pierre Coste's French translation of Chapter XXVII from 1700, and Balibar's new French translation. In an extensive 'Glossary', comprising thirty-one substantial entries, altogether almost as long as Balibar's main essay itself, the philosophical argument is continued. The book concludes with a dossier of extracts from texts, cited in the development of Balibar's argument, by René Descartes, Louis De La Forge, Nicolas Malebranche, Ralph Cudworth (in English, and with French translation), Pierre-Sylvain Régis, Gottfried Leibniz and Étienne Bonnot de Condillac.

Along with this essay, the present volume comprises Warren Montag's translation of Balibar's 'Introduction' (Part I of the original), sixteen of the thirty-one Glossary entries (parts of Part III) and a new Preface and Postscript by Balibar. Thus it is not, straightforwardly, an English edition of the French text; it is a different book. This difference is, in part, an acknowledgement that the conditions must be created for a reception of *Identity and Difference* into English. For if *Identity and Difference* has, to this point, yet to make a significant Channel or Atlantic crossing, this has less to do with it having hitherto only been available in French than with some of the consequences of the historical antagonism in the English-speaking intellectual world between 'analytic' and 'continental' philosophy.

---

1   John Locke, *Identité et différence: L'invention de la conscience*, introduced, edited and translated by Étienne Balibar, Paris: Éditions du Seuil, 1998. Henceforth referred to as *Identity and Difference*; citations in the text (*ID*) refer to the page numbers of the English translation in this volume.

The writing of this essay and this English edition of *Identité et différence* were made possible by the award of a five-month fellowship from the UK Arts and Humanities Research Council in 2012.

In the Anglophone world, Locke's *Essay* is 'owned' by the analytical tradition and effectively ignored by the continental. Despite a glowing review by John Yolton (one of the foremost British Locke scholars of the twentieth century), the 'continental' origin of *Identity and Difference* seems to have precluded its being read by the predominantly analytical readers of Locke's *Essay*.[2] What is perhaps the most original of recent interpretations of the *Essay*'s most famous chapter has thus not been registered in Anglophone studies of Locke. On the other hand, the 'continental' readership familiar with Balibar's work on Marx and Marxism, on nation, class and race, on Spinoza, on the philosophy of the subject, and on Europe and citizenship has perhaps been nonplussed by the idea of a book on John Locke, arch liberal, bourgeois apologist and (allegedly) naïve pre-Kantian empiricist.[3] Thus have the presumptions of a certain audience forestalled the reading of a work that would precisely puncture them. For Balibar's *Identity and Difference* makes a good case for a 'continental' John Locke, in more ways than one.

Locke's chapter on personal identity is a standard topic of study in Anglophone undergraduate philosophy programmes, positioned as the first detailed argument for what constitutes personal (as opposed to material or biological) identity over time. Since just after the middle of the twentieth century, 'personal identity' has also become a discrete topic in analytical philosophy. A typical syllabus on personal identity would start with Locke, work through the famous objections from Joseph Butler and Thomas Reid in the eighteenth century (the basic forms of which still dominate in contemporary criticism of Locke), and then move into the twentieth century with trenchant criticism from A.J. Ayer, sympathetic commentary and criticism from John Yolton and J.L. Mackie, the proposal of new theories from H.P. Grice, Derek Parfit, Sydney Shoemaker, David Wiggins and most recently the renewed interpretations and criticism of Michael Ayers and Galen Strawson.[4] *Identity and Difference* suggests the construction of a very different, multi-branching, Franco-German philosophical lineage from Chapter XXVII of Locke's *Essay*, one that moves in the stream of the 'continental' philosophy of the subject,

---

2   For Yolton's review see *British Journal for the History of Philosophy* 10: 2, June 2002: 'In my opinion, this is one of the best books on the *Essay* to be published in recent times.' (312) Much of the misunderstanding that so astonishes Galen Strawson in his recent book on Locke is signally absent from Balibar's book, yet he makes no mention of it. (Strawson, *Locke on Personal Identity: Consciousness and Concernment*, Princeton, NJ: Princeton University Press, 2011.)

3   Louis Althusser identified this problem as an obstruction to the French reception of Locke. See Warren Montag, 'On the Function of the Concept of Origin: Althusser's Reading of Locke', in Stephen Daniels, ed., *Current Continental Theory and Early Modern Philosophy*, Evanston, IL: Northwestern University Press, 2006.

4   For an explanation of the nineteenth-century hiatus in serious studies of Locke see Hans Aarsleff, 'Locke's Reputation in Nineteenth-Century England', in Richard Ashcraft, ed., *John Locke: Critical Assessments*, Vol I, London and New York: Routledge, 1991.

starting with Kant, through Hegel and Marx to the twentieth-century philosophies of the subject, notably in France.

It would be presumptuous to suggest that *Identity and Difference* cannot
speak for itself – or at least speak here through Warren Montag's discerning
translation. It is less presumptuous, perhaps, to imagine that it is nevertheless
possible to facilitate its being heard. To this end, this essay will begin with a
brief reprise of Balibar's main argument concerning Locke's role in the 'invention of consciousness' and will draw out from Balibar's multi-faceted interpretation of Locke on personal identity what I take to be its most important aspects.
After a condensed overview of the main trends in the mainstream interpretation and criticism of Locke's argument, focusing in particular on the two major
objections that continue to be levelled against Locke's account, I will then relo-
cate Locke's argument and Balibar's interpretation of it within the context of
recent work on the philosophical history of the concept of the subject. This new
context for the interpretation of Locke allows us both to understand the dogged
persistence of the main criticisms of Locke – from the earliest to some of his
most recent 'analytical' critics – in a new way and to form a connection between
this part of the *An Essay Concerning Human Understanding* and Locke's political philosophy.

1. THE INVENTION OF CONSCIOUSNESS

Balibar's central thesis in *Identity and Difference* is that Locke is the crucial
figure ('*le grand protagoniste*') in the invention of the (European) philosophical
concepts of consciousness and of the self in the second half of the seventeenth
century. (*ID*, 1, 115–16) Regarding the concept of consciousness in particular,
this is no small claim. Received opinion teaches that Descartes was the first
philosopher of consciousness, or of the primacy of consciousness. Balibar's
thesis, if accepted, thus knocks off balance a central orienting point of our
understanding of the history of Western philosophy. The justification of this
thesis is an intricate matter of philosophical interpretation. The English word
'consciousness' was a seventeenth-century neologism, first used with a specific
philosophical meaning by the Cambridge Platonist Ralph Cudworth in his *The
True Intellectual System of the Universe*, published in 1678 (Locke's *Essay* was
first published in 1690; Chapter XXVII, 'Of Identity and Diversity', was added
to the second edition in 1694). Locke was close to Cudworth, and most likely
took the word 'consciousness' from him, although he gave it a new meaning and
a new philosophical role.[5] As we know, the French *conscience* is used to translate

---

5   Locke refers to Cudworth and uses the word 'consciousness' in a journal entry from 1682,
an entry that anticipates the later theory of personal identity. See K. Joanna S. Forstrom, *John Locke
and Personal Identity: Immortality and Bodily Ressurection in 17th-Century Philosophy*, London

the two now-distinct English concepts of 'conscience' and 'consciousness'.[6] *Conscience*, in the 'moral' sense usually translated by the English word with the same spelling, was in established use well before the seventeenth century. More importantly, *conscience* in a different sense, plausibly translated as 'consciousness', appears a few times in Descartes' philosophical work. The significance of these few references in Descartes is disputed, but a concept of *conscience* that is *not* primarily moral unarguably figures prominently – as Balibar discusses – in the work of the French Cartesians Louis de la Forge (in 1666), Nicolas Malebranche (in 1674 and 1678), and Pierre-Sylvain Régis (in 1690);[7] that is, earlier than and independently of Locke's (and indeed Cudworth's) 'consciousness'. Matters are further complicated by the – admittedly infrequent – appearance of the Latin *conscientia* and *conscius esse* in Descartes. So why does Balibar claim such a central position for Locke? How do these earlier French conceptions of 'consciousness' differ from Locke's, or what is the philosophical specificity – and hence historical originality – of Locke's conception?

Identity and Difference introduces us to the argument that justifies its thesis by way of a kind of narrative. This narrative should not be mistaken for the argument itself, but neither is it incidental to it. The thesis emerges, Balibar writes, on the back of a 'philological encounter', rather than a philosophical argument – the encounter with a puzzle in Pierre Coste's 1700 French translation of Locke's *Essay*. When Locke uses the word 'consciousness' before Chapter XXVII of Book II, Coste translates it with various different phrases, avoiding the use of the word 'conscience' and its cognates. For example, Locke's 'definition' of consciousness in Book II, Chapter I ('Consciousness is the perception of what passes in a Man's own mind'[8]) is rendered '*cette conviction n'est autre chose que la perception de ce qui se passe dans l'âme de l'homme.*' (*ID*, 9) But when

---

and New York: Continuum, 2010, 13. On Cudworth see Udo Thiel, 'Cudworth and Seventeenth-Century Theories of Consciousness', in Stephen Gaukroger, ed., *The Uses of Antiquity: The Scientific Revolution and the Classical Tradition*, Dordrecht: Kluwer Academic, 1991. Thiel explains that Cudworth's discussion of consciousness was 'mostly, not part of an analysis of human subjectivity, but of a metaphysical account of reality in general – an account which affirms the traditional idea of a scale of nature, drawing heavily on Plotinus.' (87) See also Balibar, 'Conscience', in Barbara Cassin, ed., *Vocabulaire européen des philosophies*, Paris: Seuil/Le Robert, 2004, 266–7.

6   To the extent that Chapter XXVII of Locke's *Essay* argues for a *moral* understanding of personal identity as constituted through consciousness, the meanings of the two English words 'conscience' and 'consciousness' are still, there, very closely related. And, indeed, as Catherine Glyn Davies points out, the meanings of the two words were still used interchangeably in the eighteenth century and after. See Glyn Davis, *'Conscience' as Consciousness: The Idea of Self-Awareness in French Philosophical Writing from Descartes to Diderot*, Oxford: The Voltaire Foundation, 1990, 3.

7   Louis de la Forge, *Traité de l'Esprit de l'Homme* (1666); Nicolas Malebranche, *De la Recherche de la Vérité* (1674) and *Éclairissements sur la Recherche de la Vérité* (1678); Pierre-Sylvain Régis, *Système de philosophie* (1690).

8   John Locke, *An Essay Concerning Human Understanding*, Peter H Nidditch, ed., Oxford: Clarendon Press, 1975, II.i.19. This reference refers to Book II, Chapter I, Section 19. All future references to the *Essay* will follow this form.

Locke postulates consciousness as the criterion for personal identity in Chapter XXVII, Coste introduces what he seems to regard as a neologism and justifies it with two long footnotes. Locke writes: 'consciousness always accompanies thinking, and 'tis that, that makes everyone to be, what he calls *self*; and thereby distinguishes himself from all other thinking things, in this alone consists *personal Identity*, *i.e.* the sameness of a rational Being'.[9] Here, Coste translates 'consciousness' as '*con-science*', and apologizes profusely for it: 'one is not only permitted, but obliged to employ new words or use words differently than they are customarily used when there is nothing that will express the author's precise idea.' (*ID*, 6) Thus Coste made a considered decision to introduce a new word, or to coin what he thought of as a new usage for an old word, to translate what was evidently for him a new idea in Locke's *Essay* at this point (bearing in mind that one of the strongest positions in the *Essay* is that words are signs of ideas, not of things).[10] Coste worked closely with Locke on the French translation of his *Essay*; both men knew the work of Descartes and the French Cartesians well. The puzzle then, for Balibar, is this: if Descartes' philosophy and that of his followers had already furnished the discourse with the idea of consciousness that Locke employed, straightforwardly able to be rendered in French as *conscience*, why did Coste not use the word earlier, and why make such a fuss about *con-science*?

If this is the highly suggestive 'enigma' (*ID*, 2) of Coste's translation, the justification of Balibar's thesis concerning Locke's role in the 'invention' of the concept of consciousness lies, on the one hand, in Balibar's detailed discussions of Descartes and the seventeenth-century French philosophers inspired by him, and on the other in his new interpretation of Locke's Chapter XXVII. If we can, for the purposes of an introduction, reduce these discussions to their headlines, they are as follows. First, the French word '*conscience*' in the sense of anything like 'consciousness' appears only twice in Descartes' published work, and even then apparently only casually. Further, Descartes very rarely uses the Latin terms from which both the French and English words derive, and not at all in the famous text that would retrospectively be considered foundational from the point of view of the presumption of Descartes' place as the first philosopher of consciousness, the *Meditations*. (*ID*, 13) Balibar is careful, nevertheless, to point out that although some attribute the introduction of the term 'consciousness' in the new sense – distinguished from its moral meaning – to Descartes, his fame as the first of the great philosophers of consciousness does not necessarily rest on this. For even if the word were absent, this would not exclude the possibility,

---

9   Locke, *Essay*, II.xxvii.9.

10   Coste did not do this lightly: '*Je suis choqué moi-même de la liberté que je prends.*' (Coste quoted in *ID* 5) 'I am myself shocked at the liberty that I am taking.' Locke (*Essay*, II.x.2) criticized the introduction of new words by 'the several *Sects* of Philosophy and Religion', which, 'when they come to be examined, may justly be called *insignificant Terms*', 'empty Sounds'.

as Balibar says, that 'Descartes conceived, and even placed at the centre of his philosophy, a "thing" in which we would retrospectively recognise what we call "consciousness"'. (*ID*, 3) Is not the 'cogito' (the name we give to the argument that concludes, in the second of Descartes' *Meditations*, 'cogito, sum' – 'I think, I am'[11]) 'another name for consciousness?' (*ID*, 20)[12] Is the idea of consciousness not implicit in the method of introspection and its result, in the discourse of the certainty of the cogito and of the certainty of the thinking thing's thoughts qua thoughts?

Balibar's answer to these questions lies in a close examination of Descartes' few uses of the Latin *conscientia* and in an unfolding of the extent of the conclusions of the cogito. We can perhaps understand the main thrust of his argument in terms of the difference between a philosophy of consciousness (properly attributed to Locke) and Descartes' philosophy of *certitude*. (*ID*, 19) As we know, Descartes discovers a first moment of certainty in his own existence, for even if he is deceived (about the existence of the external world, for example) the mere fact of his being deceived means that he certainly exists. Or at least '*I am, I exist*, is necessarily true whenever it is put forward by me or conceived in my mind'; that is, he exists *for so long as he is thinking*, effectively equating his existence with thinking, such that 'I am' becomes equivalent to 'I think'. 'Thinking' encompasses 'a considerable list' for Descartes, including: doubting, willing, understanding, affirming, denying, imagining and 'having a sensory perception'.[13] Balibar calls the 'I think', which is equivalent to 'I am', the '*general equivalent*' of all of these infinitely diverse modalities of thought', (*ID*, 21) because what is certain in each of these modalities on each occasion is always the same: I think, I am – it is always the same 'I' who doubts, imagines, has sensory perceptions and so on.[14] Descartes also says, of course, that he is 'a *thing that thinks*', 'a thinking *thing*'. Balibar understands this claim as an assertion of

---

11   René Descartes, *Meditations on First Philosophy*, trans. John Cottingham, Cambridge: Cambridge University Press, 1996, Second Meditation, 17. The form in which the argument has become a slogan – 'I think, therefore I am' – appears in the *Discourse on Method*.

12   As Alain de Libera points out (*Archéologie du sujet*, Vol. I: *Naissance du sujet*, Paris: Vrin, 2010, 28) the idea of *the* cogito is an invention of post-Cartesian philosophical readings of Descartes.

13   Descartes, *Meditations*, Second Meditation, 17, 19.

14   Descartes, *Meditations*, Second Meditation, 19: 'The fact that it is I who am doubting and understanding and willing is so evident that I see no way of making it any clearer. But it is also the case that the "I" who imagines is the same "I". For even if, as I have supposed, none of the objects of imagination are real, the power of imagination is something which really exists and is part of my thinking. Lastly, it is also the same "I" who has sensory perceptions, or is aware of bodily things as it were through the senses.' This is *not*, however, a claim about personal identity. Descartes' point is that even the apparent sensuousness of perception is epistemologically reducible to the 'I think'. When I am asleep I seem to see things; this 'seeming to see' is indubitable whatever the relation of that 'seeming' to things existing outside of me: 'I certainly *seem* to see, to hear, and to be warmed. This cannot be false; what is called "having a sensory perception" is strictly just this, and in this restricted sense of the term it is simply thinking.' (Second Meditation, 19)

the fact that *from the first person point of view* – the only point of view that there is at this stage in the *Meditations* – thought and existence are immediately identified. In the meditation on myself as a thinking thing, 'the subject (*ego*) recognises itself as the author of all its thoughts': this 'thing' that thinks in me is *nothing other* than me, I am certain that it is *me* who thinks in me and that no one else, 'not even God – perhaps especially not God', thinks 'in my place'. (*ID*, 21) What is important, then, is not so much that I am a *thing* that thinks, but that *I* am the thing that thinks – that it is *me*.

If I am the thing that thinks, what can I know of thinking, and thus of myself? Balibar refers us to the passage from Descartes' *Principles of Philosophy* where it is asked 'What is thought?' and the answer given: 'By the word "thought" I understand all that which happens in us that we can immediately apperceive or know ourselves.'[15] As Descartes' Latin here introduces the word '*conscientia*', this is the passage that is often cited as proof of his introduction of the idea of consciousness.[16] So what is this apperception, or this immediate knowledge? Balibar argues that, far from equating thought with consciousness here, Descartes isolates this consciousness (apperception, knowledge) as one thought among others, a thought about thoughts, albeit one which is present at every thought (for we cannot think without knowing that we think). This thought about thought is the thought that relates each thought to the 'I' that thinks it and inscribes the 'objective' thought of the 'I' within the world of thought itself; that is, it locates the 'I' as interior to thought, not something exterior to it. This being so, to what does this thought (this consciousness or this knowledge) amount? What is it that it knows? Balibar answers: very much, very little. Its domain is both infinitely rich (it extends to every possible thought) and extremely poor, as each time it amounts to one and the same thing: to the fact that we are thinking under such and such a modality, or that to conceive, to perceive, to will and so on are thoughts that attach to the 'I' as their author, who thus necessarily exists at the moment of thought. Thus knowledge or consciousness of thinking gives rise to no programme of investigation of consciousness, of the faculties of the soul or to any analysis of its operations – no 'rational psychology' in Kant's sense. (*ID*, 22–3)[17]

The fact that at each moment thought is necessarily known as thought and as such referred to the thinking thing that thinks it does no more than

---

15   Descartes, *Principles of Philosophy*, quoted in *ID*, 22.

16   The dossier in *Identity and Difference* includes the full passage in Latin with Descartes' approved translation (by l'abbé Picot) into French. 'Cogitationis nomine intelligo illa omnia quae nobis consciis in nobis fiunt, quatenus eorum in nobis conscientia est.' 'Par le mot penser, j'entends tout ce qui se fait en nous de telle sorte que nous l'apercevons immédiatement par nous-mêmes'.

17   This also explains, Balibar writes, why Descartes claims that the soul is easier to know than the body, and why this extraordinary claim is given so little justification in the *Meditations* – thinking cannot but immediately know itself as itself and as the thought of the 'I' each time it thinks. See *ID*, 23, 27–8. On early translations of Descartes' use of *conscientia* into French see Glyn Davies, *'Conscience' as Consciousness*, 8–9.

repeatedly re-demonstrate the first moment of certainty in the *Meditations*: I think, I am – *'the conclusion is always the same.'* (*ID*, 28) Furthermore, knowledge or consciousness of thinking is always punctual and singular – restricted to the first person – not impersonal knowledge of the generic features of any mind. As punctual, knowledge or consciousness of thought exists always 'in the moment' or 'in the present' (*actuellement*), has no essential relation to memory and thus does not for Descartes constitute any psychological identity over time. Its immediacy refers not only to its transparency, but also to the formal identity of the 'I' and its thoughts. That is, thoughts do not *turn back* on the 'I'; rather, they are immediately identified with it. Thus there is no *reflexive* relation in knowledge or consciousness of thought – no gap or crack or split or doubling – and it opens no windows on the workings of the mind. This is, as we shall see, point-by-point not just different but contrary to Locke's introduction of consciousness into his account of personal identity.

2. CONSCIOUSNESS, THE SELF AND PERSONAL IDENTITY

The major aim of Balibar's discussion of Descartes is to contest the attribution of the 'invention' of the concept of consciousness to him – to contest Descartes' 'fictive paternity' of the concept. (*ID*, 2) This is not to suggest that Descartes did not play a very important part in the European invention of consciousness; on the contrary: 'Without Descartes there would not have been any invention of *conscience* (and before it consciousness), not because he invented it, but because it emerged as a response to the difficult problems posed by the interpretation of his doctrine.' (*ID*, 13) It is also not to say that the concept then sprang fully formed from Locke's head, but rather that its 'invention' is a trans-linguistic play in several acts, (*ID*, 17) in which Locke's *Essay* forms a dramatic climax and in which Coste, too, is an important player.[18] Neither does Balibar claim that the various appearances of the concept of *conscience* as consciousness in French Cartesianism are the stages of a progressive development of the concept, culminating in Locke's *Essay*. Balibar's discussion of La Forge, Régis and Malebranche concerns the emergence of something more like a constellation of different but very closely related uses of the concept of *conscience* – both metaphysical and psychological – and other philosophemes, notably *sentiment intérieur*, with

---

18   On this point see also Balibar, 'L'invention de la conscience: Descartes, Locke et les autres', in Jacques Moutaux et Olivier Bloch, eds, *Traduire les philosophes*, Paris: Publications de la Sorbonne, 2000, especially 293–5 and 305 (in the discussion following the formal presentation): 'concerning a problem like that of the European invention of consciousness, the field from which we must depart is not first of all the field of French, and then the field of English, and so on. It is a field which is always already transnational, because each author speaks the different languages simultaneously and puts those languages to work.' See also Balibar's entry on 'Conscience' in Barbara Cassin, ed., *Vocabulaire européen des philosophies*.

which *conscience* was often identified. Nevertheless, the fact remains that Coste was extremely reticent to translate 'consciousness' as *conscience* in 1700. Correlatively, in Locke's own critical writing on Malebranche, he declares the French *sentiment* to be untranslatable, if not incomprehensible. (*ID*, 36–7)[19] For Balibar these translational difficulties are to be interpreted philosophically. They bear witness not merely (and certainly not primarily) to the empirical limitations of different languages but more importantly to 'the incompatibility of the problematics of consciousness' and to the linguistic specificity of the different problematics. (*ID*, 37) (In the series editors' accompanying paragraph to *Identity and Difference*, this point is made in a quite general form – summing up a claim from Schleiermacher on translation, Alain Badiou and Barbara Cassin write: 'there is more than one philosophical order because one philosophises in a particular language'.[20])

It is in terms of the specificity of the philosophical problematic of consciousness in Locke's *Essay* that Balibar then attempts to explain the fact that the first edition of Coste's translation introduced *con-science* very late, and that its introduction, in Chapter XXVII, was of moment to Coste. One might imagine that Coste's claim that the new use of the word was necessary at just this point to explain 'the *precise* idea of the Author'[21] suggests that Locke himself employed the idea of consciousness in Chapter XXVII in a more technical way than previously in the *Essay*. But as Balibar points out, 'consciousness' was used as early (in the first edition) as Chapter I of Book II and 'not in a vague or episodic fashion, but in a conceptually systematic way.' (*ID*, 8) What is it, then, in Chapter XXVII that demands this new linguistic mark? Balibar suggests that Coste feels the need for the linguistic innovation precisely here, in the section that first deals with the question of personal identity, because it is here, for the first time, that we see the conjunction of *two* fundamental theoretical terms in the *Essay*: 'consciousness' and 'the self'. (*ID*, 9) The latter, in this substantival form, if not actually coined here by Locke, is certainly highly novel in English.[22] For Locke, consciousness is the principle or criterion of personal identity or of 'the self'. For Balibar, this conjunction of the concept of consciousness with that of the self is 'the decisive moment in the *invention of consciousness* as a philosophical concept'. (*ID*, 1) Locke's *Essay* identifies 'consciousness' as precisely that aspect of human understanding that allows for the isolation of the sphere of the

---

19   See John Locke, *An Examination of P. Malebranche's Opinion of 'Seeing all Things in God'*, *Locke's Philosophical Works*, Vol. II, London: George Belt and Sons, 1894, 437.

20   A point nicely proved by the impossibility of translating Badiou and Cassin's point into English elegantly: 'il y a *des* ordres philosophiques parce qu'on philosophe en langue.' (*ID*, 7). And the point is perhaps one that will only be accepted from within certain of these 'philosophical orders'.

21   Coste, quoted in *ID*, 6.

22   See also Vincent Carraud, *L'invention du moi*, Paris: PUF, 2010, 131.

mental[23] (an inner theatre distinct from the outer theatre of sensation) and the simultaneous emergence of the 'self'. In so doing he offers a new account of the nature of the identity of a person or a 'self' (the two terms are often used together) quite independent of any concept of substance or of the soul. Thus the originality of the conception of consciousness in the *Essay* – which marks it out clearly from any conception of *conscience* in Descartes' work – lies in its *relation to* the conception of the person or the self and, as we shall see, in the conception of the nature of this relation.

So what, for Locke, is consciousness? Locke first defines consciousness as 'the perception of what passes in a Man's own mind'.[24] Perception is 'the first faculty of the Mind, exercised about our *Ideas* . . . and is by some called Thinking in general'. As 'thinking consists in being conscious that one thinks' and there is no thinking without ideas (*'where-ever there is Sense, or Perception, there some Idea is actually produced, and present in the Understanding'*),[25] Locke thinks it self-evident that there cannot be an idea in the mind of which the mind is not conscious, which is effectively equivalent to the claim that we 'cannot think at any time waking or sleeping, without being sensible of it . . . without being conscious of it'.[26] Further, the idea of perception is 'the first and simplest *Idea* we have from Reflection',[27] which is as much to say – with Descartes – that the thought of thought necessarily accompanies all thought. But *contra* Descartes, for Locke thinking is not the essence of the mind but one of its actions or operations.[28] As such, there is no difficulty in denying that the soul always thinks (an interruption in thinking does not affect the existence of the soul by depriving it of its essence) and the *necessary* tie between, on the one hand, thinking, perception and consciousness, and on the other, immaterial substance, is broken.

The Cartesian claim that we cannot think without knowing that we think is the core of the argument, in Book I of Locke's *Essay*, against the doctrine of innate ideas (which doctrine requires us, precisely, to have ideas of which we are not conscious).[29] It is also in defending this claim that the question of personal identity arises in the form in which it will later be discussed at length, for 'if it be possible, that the Soul can, whilst the body is sleeping, have its Thinking,

---

23   See *ID*, 41 ff.

24   Locke, *Essay*, II.i.19. It is notable that in a section added to Book I in the second edition (I, iv.20) the word 'consciousness' appears frequently.

25   Locke, *Essay*, II.ix.1; II.i.19; II.ix.4. See also II.i.9: 'To ask, *at what time a Man has first any Ideas*, is to ask, when he begins to perceive; having *Ideas*, and Perception being the same thing.'

26   Locke, *Essay*, II.i.10.

27   Locke, *Essay*, II.ix.1.

28   See, for example, Locke, *Essay*, II.i.9.

29   The proponents of the doctrine of innate ideas are forced, Locke argues, to hold that truths are imprinted on the souls of infants, for example, even though those infants know nothing of those truths. For Locke, this is manifestly unintelligible: 'No proposition can be said to be in the Mind, which it never yet knew, which it was never yet conscious of.' *Essay*, I.ii.5.

Enjoyment, and Concerns, its Pleasure or Pain apart, which the Man is not conscious of, nor partakes in: It is certain that *Socrates* asleep, and *Socrates* awake, is not the same Person',[30] though for Locke he may well be the same man. On the prompting of his friend William Molyneux, Locke expanded upon this brief reference to personal identity in the new Chapter XXVII added to the second edition of the *Essay*, via a reflection on the idea of identity itself.

For Locke, the criterion for identity is relative to the thing – or more properly the idea of the thing – whose identity is in question. He moves quickly through the specification of the principle of identity of a mass of matter (which identity consists in the continued existence together of the same atoms that make up that mass) and the principle of identity of living bodies – plants, animals and 'man' – which is participation in the same continued life, with 'fleeting' particles of matter 'in succession vitally united to the same organized Body'.[31] The idea of a man is nothing more, according to Locke, than that of 'an Animal of such a certain Form',[32] having nothing to do with rationality; but the idea of a *person*, he writes, is the idea of

> a thinking intelligent Being, that has reason and reflection, and can consider it self as it self, the same thinking thing in different times and places; which it does only by that consciousness, which is inseparable from thinking, and as it seems to me essential to it: It being impossible for anyone to perceive, without perceiving, that he does perceive. When we see, hear, smell, taste, feel, meditate, or will anything, we know that we do so. Thus it is always as to our present Sensations and Perceptions: And by this everyone is to himself, that which he calls *self*: It not being considered in this case, whether the same *self* be continued in the same, or divers Substances. For since consciousness always accompanies thinking, and 'tis that, that makes everyone to be, what he calls *self*; and thereby distinguishes himself from all other thinking things, in this alone consists *personal Identity*, i.e. the sameness of a rational Being: And as far as this consciousness can be extended backwards to any past Action or Thought, so far reaches the Identity of that *Person*; it is the same *self* now it was then; and 'tis by the same *self* with this present one that now reflects on it, that the Action was done.[33]

Until recently, it was not unusual to see this referred to as a 'memory theory' of personal identity. (In John Perry's popular collection *Personal Identity*, Locke

---

30   Locke, *Essay*, II.i.11. The passage continues, a little later: 'For if we take wholly away all Consciousness of our Actions and Sensations, especially of Pleasure and Pain, and the concernment that accompanies it, it will be hard to know wherein to place personal Identity.' An earlier, brief discussion of the problem of personal identity can be found at I.iv.4–5, concerned specifically with the question of resurrection.

31   Locke, *Essay*, II.xxvii.6.

32   Locke, *Essay*, II.xxvii.7.

33   Locke, *Essay*, II.xxvii.9.

comes under the heading of 'Versions of the Memory Theory'.[34]) For A.S. Pringle-Pattinson, editor of the once-standard 1924 edition of Locke's *Essay*, consciousness and memory are simply the same thing in Locke's argument.[35] In 1951 Anthony Flew wrote that 'in [Locke's] main statements of his position "consciousness" is simply equivalent to "memory"'.[36] Much more recently, in 1999, Nicholas Jolley felt able to say: 'Although in explaining his doctrine Locke tends to talk of consciousness, it is generally accepted that his theory offers an analysis of personal identity in terms of memory'.[37] Conceiving 'consciousness' as a series of mental states, this once-dominant interpretation of Locke takes him to understand personal identity as the empirical unity of these states gathered, or at least potentially gathered, in memory. Thus Robert C. Solomon ascribes to him 'an empirical concept of self as introspectible memories'.[38] This interpretation gives rise to the various problems connected with the fallibility of memory, especially the so-called 'transitivity of identity' problem – as, for example, in Thomas Reid's famous objection (1785) concerning the elderly general who remembers being the brave young officer but not the schoolboy flogged for robbing an orchard, though the young officer remembered being the boy. (George Berkeley had already made this objection in his *Alciphron* in 1732.)[39]

But behind this objection is a greater one, one which appears in the very earliest criticisms of Locke and the puzzle of which is still at the basis of much of the contemporary literature, including Michael Ayers's in many ways unsurpassed book on Locke from 1991.[40] This objection takes the form of a charge of circularity – reduced to its barest form, the charge that Locke presupposes the very thing, personal identity, that he sets out to explain. As Joseph Butler

---

34   John Perry, ed., *Personal Identity*, Berkeley: University of California Press, 1975. In 1785 Thomas Reid asserted the identity of consciousness and memory in Locke's *Essay*. See the extract from Reid's *Essays on the Intellectual Powers of Man* (1785), in Perry, ed., *Personal Identity*, 115.

35   See Pringle-Pattinson's footnote on p. 187 in Locke, *An Essay Concerning Human Understanding*, Abridged and Edited by A.S. Pringle-Pattison, Oxford: Clarendon Press, 1967 (first edition 1924).

36   Flew, 'Locke and the Problem of Personal Identity', in C.B. Martin and D.M. Armstrong, eds, *Locke and Berkeley: A Collection of Critical Essays*, London: Macmillan, 1968, 159.

37   Jolley, *Locke: His Philosophical Thought*, Oxford and New York: Oxford University Press, 1999, 113. See also Jolley, *Liebniz and Locke: A Study of the New Essays on Human Understanding*, Oxford: Clarendon Press, 1984, 128; David Wiggins, *Sameness and Substance*, Oxford: Blackwell, 1980, 188; Richard Swinburne, 'Personal Identity: The Dualist Theory', 8 and Sydney Shoemaker 'Personal Identity: A Materialist's Account', 85, both in Shoemaker and Swinburne, *Personal Identity*, Oxford: Blackwell, 1984.

38   Solomon, *Continental Philosophy Since 1970: The Rise and Fall of the Self*, Oxford: Oxford University Press, 1998, 17–18.

39   See Reid in Perry, ed., *Personal Identity*, 114; George Berkeley, *The Works of George Berkeley, Bishop of Cloyne*, Volume Three, *Alciphron or The Minute Philosopher*, ed. T.E. Jessop, London: Thomas Nelson, 1950, 298–9.

40   Michael Ayers, *Locke: Epistemology and Ontology*, London and New York: Routledge, 1991.

famously put it in 1837: 'one should really think it self-evident, that consciousness of personal identity presupposes, and therefore cannot constitute, personal identity, any more than knowledge, in any other case, can constitute truth, which it presupposes.'[41]

Now, as many people have pointed out, Butler's objection is wrong to assume that Locke claimed that *consciousness of* personal identity constitutes personal identity – that would indeed be circular. But even when Locke's position is more accurately rendered as the claim that the consciousness that always accompanies thoughts and perceptions (two terms taken by Locke, following Descartes, to refer here to the same thing) 'makes everyone to be what he calls *self*'[42] the problem is still not, for most commentators, avoided, and this because of two things. First, the strict problem of circularity remains: personal identity (my self) is presupposed in identifying present thoughts and memories *as mine*. In John Sargeant's words, from 1697: 'A Man must *be* the same, ere he can *know* or *be Conscious* that he is the same.'[43] And second, understanding consciousness as *consciousness of* thoughts and perceptions, consciousness is understood to be a quality, an operation, an attribute, an accident, a sign or – in the terminology of a certain enduring ontology – a *mode* which presupposes the substance of which it is an accident, a mode, and so on. Henry Lee made the objection in this form in 1702: '*Consciousness* alone can't unite the several Acts of an intelligent Being, without the *Substance* of which it is only the Mode or Power.'[44] For many of Locke's earliest critics this problem was proof that, contra Locke, we do have to posit a permanent substance (mostly, the immaterial substance of the immortal soul) in the explanation of personal identity. If we do not, the self becomes, as Berkeley has Hylas say, 'a system a floating ideas',[45] a conception of the self that is compelling to some – famously, of course, Hume – but intolerable to those concerned with the issue of resurrection on the day of judgment, which is the single most significant aspect of the historical-intellectual context of Locke's discussion.[46]

---

41   See the extract from Butler's *The Analogy of Reason* (1736) in Perry, ed., *Personal Identity*, 100. Butler does not mention Locke by name here (though he does later) but it is clear that Locke is the target of the criticism.

42   Locke, *Essay*, II, xxvii, 9.

43   John Sargeant, *Solid Philosophy Asserted Against the Fancies of the Ideists: Or, The Method to Science. Farther Illustrated with Reflexions on Mr Locke's Essay concerning Human Understanding*, London: Roger Clavil, 1697, 265.

44   Henry Lee, *Anti-Scepticism, Or, Notes Upon Each Chapter of Mr Lock's Essay Concerning Human Understanding*, London: Clavel and Harper, 1702, 125.

45   Quoted in Christopher Fox, *Locke and the Scriblerians: Identity and Consciousness in Early Eighteenth-Century Britain*, Berkeley: University of California Press, 1988, 46.

46   J.L. Mackie (*Problems From Locke*, Oxford: Clarendon Press, 1976, 178) presents these two alternatives.

3. BALIBAR'S INTERPRETATION

This second form of objection – that Locke presupposes what he sets out to explain, leading to the idea that we must, after all, posit a substantial basis for personal identity – is still the focus of much contemporary discussion of Locke on this issue. But Balibar's interpretation of Locke cuts right across this objection. This interpretation is multi-faceted; the mode of its elaboration in *Identity and Difference*, in the long 'introductory' essay and in the sequence of Glossary entries, reflects this in a material form. Its multiple, lateral arguments are difficult to summarize, but two features – strikingly original in the context of mainstream interpretation of Locke – stand out. First, the 'circle' of self and consciousness is repositioned as the object of Locke's analysis, rather than the (regrettable) structure of his argument; and second, the principle of identity itself is seen to be discovered *within* the structure of consciousness itself, rather than being problematically applied to it.

In making the first of these points, Balibar's interpretation focuses on *the identity of consciousness with itself* as the condition for the claim that identity of consciousness constitutes personal identity:

> Even before arriving at the statement of a criterion of identity for the human *person*, Locke inscribed a statement in the constitution of consciousness that renders this consciousness 'identity to oneself' [*une identité à soi*]. Without this preliminary moment, there could be no question of *founding* anything at all. Consciousness could not guarantee the identity of the person if it did not contain the principle of identity in itself. (*ID*, 47)

The *presupposition* of the identity of consciousness with itself as the condition for its being the criterion of personal identity is, of course, the basis of the classic objection that Locke presupposes the very thing (identity of self) that he sets out to explain. But Balibar argues that the 'circle' of consciousness's identity with itself is not a fault in Locke's reasoning (begging the question); rather, *it is the very object of his analysis*. In other words, the *discovery of the circle of consciousness and self* is the major achievement of Locke's account. (*ID*, 86–7, 76)

It is often said that Locke's use of the idea of consciousness is confused and equivocal, moving between a descriptive, adjectival sense (consciousness *of* mental contents) and a substantive sense (consciousness as a describable 'thing', a mental 'entity'). But in the effective identification of thinking and consciousness in the claim that we cannot think without knowing that we think, the two different senses of consciousness are simultaneous: any act of knowing that we think, any *consciousness of* thinking, is simultaneously an act *of consciousness* as identical with itself or in which consciousness constitutes itself as self-identical.

Consciousness *is* identity with itself *as* consciousness *of* thinking and 'the self' is the name for the self-identity of consciousness, 'personal identity' being its formal *general* title.[47] This is what Balibar calls, in contradistinction to Descartes' first-personal 'I' – about which nothing can be said beyond the affirmation of its punctual existence – an 'impersonal' conception of the self; that is, a generic term. That this self as identity to self is always in some sense *presupposed* in the discussion of personal identity is not the mark of Locke's logical failure; it is, in part, the consequence of its elaboration as a proto-transcendental concept.

Foregrounding the relation between the concepts of consciousness and 'the self' and explicating 'the self' as consciousness of self (to say '*mere* consciousness of self' would betray a substantialist prejudice) Balibar's interpretation brings the inherent *reflexivity* of Locke's conception of consciousness more clearly into view. This complicates the relation between the concepts of consciousness and reflection in the *Essay*. In Book II, Chapter I, 'Of Ideas *in general, and their Original*', Locke identifies sensation and reflection as the only two possible origins of ideas. Sensation is perception of external, sensible objects; reflection is 'the *Perception of the internal Operations of our Minds* within us'. Reflection is not second to sensation ontologically – it is as immediate as sensation – and it is not reflection on the ideas of sensation but 'on its own Operations within it self', 'as it is employ'd about the *Ideas* it has got' through sensation. Reflection is 'that notice which the Mind takes of its own Operations'; that is, reflection is the mind reflecting on itself, the mind turning back upon itself or 'turning inwards upon itself'.[48] Although consciousness is similarly reflexive, it is not identical with reflection in the sense specified by Locke; that is, it is more than attentive contemplation of the operation of the mind. When the identity of consciousness to itself and its making of 'the self' is stressed over its interpretation as transparent awareness of perceptual or ideational content, Balibar suggests that the concept of consciousness in the *Essay* 'doubles' that of reflection, encompassing within itself both the distinction between sensation and intellectual operation (passivity and activity) that marks reflection off from sensation, and functioning as the condition of possibility for the 'understanding' that is the object of Locke's study. (*ID*, 54–5)

However this may be, it is clear that, for Balibar, it is the inherent reflexivity of consciousness and its being that by which 'every one is to himself, that which

---

47   Locke, *Essay*, II.xxviii.26: '*Person*, as I take it, is the name for this *self.*' With full respect to Locke's attempt to void the discussion of any reference to substance, one might say that consciousness is the constituting movement-action, the inward folding that *is* the self.

48   Locke, *Essay*, II.i.3; II.i.4; II.i.8. Locke also says that, although this source of ideas 'be not Sense, as having nothing to do with external Objects; yet it is very like it, and might properly enough be call'd internal Sense. But as I call the other *Sensation*, so I call this *REFLECTION*, the *Ideas* it affords being such only, as the Mind gets by reflecting on its own Operations within itself.' (II.i.4)

he calls *self* [49] that distinguishes it most clearly from any concept of consciousness in Descartes. Vincent Carraud, who ostensibly disputes Balibar's reading of Locke's place in the history of the 'invention' of consciousness, fully affirms this difference. In his book *L'invention du moi*, Carraud's distinction between Descartes' idea of *conscience* and Locke's notion of consciousness hinges principally on the immediate and non-reflexive nature of the former as opposed to the reflexive nature of the latter. Carraud follows Balibar (though he does not acknowledge this) in explaining Coste's decision to translate 'consciousness' as '*con-science*' for the first time in Chapter XXVII by noting the simultaneous introduction of the innovative substantivisation of 'the self'.[50] Like Balibar, Carraud also distinguishes between the first personal status of *le moi* in Descartes and the 'impersonal' conception of the self in Locke. But appearing to interpret Balibar as claiming that *Locke alone* invented the concept of consciousness, Carraud insists on giving the credit back to Descartes. Carraud cites as proof Cudworth's use of the idea of consciousness, the few uses of *conscience* in Descartes and the far more frequent use of the word in La Forge and Malebranche, as if Balibar did not discuss precisely all these. Carraud's conclusion then seems contradictory:

> There is then not the slightest reason to strip Descartes of the credit for the invention of the concept of conscience in its non-moral sense . . . However, as we have seen, the Lockean concept of consciousness and that of Descartes are significantly different. If Lockean consciousness makes sense only as reflection and, via reflection, as constitutive of the self, being conscious is for Descartes, to have an idea, that is, to know. Reflexivity is in no way necessary for this knowledge, whatever it is – including knowledge of the *ego*.[51]

Of course, this difference is precisely Balibar's point.

If the first major aspect of Balibar's interpretation of Locke is thus the insistence that consciousness's identity with itself is not an error in Locke's argument but the novel object of his analysis, the second is closely connected to this. Balibar shows, that is, that the account of the origin of the idea of identity and thus the nature of the principle of identity itself is inseparable from the account of the identity of consciousness with itself. Balibar's reading is then able to bring to the fore an aspect of Locke's discussion of consciousness and personal identity that

---

49   Locke, *Essay*, II.xxvii.9.

50   Carraud, *L'invention du moi*, 142–5.

51   Carraud, *L'invention du moi*, 149. Carraud writes that there is even less reason 'to make the word [*conscience* in its non-moral sense] a Lockean neologism'. In fact Balibar does not claim that 'consciousness' is Locke's neologism (he refers to Cudworth's use of the word); more importantly, Balibar insists on the idea of the '*European* invention of consciousness' (*ID*, 17) precisely because of the involvement of the various actors Carraud mentions and to underline the philosophical role of translation. For Carraud, on the other hand, it seems that it may still be a question of national pride.

has hitherto gone unnoticed, which not only alters our understanding of this specific part of the *Essay* but also allows us to see a deeper relation between some of its major parts, especially between the discussion of personal identity and the refutation of the doctrine of innate ideas in Book I.

In the refutation of the doctrine of innate ideas, Locke discusses, among other things, two major candidates for the status of innate principle, namely, the two fundamental principles of logic: the principle of identity and the principle of non-contradiction, most often exemplified in the *Essay* in the form of the two claims that 'whatsoever is, is' and ''Tis impossible for the same thing to be, and not be.' If these principles were innate they would, Locke argues, enjoy universal assent, but in fact they are strictly unknown *qua* principles to 'Children and Ideots'.[52] But, Balibar argues, if these principles are not innate *in* the mind, they are rediscovered in Locke's philosophy as principles *of* the mind, inscribed in the structure of the mind itself, in the identity of the mind with itself in consciousness, and in the non-contradiction of the mind with itself (in the form of the thesis that the mind cannot think without thinking, or perceive without perceiving that it perceives).

The importance of this point is not just that it allows us to see the substitution of innate principles *in* the mind with immanent principles *of* the mind; it also allows us to see beyond the rather obviously inadequate explicit account of the origin of the ideas of identity and diversity in the *Essay* to the deeper structure of the *Essay*'s philosophical position. Towards the end of Book I, in Chapter IV, in the section titled 'Other Considerations concerning innate Principles, both speculative and practical', Locke argues that we would be less likely to believe that the fundamental principles of logic were innate if we 'considered, separately, the parts out of which those Propositions are made'; that is, the ideas of impossibility and of identity.[53] That the idea of identity is not innate is proved, Locke suggests here, by the fact that it is nowise clear and obvious to us what constitutes identity, especially as concerns the identity of 'a Man, being a creature, consisting of Soul and Body', and also the identity of 'Persons' when reflecting on the resurrection and the day of judgment.[54] From the very beginning, then, the question of the origin of the idea of identity is bound up with the puzzle of what constitutes *personal* identity. But if the question of its origin is at first dealt with only negatively – the idea of identity is *not* innate – Locke stumbles in attempting to say anything positive concerning its origin, as the tautological nature of his first definition of identity shows.[55] The discussion moves

---

52   See, for example, Locke, *Essay*, I.ii.4–5.
53   Locke, *Essay*, I.iv.1.
54   Locke, *Essay*, I.iv.4–5.
55   See II.xxvii.1: 'In this consists *Identity*, when the *Ideas* it is attributed to vary not at all from what they were that moment, wherein we consider their former existence, and to which we compare the present.'

quickly from the question of the origin of the idea of identity to that of the different 'sorts of *Identity*'[56] – to the question of what, the idea of identity having been somehow acquired, it refers to in the consideration of different sorts of things (or at least the ideas of different sorts of things). The question of the origin of the idea of identity thus seems to be replaced by the question of the justification for the ascription of identity in generic cases: the case of a mass of matter, of a living thing (including a man) and, of course, the case of a person.

From one perspective, then, the question of the origin of the idea of identity is simply lost; but from another (Balibar's) it is rather that the discussion involutes. The question of the origin of the idea of identity is sucked into the discussion of personal identity and is regurgitated in the changed form of the implicit conclusion that the idea of identity itself emerges from the recognition of a self by itself. (*ID*, 74)

Perhaps, at this point, *An Essay Concerning Human Understanding* gives a foretaste of the science of the experience of consciousness? Locke's first tautological definition of identity says, in effect, that the identity of an idea consists in its being identical to itself, or not different from itself: there is identity where there is no difference. The more philosophically sophisticated idea that emerges from the discussion of personal identity concerns, instead, identity *within* difference, as consciousness is, in Balibar's words, '*a self-identity that is maintained, or better, reiterated through difference*' (*ID*, 55) – differences between sensation and reflection, activity and passivity, past and present. This, we may say, is the point at which the interpretative track is most obviously shifted away from the analytical path, forging Locke's place in a different philosophical history by virtue of his

> having . . . identified identity with the active recognition of a 'self' by itself, operating in the element of consciousness. Without Locke's contribution, neither Kant, nor Fichte, nor Hegel, nor even Husserl would have been possible, even as they took Locke as an empiricist, if not a naturalist, philosopher and turned away from him in favour of a more or less mythical Cartesianism. (*ID*, 74)

Balibar's interpretation has now brought us very far from the 'empirical concept of self' often attributed to Locke. Indeed, we might see Locke's notion of 'self' as the fundamental *rationalist* core of *An Essay Concerning Human Understanding*. This is not just because it is, as Balibar says, perhaps the first true 'rationalist psychology', in which the possibility of knowledge of the self is inscribed within the structure of the mind itself. It is also because the principle of identity, discovered in the recognition of a self by itself, or discovered as the identity of consciousness, is the foundation, ultimately, for *all* knowledge to the

---

56   Locke, *Essay*, II.xxvii.7.

extent that the principle of personal identity is necessary for the experience of duration which furnishes us with the concept of time necessary for the identification of the identity of matter and living things across time.[57] Thus the principle of personal identity, ostensibly an afterthought, added to the second edition, on the prompting of Molyneux, actually forms the philosophical heart – logical, epistemological, and as we shall see moral and political – of the *An Essay Concerning Human Understanding*. Such, anyway, is its retrospective significance, revealed in Balibar's interpretation.

4. THE SUBSTANCE PROBLEM

If, as I have argued, Balibar's interpretation of Locke cuts across the classic objection of circularity and its concomitant claim, contra Locke, that we must posit a substantial basis for identity, what is the philosophical context that makes Balibar's interpretation possible? What are the philosophical presuppositions that drive the classic objections in the mainstream literature, and what explains their persistence? What, on the other hand, allows Balibar to approach the whole question of personal identity in Locke differently?

For Locke's contemporary critics and their heirs today, the problem that Locke's theory seems to presuppose the substance of which consciousness is a mode has tended either to prove that Locke's argument fails, or to lead to the postulation of another candidate for the place of the immortal soul, for example in E.J. Lowe's postulation of a '*psychological* substance'.[58] For Michael Ayers, however, the objection misses the point that Locke 'held that a person is a substance in the sense in which a horse or oak is a substance';[59] and that consciousness is the 'non-substantial principle of substantial unity' of the person, a position which requires that 'rational consciousness is not a mere power or accident'.[60] But this is not to say that Ayers advocates Locke's position; not at all. Locke's position is the attempt to pull off a philosophical 'trick', according to Ayers, and we must ask whether it works, and we must answer that it does not, because, according to Ayers – denying Locke's distinction between man

---

57   See *ID*, 83–4. Of course Locke doesn't explicitly say this, but see II.xiv.16–17. See also Reid in Perry, ed., *Personal Identity*, 107: 'The conviction which every man has of his identity . . . is indispensably necessary to all exercise of reason. The operations of reason, whether in action or in speculation, are made up of successive parts. The antecedent are the foundation of the consequent, and, without the conviction that the antecedent have been seen or done by me, I could have no reason to proceed to the consequent, in any speculation, or in any active project whatsoever.'

58   Lowe, *Subjects of Experience*, Cambridge: Cambridge University Press, 1996, 32. See also Lowe, *Locke on Human Understanding*, Abingdon, Oxon.: Routledge, 1995, Ch. 5.

59   Ayers, *Locke*, 276. Locke claims that we have two kinds of ideas of substances: 'one of single Substances, as they exist separately, as of *a Man*, or *a Sheep*; the other of several of those put together, as an *Army* of men, or *Flock* of Sheep'. (II.xii.6)

60   Ayers, *Locke*, 263.

and person – any substantial unity that the person enjoys is due to its being a materially unitary thing, a bodily self.[61] What Ayers says rests on his claim that, for Locke, a person is a substance. It also rests on Ayers's own defence of a traditional distinction between substance and non-substance, where substances 'or material objects characteristically have a kind of natural or given individuality, unity and continuity which non-substances cannot have. The individuality of substances is real, and prior to their individuation by us'.[62] For Ayers, persons are substances in this sense; really, materially individuated. Thus, he writes, 'the idea that psychological unity [Locke's 'consciousness'] serve as the principle of individuation of a sort of substances, persons, is as wrong-headed and ineffectual as it would be to insist that we can arbitrarily make its heat the principle of individuation of something as substantial as a hot-cross-bun'.[63] So, for Ayers, although Locke may have postulated persons as substances – an interpretation of Locke that separates Ayers from the critics mentioned above – he shares their view that consciousness is a mere mode, and he shares the basic terms of their underlying ontology: things are to be distinguished as being either substance or mode.

But a recent strand in the study of Locke has begun to take a different tack, to propose a different understanding of the account of the person which obviates the objection of circularity or the problem that Locke's theory seems to presuppose the substance of which consciousness is a mode. This strand emerged in work by intellectual historians, not analytical philosophers. The work of Udo Thiel is probably the most important in this regard.[64] Thiel's interpretation of Locke is part of his extensive work on seventeenth- and eighteenth-century theories of self-consciousness and personal identity. Speaking in broad terms, Thiel's historical orientation brings two contextual aspects to the fore: first, the context of the theological debates that are the background to Locke's discussion of personal identity; and second, the history of the concept of the 'person'. The theological context is twofold, concerning the nature of the trinity ('There is but one living and true God . . . And in the unity of this Godhead there be three Persons') and the resurrection of the dead, which is what really concerned Locke. In debates on the trinity, the question of what makes a person

---

61   Ayers, *Locke*, 263, 288–9.

62   Ayers, *Locke*, 295.

63   Ayers, *Locke*, 289. Ayers also criticizes the view that Locke's 'person' is a mode. See 281 ff.

64   Udo Thiel, 'Locke's Concept of Person', in Reinhard Brandt, ed., *John Locke* (Symposium Wolfenbuttel), Berlin and New York: Walter de Gruyter, 1981; 'Cudworth and Seventeenth Century Theories of Consciousness' in S. Gaukroger, ed., *The Uses of Antiquity*, Dordrecht: Kluwer, 1991; 'Personal Identity', in Daniel Garber and Michael Ayers, eds, *The Cambridge History of Seventeenth-Century Philosophy*, Vol. 1, Cambridge: Cambridge University Press, 1998; *The Early Modern Subject: Self-Consciousness and Personal Identity from Descartes to Hume*, Oxford: Oxford University Press, 2011.

One was central.[65] Connected to this, the debates on the resurrection of the dead concerned the form in which the dead would be resurrected (whether in the same body, or as the same immortal soul) and what therefore one needed to believe about the immortality of the soul, for example, in order to believe in this article of Christian faith.

Locke's Chapter XXVII was in great part a contribution to the debate on resurrection, with an answer to the question: what kind of continuity is necessary in order that men and women be justly judged and rewarded or punished on the day of judgment? His answer: neither the continuity of a material nor of an immaterial substance (neither body nor soul) but the continuity of the *person*, where that is a

> Forensick Term appropriating Actions and their Merit; and so belongs only to intelligent Agents capable of a Law, and Happiness and Misery. This personality extends it *self* beyond present Existence to what is past, only by consciousness, whereby it becomes concerned and accountable, owns and imputes to it self past Actions . . . [and] at the Great Day, when every one shall *receive according to his doings, the secrets of all Hearts shall be laid open.* The Sentence shall be justified by the consciousness all Persons shall have, that they *themselves* in what Bodies soever they appear, or what Substances soever that consciousness adheres to, are the *same*, that committed those Actions, and deserve that Punishment for them.[66]

With this concept of the person, Locke breaks with what Thiel calls the 'traditional "ontological" view',[67] invoking, if anything, the ancient Roman concept of *persona*, distinguished from *res* (thing), where *persona* refers 'to the individual human being in so far as he or she stands in a relation to legal matters' and later refers to the bearers of rights and duties.[68] Recognizing this, other recent work on Locke, along with Thiel, has begun to stress the primarily moral or practical and affective nature of his concept of a person, with attention focusing on Locke's talk of 'concernment' and 'accountability'.

Of course, accountability has always been a part of the discussion of Locke, for example in the discussion of puzzle cases where people might typically ask: if personal identity consists in consciousness or memory, can a person be held accountable for actions of which she has no memory? But in these cases we are asked to make a judgment on the basis of whether a person, already assumed to exist, should be held accountable for a particular action, whereas Thiel's different claim is that being-accountable brings the person into existence. On this

---

65 As in, for example, William Sherlock, *A Vindication of the Doctrine of the Holy and Ever Blessed Trinity and the Incarnation of the Son of God*, London: W. Rogers, 1690, 47–9, 267.

66 Locke, *Essay*, II, xxvii, 26.

67 Thiel, 'Personal Identity', 888.

68 Ibid., 869.

interpretation, the appropriation (or 'owning') of experiences and actions actually constructs the person as self across time, giving what Marya Schechtman calls a 'self-constitution' theory of personal identity,[69] sometimes also called 'narrative identity'.[70] Thus, rather than a person being a unity that is known as such through consciousness, or the component parts of which are identified as such by being accompanied by consciousness, consciousness – 'whereby [the self] becomes concerned and accountable, owns and imputes to it *self* past Actions'[71] – constitutes the person as a moral entity.[72] Drawing on Thiel and Schechtman, Galen Strawson's recent book about Locke on personal identity (2011) also stresses the forensic nature of Locke's concept of person, interpreting it as a theory of moral and legal responsibility.

This recent and still-small body of literature represents, as I have said, a significant shift in the interpretation of Locke on personal identity, and it is significant in countering the two main forms of objections to Locke. They completely do away with the fallibility of memory objections (because a person is neither the empirical sum of memories nor the principle of connection between them) and, more importantly, it answers the charge of circularity. That objection – that consciousness presupposes, and so cannot constitute, personal identity – itself presupposes precisely what Locke's theory denies, that is, it presupposes that the person is a thing (*res*, in some sense, material or immaterial) of which we are conscious, when Locke argues that a person is constituted as such through consciousness.[73] That is, the objection surreptitiously presupposes the very thing that this concept of the person is meant to deny: that the person is (must be) a substance, whereas consciousness is (only) a mode. But according to Thiel et al., and contra Ayers, Locke's 'person' is the idea of something that is *neither* a substance *nor* a mode.

Note that this interpretation does not deny that persons are or may be ontologically dependent. For Thiel, Locke's concept of the person presupposes thinking substance or the man as the agent who thinks, consciousness and appropriation of these acts and thoughts being, precisely, the constitution of personal, i.e. moral, identity. For Strawson, the idea of the person *includes* 'a

---

69   Marya Schechtman, *The Constitution of Selves*, Ithaca and London: Cornell University Press, 1996, 17, 106. See also Raymond Martin, 'Locke's Psychology of Personal identity', in Peter Anstey, ed., *John Locke: Critical Assessments*, Vol. III, Metaphysics, London and New York: Routledge, 2006.

70   See also Kim Atkins, *Narrative Identity and Moral Identity: A Practical Perspective*, London and New York: Routledge, 2008, 15, 17.

71   Locke, *Essay*, II, xxvii, 26. See also Strawson, *Locke on Personal Identity*, 48.

72   Udo Thiel, 'Locke's Concept of Person', 184.

73   As Raymond Martin points out ('Locke's Psychology of Personal Identity', 387), circularity is not a weakness in this argument; rather, it is built into its very structure, it is part of the very nature of the reflexivity of consciousness. See also Udo Thiel, 'Personal Identity', in Savonius-Wroth, Schuurman and Walmsley, eds, *The Continuum Companion to Locke*, London and New York: Continuum, 2010, 198.

whole human *material* body', similar to Locke's 'man'.[74] But this does not mean that the moral entity 'person' is conceptually identical with her body or with the natural agent, any more than the dependency of ideas on the human beings who think them makes those ideas conceptually identical with those humans. This, however, is precisely what the circularity objection does presuppose: that the person is identical with the substance.

5. FROM SUBSTANCE TO SUBJECT

When the main thrust of Locke argument is to deny that the person must be thought in terms of substance, why have so many of his readers – from his earliest critics to those in the late twentieth century – repeatedly pressed against him the charge that, after all, his conception of the person was such that it was – must be – *constitutively* substantial? When Locke's main point was to separate the idea of a person from the idea of substance, why have so many read him as surreptitiously – and necessarily – presupposing their identity? Strawson asks this very question, but does not have an answer to it other than to blame certain influential commentators.[75] Strawson is also, of course, unaware of Balibar's interpretation, and the two points are not unconnected. For the answer to the question lies in an aspect of the 'continental' tradition of philosophy – in the philosophical history of the concept of the subject to which Balibar has been a major contributor and which is a crucial part of the philosophical context of Balibar's interpretation of Locke. From the perspective of this context, Locke's shifting of the centre of the analysis of the person to consciousness and away from substance clears the way for the point of view of the *subject*, understood in a specific sense (*ID*, 210, 221). It allows Locke to think

> mental reality, in its intelligible structure, as distinct from the structures of living organisation (the mental is opposed to the vital) as from those of language (the mental is opposed to the verbal); to think it as an *action without substance* (at least, without a *determinate* substance, whether material, spiritual, etc). But not, obviously, as an *action without a subject*. (*ID*, 94)

Indeed, for Balibar, Locke's treatise 'forms an essential moment in the invention of the modern subject, a moment from which the theorizations of the subject and the moral person, such as those of Kant and Hegel, are directly derived'.[76]

---

74   Strawson, *Locke on Personal Identity*, 9.

75   See Strawson, *Locke on Personal Identity*, 1; also 4.

76   *ID*, 104, emphasis added. This argument is also made by Alain de Libera in his *Archéologie du sujet*, Vol I, *Naissance du sujet*, 98–119. The fourth volume of *Archéologie du sujet* is projected to include de Libera's most significant discussion of Locke (see *Naissance du sujet*, 123).

But what exactly do we mean here by 'subject'? Within the constellation of possible meanings of the term, to which specifically do we refer here, and what is its relation to the other meanings? Recent work in French on the philosophical history of the concept of the subject has illuminated but also considerably complicated our understanding of the emergence of 'the modern subject'.[77] The entry on 'Subject', co-authored by Étienne Balibar, Barbara Cassin and Alain de Libera, in the *Vocabulaire européen des philosophies* published in 2004, offers a distilled introduction to the topic.[78] The 'Subject' essay distinguishes between three main groups of meaning of 'subject' in the history of philosophy. First is the ontological and logical meanings of subject as 'subjectness' (*subjectité*, *Subjektheit*),[79] traced back to the classical Greek concept of the *hupokeimenon*, translated with the Latin *subjectum* – denoting that which underlies, either in the sense of substance or of logical subject. Most importantly for our purposes here, this picks out the meaning of *subject as substance*: that in which there are accidents, the material or immaterial substance which underlies its accidents or qualities or modes, which is connected to the meaning of the logical and/or grammatical subject – that to which predicates are attached.[80]

Locke uses the word 'subject' in this sense in the *Essay*, for example in the section dealing with the distinction between primary and secondary qualities. Both sorts of qualities are for Locke 'powers' to produce ideas in the mind of the perceiver, powers belonging to the 'Subject' and not to the perceiver: 'Whatsoever the Mind perceives in it self, or is the immediate object of Perception, Thought, or Understanding, that I call *Idea*; and the Power to produce any *Idea* in our mind, I call *Quality* of the Subject wherein that power is.'[81] Although the secondary qualities are said to be 'nothing in the Objects themselves', Locke is keen to stress that they, and indeed the 'third sort' of qualities – for example 'the power in Fire to produce a new Colour, or consistency in Wax or Clay' – are 'real Qualities in the Subject', that is, *not* the mere productions of the perceiver.[82] Later, in the chapter on power, Locke attempts to distinguish the subject *in this sense* from the idea of an agent. Our two sorts of ideas of action – motion and thinking – sometimes lead us to consider as actions what are really passions, that is,

---

77 This work includes various essays by Balibar, most of which are collected in his *Citoyen sujet et autres essais d'anthroplogie philosophique*, Paris: PUF, 2011. The two main essays in English translation are 'Citizen Subject' in Eduardo Cadava, Peter Connor, Jean-Luc Nancy, eds, *Who Comes After the Subject?*, London and New York: Routledge, 1991; and 'Subjection and Subjectivation', in Joan Copjec, ed., *Supposing the Subject*, London and New York: Verso, 1994.

78 Hereafter referred to as Balibar et al., 'Subject'. English translation: *Radical Philosophy* 138, July/August 2006. Page references refer to this translation.

79 'Subjectness' translates *subjectité* and *Subjektheit*; all three terms are neologisms, the French and the English derived from Heidegger's German. See Balibar et al., 'Subject', 15.

80 Balibar et al. call the 'suture' of these two meaning 'onto-logical' (16).

81 Locke, *Essay*, II.viii.8.

82 Ibid., II.viii.9.

the effects barely of passive Powers in those subjects, which yet on their account are [mistakenly] thought *Agents*. For in these instances, the substance that hath motion, or thought, receives the impression whereby it is put into that *Action* purely from without, and so acts merely by the capacity it has to receive such an impression from some external Agent; and such a *Power* is not properly an Active Power, but a mere passive capacity in the subject.[83]

Some subjects may also be agents, but the idea of the subject in this sense and the idea of the agent are not identical. The passive capacity or power of the subject in this sense includes the passive power of thinking: 'a Power to receive *Ideas*, or *Thoughts*, from the operation of any external substance.'[84] Further, the subject in this sense can also be used to denote what we would now call the object, for example:

> *Power* being the Source from whence all Action proceeds, the Substances wherein these Powers are, when they exert this Power into Act, are called *Causes*; and the Substances which thereupon are produced, or the simple *Ideas* which are introduced into any subject by the exerting of that Power, are called *Effects*. The *efficacy* whereby the new Substance or *Idea* is produced, is called, in the subject exerting that Power, *Action*; but in the subject, wherein any simple *Idea* is changed or produced, it is called *Passion*.[85]

The second group of meanings identified by Balibar et al. in the 'Subject' essay is that of the *subject as subjectivity* (*subjectivité*): the subject understood as the *antonym* of the object, co-emergent with the idea of the sphere of the psyche or the mental as opposed to the sphere of objectivity. This is the idea of the subject as ground of representation, or of the idea of what Alain de Libera calls the '*sujet agent*', which comes to assume the status of unique title-holder for all 'the power, or the functions, of the I, of the individual and of the person: the speaking subject, thinking subject, willing subject – in a word: *agent* subject'.[86] The complex intellectual conditions for the emergence and, as it were, 'triumph'

---

83   Locke, *Essay*, II.xxi.72. The use of 'subject' and 'substance' as synonyms is also common in the chapter on complex ideas of substances (II.xxiii).

84   Ibid., II.xxi.72.

85   Ibid., II.xxiii.11. See also II.x.11: although even 'Vegetables have, many of them, some degrees of Motion . . . Yet, I suppose, it is all bare Mechanism; and no otherwise produced, than the turning of a wild Oat-beard, by the insinuation of the Particles of Moisture; or the short'ning of Rope, by the affusion of Water. All of which is done without any Sensation in the Subject, or the having or receiving any *Ideas*.'
This is not quite the same as the idea of the subject as object identified in Balibar et al., 'Subject': 'A third meaning makes subject synonymous with object, as when we evoke the "subject" of a book or science' (15); in English 'subject matter'.

86   Libera, *Naissance du sujet*, 12. '*Sujet agent*' might also be translated as 'subject-agent'.

of the 'agent subject' are traced in great detail in de Libera's *Archéologie du sujet*, from the starting point of the unobviousness of the eventual synonymity of the terms 'subject' and 'agent'.[87] This complexity notwithstanding, Kant's role in the 'birth' of the modern subject is decisive. Although the idea of 'subjectivity' in the sense used in Baumgarten's *Aesthetics* (the 'merely' subjective field of phenomena that are the effect of the sentient being's own dispositions) is an important part of the background to Kant's philosophical work,

> It is ... only in the *Critique of Pure Reason* that *das Subjekt* (qualified in different ways as the logical subject, the empirical subject, the rational subject, the transcendental subject or the moral subject) becomes the key concept in a philosophy of subjectivity. Kant's philosophy therefore simultaneously 'invents' the problematic of a thought whose conditions of access to both the objectivity of the laws of nature and the universality of ethical and aesthetic values lie in its own constitution (the so-called 'Copernican revolution'), and gives the name 'subject' (i.e. the opposite of 'object') to the generic individuality inherent in the interplay between the faculties of knowledge.[88]

When Balibar says that Chapter XXVII of Locke's *Essay* 'is an essential moment in the invention of the modern subject' (*ID*, 104), it is the subject in this sense to which he refers.

In proposing a definition of the idea of a person that is notable, primarily, for being distinguished from any idea of substance, Locke does seem to be talking about what we now call 'subject' in this sense, even though he never uses the word like this in *An Essay Concerning Human Understanding*.[89] In urging a non-substantial notion of 'person', Locke was rejecting the widely accepted, *theological* definition of his contemporaries. As Stillingfleet put it: 'a person is a complete intelligent substance with a peculiar manner of subsistence'.[90] In reasserting this definition against Locke, many of Locke's earliest readers effectively identified the concepts of subject and substance, or 'subject' was implicitly and explicitly understood ontologically to mean the material or immaterial substrate of accidents. The ease of this identification might explain why Locke avoided the use of the word 'subject' in the discussion of personal identity, having used it in the sense of substance elsewhere in the *Essay*. But the word was frequently used to argue against Locke, the identification of subject and substance being implicit in all claims that consciousness could not be the principle of unity of a person,

---

87   A conjunction no more (im)probable, de Libera says (*Naissance du sujet*, 15), than that of a sewing machine and an umbrella on a dissecting table.

88   Balibar et al., 'Subject', 30, translation modified.

89   Cf de Libera, *Naissance du sujet*, Vol I, 87: 'Le sujet peut être caché sous le masque de *personne*.'

90   See ibid., 102.

because that principle of unity must be substantial. We can see this, for example, in John Sargeant's claim in 1697 that consciousness of any action is an 'Accident' of the 'Subject or Knower'.[91] We can see it in Samuel Clarke's claim in 1707 that '*Consciousness* is . . . *a real Quality, truly and properly inherent in the Subject itself, the thinking Substance*'.[92] It is common in the debates sparked by Locke's claim that it is possible for God to so arrange things that matter can think, where the question then becomes – as for example in Anthony Collins's reply to Clarke in 1707 – whether the subject of thinking must be material or immaterial substance.[93] And it is still perfectly explicit in Victor Cousin's *Elements of Psychology* in 1851:

> Now your personal existence, the *self* which you are and which reason reveals to you – what is it, relatively to the operations which consciousness and memory attest to you? It is the *subject* of these operations, of which the operations themselves are the characteristics, the signs, the attributes. These operations are perpetually changing and renewing; they are accidents. On the contrary, your personal existence subsists always the same; amidst the perpetual diversity of your acts, you are to-day the same that you were yesterday, and that you will be to-morrow. Personal identity is the unity of your being, your *self*, opposed to plurality of consciousness and memory. Now being, one and identical, opposed to variable accidents, to transitory phenomena, is substance . . . Here you have personal substance.[94]

Given the effective equation of the concepts of subject and substance in these examples, we can see how Locke's non-substantial notion of the person functions

---

91   John Sargeant, *Solid Philosophy*, 265: '*Consciousness* of any *Action* or other Accident we have now, or have had, is nothing but our *Knowledge* that it belong'd to us; and since we both [Sargeant and Locke] agree that we have no *Innate Knowledges*, it follows that both Actual and habitual Knowledges are *Acquir'd* or *Accidental* to the Subject or Knower, wherefore the Man, or the Thing which is to be the *Knower*, must have had Individuality or Personality from *other* Principles, *antecedently* to this Knowledge call'd *Consciousness* . . . A Man must *be* the same, ere he can *know* or *be Conscious* that he *is* the same.'

92   Samuel Clarke, *The Works of Samuel Clarke*, Vol. III, John and Paul Knapton, 1738, 797. See also 795: 'Every *real Quality* inheres in some Subject. This is also, I think, granted by All. For whatever is called a *Quality*, and yet inheres not in any *Subject*, must either subsist of itself; and then it is a *Substance*, not a *Quality*; or else it is nothing but a *mere Name*.'

93   Anthony Collins, *A Reply to Mr. Clark's Defence of his Letter to Mr Dodwell*, London, 1707, 25–6.

The presumption is also revealed in jest. The satirical *Memoirs of Scriblerus* (first published 1741 but composed from 1713), includes the following: 'When he was told, a substance was that which was subject to accidents; then soldiers (quoth Crambe) are the most substantial people in the world. Neither would he allow it to be a good definition of accident, that it could be present or absent without the destruction of the subject; since there are a great many accidents that destroy the subject, as burning does a house, and death a man.' Quoted in Fox, *Locke and the Scriblerians*, 98.

94   Victor Cousin, *Elements of Psychology, Included in a Critical Examination of Locke's Essay on the Human Understanding*, trans. C.S. Henry, London: Thomas Delf, 1851, 97.

as a 'conceptual interchange' (to use de Libera's phrase)[95] in the birth of a new figure of the subject. However, this new figure seems to play no part in mainstream Anglophone commentary on Locke, which still tends to equate the concepts of subject and substance. In 1999, Nicholas Jolley claimed that the 'happy' view of the person is one in which 'the body is intermittently the subject of mental states or properties', and to assume an immaterial 'subject of consciousness' – that is, an immaterial soul – 'may seem an unpardonable metaphysical extravagance'.[96] E.J. Lowe, in his 1996 book *Subjects of Experience*, argues that 'a person or subject of mental states must be regarded as a substance of which those states are modes . . . a psychological substance'.[97] The presupposition of the identity of subject and substance is also at work in Michael Ayers's claim that consciousness should only be understood as a mode of the substance 'person'. For Ayers, as we have seen, Locke's position is that a person is a substance in the same way that a horse or an oak is a substance, as a particular substance. Contra Locke, Ayers holds a traditional view of substance as, to quote the relevant passage again, 'material objects which characteristically have a kind of natural or given individuality, unity and continuity which non-substances cannot have . . . The individuality of substances is real, and prior to their individuation by us'.[98] If a person is a substance and a substance is naturally individuated, we can see why Ayers must also claim, again contra Locke, that a person is, after all, the same as a man. This means that there is no space at all in Ayers's view (or in his interpretation of Locke) for anything like the concept of the subject as subjectivity, it being meaningless, for him, to speak of 'a subject of thinking or speaking'[99] outside of its being identical with a natural substance. Udo Thiel stresses that the various objections to Locke from Henry Lee, Sargeant, Butler and Reid are 'based on an understanding of "person" as substance'[100] – the very understanding that Locke denies. But even Thiel glosses Locke's position as the claim that 'consciousness does not bring about the identity of the human subject as soul or man', that is, as the immaterial or material subject-substance.[101]

---

95   Libera, *Naissance du sujet*, 87.

96   Jolley, *Locke*, 93, 95. Mackie also implicitly equates subject and substance in his criticism of Locke and his view that the question of what underlies and thus makes possible the unity of consciousness is an empirical one. See Mackie, *Problems from Locke*, 178–202.

97   E.J. Lowe, *Subjects of Experience*, 32. See also E.J. Lowe, *Locke on Human Understanding*, Chapter 5, where Lowe argues that the vicious circularity of Locke's argument can only be overcome with recourse to an idea of a substantial self.

98   Ayers, *Locke*, 295. Whereas for Locke particular substances 'are nothing but several Combinations of simple *Ideas*, co-existing in such, though unknown, Cause of their Union, as makes the whole subsist of itself,' which combination of ideas we are apt to suppose to 'rest in, and be, as it were, adherent to that unknown common Subject, which inheres not in anything else.' *Essay*, II.xxiii.6.

99   Ayers, *Locke*, 284.

100   Thiel, 'Personal Identity', 903. See also Thiel, 'Locke's Concept of a Person', 183.

101   Thiel, *The Early Modern Subject*, 122. Despite the title of Thiel's book, the concept of the subject itself is not investigated but mostly used in this way to refer to the substrate of consciousness.

One last example will show the nature of the problem here. For Strawson, 'Locke requires – or rather takes for granted – the continuity of a subject of experience [S],'[102] where '[S]' 'may be constituted of other substances at other times, but must always be constituted of some substance or substances at any time that it exists.'[103] With this Strawson distinguishes between the category of the subject and the concept of substance, but remains unable to fully separate them conceptually. Strawson reads Locke as presupposing that substance is a component of the subject or the person, as if the question animating Locke's discussion was: in what does the person (subject) consist? Which components make up the person or subject – of what is it made? This already thinks subject as object-like, such that the same kinds of questions are asked of it as are asked of other objects. The possibility that Locke's discussion of personal identity develops – or at least broaches – a wholly different problematic of the subject is not considered. The subject as subjectivity is distinguished from the sense of the subject as substance precisely because it is the concept of a subject that can *consider itself* as subject, which can *assume* the position of subject. This is an idea of a different philosophical order than that of the object-subject that Ayers and Strawson analyse.

6. THE PERSON AND THE SUBJECT OF POLITICS

Having distinguished between these two groups of meaning of 'subject' – the subject as substance and the subject as subjectivity – we are better able to understand how Balibar's characterization of Chapter XXVII of Locke's *Essay* as 'an essential moment in the invention of the modern subject' locates Locke in relation to a Kantian and post-Kantian, Franco-German philosophical tradition to which 'subjectivity' is central. We can also see how the confusion of these two meanings of the subject has blocked a certain understanding of Locke's account of the person and condemned criticism of it to the repetition of hoary objections, in particular the objection of circularity and its concomitant reliance on, or recourse to, a notion of substance. With Balibar's interpretation of Locke, a twist of the theoretical kaleidoscope leaves us with a much-altered picture of Locke's achievement in Chapter XXVII of the *Essay* and of his role in the development of modern European philosophy.[104]

---

102   Strawson, *Locke on Personal Identity*, 79.
103   Ibid., 59.
104   To say nothing, in detail, of the *bouleversement* of the received history of Western philosophy, the unseating of Descartes as the first philosopher of 'subjectivity'. Elsewhere Balibar explains in more detail how Kant's projection onto Descartes of his own conception of the transcendental subject, and the accusation (in the Paralogisms of Pure Reason) concerning the illegitimate substantialisation of the transcendental subject, established this received history – a history promulgated, notably, by Heidegger. See Balibar, 'Subjection and Subjectivation', 5–6; Balibar et al., 'Subject', 29–32'; Balibar, 'Citizen Subject', 33–7.

But Balibar also claims that one of the aims of *Identity and Difference* is to indicate how the discussion of personal identity allows us to understand the 'general economy' of the *Essay*, and in particular its moral and political dimensions. (*ID*, 2) The overarching terms of this general economy extend beyond the *Essay*, perhaps most importantly to the *Two Treatises of Government*. They are constituted via a mobile constellation of concepts that deserve a study of their own: *appropriation, property, ownness, propriety, concernment, accountability* and the *inalienable*. Since the publication of *Identity and Difference*, Balibar has continued to worry away at these concepts in his ongoing interrogation of Locke. One of the central arguments that crystallizes across this work concerns the emergence of identity, in Locke's writings, as an *effect of* appropriation and the inalienable, rather than its (logical, ontological or social) condition of possibility.[105] This argument goes behind the abstract distinction between, on the one hand, the realm of politics and civil society, and, on the other, the domain of the private individual. Deeper than Macpherson's identification of Locke's 'social assumptions' (concerning a market economy) with the possessive individual, Balibar's unpicking and re-stitching of Locke's conceptual fabric reveals a conception of the individual identified in/as his/her property, the idea of having 'a property in one's own person' being 'the ultimate point where *propriety* meets with *property*, where to "be" rejoins "to have", the point *from which* persons and things will start to diverge, to become opposite terms'.[106]

This means, of course, that politics seeps into *An Essay Concerning Human Understanding* – or perhaps seeps out of it. Traditionally, commentary and criticism of Locke has tended to treat the *Essay* as separate from Locke's political philosophy, and indeed has often seen the central epistemological premises of the *Essay* as basically irreconcilable with the political theory of the *Two Treatises*

---

105   As well as the entries in the Glossary covering some of these terms (particlarly Appropriate; Concern, To Be Concerned; Own, To Own), see also Étienne Balibar, '"Possessive Individualism" Reversed: From Locke to Derrida', *Constellations* 9: 3, 2002; 'My Self and My Own', in Bill Maurer and Gabrielle Schwab, eds, *Accelerating Possession: Global Futures of Property and Personhood*, New York: Columbia University Press, 2006.

106   Balibar, '"Possessive Individualism" Reversed', 303. Ian Harris (*The Mind of John Locke: A Study of Political Theory in its Intellectual Setting*, Cambridge: Cambridge University Press, 1998, 227) explains that the seventeenth-century meaning of *dominium* as exclusive control over self was also called *suum*, or property: 'This control referred to the qualities inhering in a person and was thought to comprise his life, limbs, liberty, and so on.' Opponents of absolutism argued that material possessions belonged with these, so property in the ordinary sense qualified as *suum*. This was 'to move property (in the concrete sense) on the conceptual map'. Locke secured it by arguing that 'a deployment of the agent's *dominium*, his property in the wider sense, produced property in the narrower one'.

The dysymmetry of this 'his/her' in the quotation from Balibar and its relation to Luce Irigaray's claim that 'any theory of "the subject" has always been appropriated by the "masculine"', is one of the major questions that any study building on Balibar's work would have now to answer. (Irigaray, *Speculum of the Other Woman*, trans. Gillian C. Gill, Ithaca, NY: Cornell University Press, 1985, 133–46.)

of Government.[107] But Balibar's explicit excavation of the relation between property and propriety (ownness) draws the *Essay* and the *Two Treatises* closer together. Balibar acknowledges that in this, the spirit of *Identity and Difference* is indebted to C.B. Macpherson's now-classic study from 1962, *The Political Theory of Possessive Individualism*, despite the fact that Macpherson says next to nothing there about Locke's *Essay*. (*ID*, 72) Macpherson argued that Locke's political theory (specifically the *Two Treatises of Government*) read back into the idea of the state of nature certain 'social assumptions', 'preconceptions about the nature of seventeenth-century man and society which he generalized quite unhistorically'. These assumptions correspond to 'the actual relations of a market society'. Locke, that is, assumes that individuals pre-exist society and that the individual is to be defined as, by nature, a property owner, albeit first of all 'the sole proprietor of his own person and capacities – the absolute proprietor in the sense that he owes nothing to society for them – and especially the absolute proprietor of his capacity to labour'. With a 'natural propensity to unlimited accumulation', individuals *naturally* acquire unequal amounts of property in the state of nature, an inequality which it is the role of government to protect.[108]

Despite Macpherson's identification of the 'possessive quality' of seventeenth-century individualism in 'its conception of the individual as essentially the proprietor of his own person or capacities',[109] he does not attempt to link this with Locke's discussion of the idea of the person in the *Essay*. However, we can imagine what would have happened if he had. Macpherson's assumption of the idea of 'self-proprietorship' as an essentially economic concept would no doubt have made the 'person' of the *Essay* a *persona economicus*, modelled on the idea of the possessive individual – an approach in which the philosophical aspects of the *Essay* would, essentially, be thought as determined by Locke's politics, or at least his veiled political assumptions. This is the approach taken by Neal Wood in *The Politics of Locke's Philosophy* (1983), where aspects of Locke's *Essay* are explained according to their being 'rooted in a particular social outlook' which includes, notably, the bourgeois ideal of the rational individual as the basis of society. For Wood, this means that Locke conflates the acquisitive self of bourgeois individualism (the 'conative self') with the 'cognitive self', producing a market-model theory of knowledge as acquisition.[110] Ellen Meiksins Wood's

---

107   See, for example, Peter Laslett's Introduction to his edited edition of Locke's *Two Treatises of Government*, Cambridge: Cambridge University Press, 1960, especially 79–92. The notable exception in English is Neal Wood's *The Politics of Locke's Philosophy: A Social Study of An Essay Concerning Human Understanding*, Berkeley: University of California Press, 1983.

108   C.B. Macpherson, *The Political Theory of Possessive Individualism: Hobbes to Locke*, Oxford: Oxford University Press, 1962, 4, 197, 231, 235.

109   Macpherson, *The Political Theory of Possessive Individualism*, 3.

110   Neal Wood, *The Politics of Locke's Philosophy*, 3, 157.

earlier *Mind and Politics* (1972) similarly identifies a politically motivated conception of human nature as the basis of Locke's political theory, a conception that she *identifies with* Locke's conception of the self in the *Essay*.[111]

The virtue of this approach is its insistence on the relationship between philosophy and politics; its weakness, though, is its tendency to see this relationship from only one side, to see philosophy as *only* the ideological outcrop of politics. This is an effect of the disciplinary specificity of these works, of their primarily political analyses. Balibar's analyses of the relation between property and propriety are, on the other hand, what we can call *transdisciplinary*: they are the elaboration of a transdisciplinary effect in which the non-economic aspects of the concepts are *also* active. Others had already pointed out that Macpherson had erred in assuming that the concept of propriety was, in the seventeenth century, a primarily economic concept.[112] But only Balibar has attempted to pursue the transdisciplinary functioning of the concept of propriety in the politico-philosophical conjuncture of Locke's work.

We also see this in relation to another episode in the adventures of 'the subject', and some of the propositions to which it has given rise in Balibar's work. The third main meaning of 'subject' identified in the 'Subject' entry of the *Vocabulaire* is one frequently employed in Locke's *Two Treatises of Government* and manifestly (but only manifestly) absent from the *Essay*. This is what we might call the 'juridico-political' concept of the subject: the *subject as subjected*, 'the subject as an individual or a person submitted to the exercise of a power, whose model is, first of all, political, and whose concept is juridical.'[113] Corresponding to the Latin *subjectus*, the subject in this sense is (at least until the French Revolution) distinguished from the slave (*servus*) in being, in some sense, voluntarily subjected to the sovereign power (the subject 'performs his own subjection'),[114] but *subjected* nevertheless. One of the most complex conceptual intrigues of modern European philosophy concerns the relation between this juridico-political subject and the subject as (autonomous) subjectivity. Balibar noted the linguistic 'enigma' of the 'historical play on words' involved here at the same moment as the enigma of Coste's translation was driving his work on Locke. In 1994 he asked: 'why is it that the very *name* which allows modern philosophy to think and to designate the *originary freedom* of the human being – the name of the "subject" – is precisely the name which *historically* meant suppression of freedom, or at least intrinsic limitation of free-

---

111   Ellen Meiksins Wood, *Mind and Politics: An Approach to the Meaning of Liberal and Socialist Individualism*, Berkeley: University of California Press, 1972, 3, 61, and passim.

112   See, for example, James Tully, *An Approach to Political Philosophy: Locke in Contexts*, Cambridge: Cambridge University Press, 1993, 81–2.

113   'Citizen Subject', 38, see also 39–43; and Balibar et al., Subject', 38.

114   Balibar, 'Subjection and Subjectivation', 10.

dom, i.e. *subjection*?'[115] This 'contradiction' between two meanings of the same word then becomes embedded in the paradoxical notion of the 'sovereign subject', what (or, rather, who) Balibar calls the 'citizen subject'.

The idea of the citizen subject is one that seeks, not to overcome the 'contradiction' between the history of subjection and the history of freedom in the concept of the subject, but to demonstrate its dialectic. For Balibar it is no coincidence that the historical moment of the philosophical production of the 'transcendental subject' (in Kant's *Critique of Pure Reason*, 1781/1787) is also the moment of the substitution of the sovereign 'citizen subject' for the subject subjected to the Sovereign (1789), 'that moment at which politics destroys the "subject" of the prince, in order to replace him with the republican citizen'.[116]

Kant's notion of the transcendental subject is a remote, philosophical registration of the revolution (a word that Kant himself does not eschew) in idealist form. With the notion of the citizen subject, on the other hand, Balibar emphasizes that the subject's freedom is concretely realized only in the civic or political realm. That is, 'the freedom of the subject' refers not to the essence of subjectivity itself, as 'an originary source of spontaneity and autonomy'; rather, '"freedom" can only be the result and counterpart of liberation, emancipation, *becoming* free: a trajectory inscribed *in* the very texture of the individual, with all its contradictions, which starts with subjection and always maintains an inner or outer relation with it'.[117] The revolutionaries of 1789 did not become conscious of a pre-existing freedom, they were not 'always already destined to liberty'. Rather, they

> were able to begin thinking of themselves as free subjects, and thus to identify liberty and subjectivity *because* they had abolished the principle of their subjection, their being subjected or subject-being in an irreversible if not irresistible manner, while conquering or constituting their political citizenship.[118]

Accordingly, what originally looked like a contradiction between two meanings of 'subject' is, in Balibar's idea of the citizen subject, the immanent inscription of the (constitutively incomplete) achievement of collective self-emancipation from subjection.[119]

---

115   Ibid., 8.
116   Balibar, 'Citizen Subject', 39.
117   Balibar, 'Subjection and Subjectivation', 9.
118   Ibid., 11–12.
119   Thus the citizen subject is an ideal: 'Citizenship is not one among other attributes of subjectivity, on the contrary: it *is* subjectivity, that form of subjectivity that would no longer be identical with subjection for anyone. This poses a formidable problem for citizens, since few of them, in fact, will achieve it completely.' Ibid., 12.

The notion of the citizen subject is one of the more obviously political conceptions of the subject in twentieth-century French philosophy. As part of a twentieth-century history it needs to be thought alongside the emphasis on the element of pure subjection in Althusser's account of the subject (the individual interpellated by ideology), the subject's subjection to the signifier in Lacan's psychoanalytical theory, and the three major aspects of the 'theory of the subject' (if such it is) in Foucault: i) subjectivity as forms of subjection; ii) the intensification of the contradiction between subjection and subjectivity in the notion of subjectivation; and iii) the self-formation of the subject through the care of the self.[120] Of these, it is the notion of subjectivation to which Balibar is closest, to the extent that it registers the dialectic of subjection and subjectivity internally. Thus the distinction between these last two meanings of 'subject' (as subjected and as subjectivity) is made only in order that their uneasy but essential conjunction in the idea of the citizen subject or of subjectivation may be marked.

What, then, is Locke's place in this? Balibar et al. hint at the 'hidden link' between the juridical concept of the person (which, as we have seen, underlies Locke's conception) and the dimension of subjection at work in the notion of the subject.[121] Can we reveal anything of this link, and its link to 'subjectivity', in Locke? Balibar notes, we may recall, the philosophical-political conjunction of the production of the 'transcendental subject' and the 'citizen subject' substituted for the subject subjected to the Sovereign. We might also note, then, the earlier conjunction of Locke's philosophical production of the idea of the 'person' in the *Essay*, and his rejection of self-constituted or natural monarchical authority in his *Two Treatises of Government*. But if the citizen is, according to Balibar, 'unthinkable as an "isolated individual", for it is his active participation in politics that makes him exist', is Locke's political subject still in essence a subjected – *because isolated* – subject? Or is the crossing of the personal subject with the political subject in Locke's works a transitional moment between subjected subject and citizen subject, part of that 'whole labour of definition of the juridical, moral, and intellectual individual'[122] that, according to Balibar, prepares for

---

120   Focussing on the relations between habit, custom, education and self-perfection in Locke's *Essay*, Tully (*An Approach to Political Philosophy*, 239, 240) understands Locke's 'self' – what Tully calls 'the penalised self' – in the first of these Foucauldian ways, produced 'by subjection to a way of governing action that aims at forming habitual mental and physical conduct . . . Locke could assume that this penalized self was constituted prior to the juridical apparatus that governs and subjects it. We should ask, rather, if this self . . . is not a product of centuries of subjection to juridical governance. Is it not a form of subjectivity that continues to be imposed on us in virtue of the juridical mode of governance being invested in our social practices?'
121   Balibar et al., 'Subject', 25.
122   Ibid., 51, 45.

the substitution? If so, it would, in part, be Locke himself who provided the intellectual materials that would contribute towards the overcoming of his own profound individualism.[123]

7. THE INCOMPLETE LOCKE

In reflecting, around the time of the publication of *Identity and Difference*, on his own philosophical practice, Balibar re-iterated the conviction that has been both one of the starting points and one of the results of his work:

> philosophy is never independent of specific conjunctures. It should be clear that I use this word in a qualitative rather than a quantitative sense, stressing by it the very brief or prolonged event of a crisis, a transition, a suspense, a bifurcation, which manifests itself by irreversibility, i.e., in the impossibility of acting and thinking as before.[124]

Although this includes individual examples, Balibar emphasizes the greater significance of the *collective* examples, that is:

> examples that show how philosophers see their discourse internally connected to one another (and connected to non-philosophical, e.g., theological, legal, scientific discourses) in the same conjuncture . . . For example . . . 'the invention of consciousness' in the conjuncture of '1690' (the mechanistic or spiritualist Cartesians, Malebranche, Leibniz, and Locke).[125]

In the same text, Balibar also writes of the 'incompleteness' proper to philosophical texts, an incompleteness which requires their constant reinterpretation (or even 'rewriting') (and, we might, add, thereby explains how the history of philosophy remains alive). Balibar refers here mainly to the incompleteness of

---

123   Any attempt to pursue this line of thought would have to take account of an important *class* of subjects in Locke's social and political world, and their place in the subject/subjection dialectic: servants. (I am indebted to Mark Neocleous for pointing this out.) In the *Two Treatises of Government* Locke famously claims that as 'every Man has a *Property* in his own *Person* . . . the Labour of his Body and the *Work* of his Hands, we may say, are properly his. Whatsoever then he removes out of the State that Nature hath provided, and left it in, he hath mixed his *Labour* with, and joyned to it something that is his own, and thereby makes it his *Property*'. (Second Treatise, Chapter V, § 25, 287–8.) As what was before common has no use prior to this inmixing of labour, Locke concludes: 'Thus the Grass my Horse has bit; the Turfs my Servant has cut; and the Ore I have digg'd in any place where I have a right to them in common with others, become my *Property*, without the assignation or consent of any body'. (Chapter V, § 28, 289.) What kind of a subject is this servant? For a discussion of the importance of this passage see Montag, 'On the Function of the Concept of Origin'.

124   Balibar, 'The Infinite Contradiction', *Yale French Studies* 88, 1995, 144.

125   Balibar, 'The Infinite Contradiction', 145.

canonical texts, but also refers to his own work as 'this incomplete investigation of the history of the concept of "subject"'.[126]

The analysis of Locke in *Identity and Difference* exhibits the 'conjuncture of "1690"' in philosophical terms mainly, but as part of Balibar's 'incomplete investigation of the history of the concept of "subject"', it allows for the incompleteness of the question of the political subject in Locke to emerge. In this sense, *Identity and Difference* does not lead us to conclusions about Locke; rather, it opens a new chapter for investigation. Read on.

---

126   Ibid., 149. See also 146.

CHAPTER ONE

Locke's Treatise on Identity

Chapter XXVII ('Of Identity and Diversity') of Book II of *An Essay Concerning Human Understanding*, added to the second edition (1694) of the work Locke had published first in 1690, would become the acknowledged or unacknowledged reference for all the great 'theories of knowledge' and 'sciences of the experience of consciousness' in Western philosophy, from Leibniz's *New Essays Concerning Human Understanding* (which is presented as a 'dialogue' with the *Essay*'s formulations) to Condillac's *Essay on the Origin of Human Knowledge*, Kant's *Critique of Pure Reason*, Reid's *Essays on the Intellectual Powers of Man*, Hegel's *Phenomenology of Spirit* and even Bergson's *Time and Free Will* and Husserl's *Ideas*. It practically constitutes an essay within the *Essay* or, as I will henceforth say, a 'treatise'.[1] Not only was it added after the fact (at the suggestion of his friend, William Molyneux), in part to confront the objections raised by the critique of the idea of a substantial soul, and in part to resolve the difficulties created by the *Essay*'s argumentation in the eyes of the author himself, but it also develops according to its own order and advances a set of arguments, which could be isolated from their context, intended to resolve the 'problem of personal identity'. As such, these arguments have determined a long succession of debates up to our own time, especially in Anglo-American philosophy, to whose originality they have greatly contributed.[2]

For my part, however, while taking advantage of this autonomy to detach the treatise, 'Identity and Difference', from a retranslation of Locke's text in its entirety, I did so not to isolate the question of the 'criterion of identity' but in order to situate it in its context. By making consciousness the criterion of personal identity, Locke was led, in effect, to revolutionize the very conception of subjectivity, as much in relation to the Aristotelian idea of the individual soul (*l'âme*) as a 'substantial form', as to the Cartesian claim of an existing and thinking 'I'. This theoretical revolution – which still governs us, up to and including our critiques of psychologism, the primacy of consciousness and the imperialism of the subject – is the decisive moment of *the invention of consciousness* as a philosophical concept, with Locke himself as the primary protagonist. On the one hand, this revolution crystallizes the different implications of the invention (the possibility of an interior

---

1   The other autonomous development (an outline of a 'Treatise on the Passions') is represented by Chapter XXI of Book II, 'Of Power', the central figure of which is the concept of 'uneasiness'. It was not simply added, but considerably expanded in the 1694 edition.

2   See the assessment proposed by H. E. Allison in 'Locke's Theory of Personal Identity', and by J. Baillie, 'Recent Work on Personal Identity', *Philosophical Books* 34, 1993, 193–206.

experience with direct access to 'mental reality', the recasting of the classical conception of time and of the relation between knowledge and responsibility). On the other, it has already established the site in which, beginning with Hume, Kant and Hegel, the critiques of self-consciousness as the effect of a 'fiction' of the imagination, as a paralogism of pure reason or as the figure of a self 'alienated from itself' will be situated. In this sense, at the very moment Locke inaugurated what has become for us the primary or first philosophical modernity, he established the conditions for the opening of a second modernity.

In the following pages I propose three objectives for our (re)reading of Locke's treatise:

1) To restore to the invention of consciousness, self and self-consciousness the force of its novelty, showing above all how, in French philosophical language (and indeed others), despite the efforts of Locke's translator, it was effaced through the attribution of a fictive paternity to Descartes.[3]

2) To situate the Lockean treatise on identity and difference in the broader history of the European invention of consciousness, several of whose episodes I have discussed elsewhere.[4]

3) To indicate how the conjunction of the questions of personal identity and of the mind's knowledge of its own operations is situated in the *Essay* and how this conjunction permits a better understanding of the general economy and articulation of the remainder of Locke's work (particularly its moral, religious and political dimension). This clarification will be further developed in the Glossary that follows this text.

1. THE ENIGMA OF TRANSLATION: PIERRE COSTE'S 'EXPEDIENT'[5]

We once believed that Descartes was the first of the great 'philosophers of consciousness'. France, even expatriated in Holland, had this glory. And we

---

3   My position on this point has already been asserted by some authors, notably Francis Jacques in his preface to the French translation of Gilbert Ryle's *The Concept of Mind*: 'but why did the author concern himself so little with establishing through a precise identification of the Cogito, an equitable imputation of responsibilities? . . . Because finally if he had wanted to present his adversary in his historical reality, he could have done so: in the person of John Locke. It was he and not Descartes who prescribed a minute examination of the states and operations of consciousness . . . It was the Anglo-Saxon philosopher who maintained that the mind could see or observe its own operations in the light that they emitted'. (*La notion d'esprit*, Paris: Payot, 1978, VI).

4   For a more precise account, see my article 'Conscience' in Cassin, ed., *Vocabulaire*.

5   The first version of the following pages was presented in 1992 at a conference on 'Translating philosophers' organized by Olivier Bloch at the University of Paris I. The present version benefitted from personal observations by Catherine Glyn Davies, author herself of the irreplaceable study *'Conscience' as Consciousness: The Idea of Self-Awareness in French Philosophical Writing from Descartes to Diderot* (Oxford: The Voltaire Foundation, 1990), to whom I am greatly indebted.

were reassured by the famous, and still recent, controversies that set in opposition interpreters (Gueroult, Alquié) who, while they diverged radically on the meaning and properties of the Cartesian 'consciousness', agreed all the more in seeing a theory of the identity of consciousness and of the subject at the heart of the 'meditation'. We also believed that we knew (as the dictionaries of philosophy repeated, echoing each other) that he had introduced the very term 'consciousness' (*conscience*) in the sense understood as metaphysical, but also as psychological, transcendental, epistemological (by means of the well-known controversies concerning the equivalence and compatibility of these terms), to distinguish it from its supposedly 'moral' meaning.[6]

The first point is undoubtedly independent of the second: it cannot be absolutely ruled out that Descartes conceived and even placed at the centre of his philosophy a 'thing' in which we retrospectively recognize what we call 'consciousness', but this can be determined only after carefully examining what distinguishes his theses from those of a Locke, a Kant, a Husserl, a Freud or a Bergson. It remains the case that the idea of an anonymous or pseudonymous concept is difficult to assume: if Descartes elaborated a doctrine of consciousness and its foundational character without giving it a name, or by giving it another name, how would we know it? If he had articulated his doctrine of consciousness by means of a diverse terminology that contained a number of only partially equivalent terms, where would the demonstration of their systematic articulation be found? Only by invoking the following tautology: Descartes' philosophy being essentially that of consciousness, the complete system of Cartesian concepts constitutes its description, and so on.

Inversely, the idea of Descartes' introduction of the term 'consciousness' into philosophy does not imply that he merits the title of philosopher of consciousness or of the *primacy* of consciousness in the sense that, for different reasons, neither Spinoza, Hegel, Comte, Nietzsche, Frege, Wittgenstein, Heidegger nor Cavaillès are so considered: we may, however, surmise that this idea owes its apparent credibility to a reading of Cartesian philosophy whose longevity and historical importance it would be futile to contest, although it would be useful to verify its claims.

For Descartes is neither the 'introducer' nor the 'inventor' of 'consciousness'. And I strongly doubt that from this point on it will be possible to see him

---

6 See F. Brémondy's entry 'Conscience' in *Les notions philosophique. Dictionnaire*. Ed. S Auroux (Paris: PUF, 1990), 432–3. A slightly different version of the story is proposed in the entry 'Bewusstsein' by A. Diemer in the *Historisches Wörterbuch der Philosophie*: 'Der moderne Bewusstseinsbegriff ist nach allgemeiner Auffassung [sic] durch Descartes konstituiert . . . vom Gewissensbegriff losgelöst . . . und umgekehrt zum zentralen anthropologischen Begriff "geworden".' The 'possible confusion' of the two meanings of *conscience* proper to French, in comparison to the German *Gewissen* and *Bewusstsein*, and the English *conscience* and *consciousness*, is also sometimes noted.

as the typical, even archetypal, 'philosopher (of the primacy) of consciousness.'
Neither in the psychological sense of the term (but where does psychology or
psychologism start or stop?), nor in the metaphysical or transcendental sense. I
do not owe this disillusion primarily to philosophical argumentation (even if
certain contemporary work around Lacan, Canguilhem and Wittgenstein might
have prepared us for it), but to a particular philological encounter with Pierre
Coste, the French translator of Locke's *Essay* in 1700, which was, until only very
recently, the only complete French translation.[7]

This archaism is, for once, fortunate in that it holds open the possibility that
any student, any French reader, may still stumble on the two translator's notes
on page 264 of the French edition, concerning paragraph 9, Chapter XXVII of
Book II:[8]

(1) Le *moi* de M. *Pascal* m'autorise en quelque manière à me servir du mot *soi, soi-*
même, pour exprimer ce sentiment que chacun a en lui-même qu'il est *le même*; ou
pour mieux dire, j'y suis obligé par une nécessité indispensable; car je ne saurais
exprimer autrement le sens de mon Auteur, qui a pris la même liberté dans sa
Langue. Les périphrases que je pourrais employer dans cette occasion, embarrasse-
raient le discours, et le rendraient peut-être tout à fait inintelligible.

Which we may translate as follows:

M. Pascal's *moi* has authorized me in a certain sense to make use of the word '*soi,*
soi-même' to express the sentiment that each has in himself that he is the same; or
rather, to put it more truthfully, I was obliged by an indispensable necessity to do
so. For I did not know how to express the author's meaning otherwise, given that he
had taken the same liberty with his own language. The paraphrases I might have
employed on this occasion would have encumbered the discourse and perhaps
rendered it completely unintelligible.

And:

(2) Le mot Anglais est *consciousness*, qu'on pourrait exprimer en Latin par celui de
conscientia, si sumatur pro actu illo hominis quo sibi est conscius. Et c'est en ce sens
que les Latins ont souvent employé ce mot, témoin cet endroit de *Cicéron* (Epist. ad
Famil. Lib. VI. Epist. 4.) *Conscientia rectae voluntatis maxima consolatio est rerum*
incommodarum. En Français nous n'avons à mon avis que les mots de *sentiment* et

---

7   A new translation of Books I and II by Jean-Michel Vienne appeared in 2001, followed
by Books III and IV in 2006 (Paris: Vrin).

8   I reproduce here the reprinted, revised and corrected fifth edition of 1755. E. Naert, ed.,
Essai philosophique concernant l'Entendement humain, traduit de l'Anglois par M. Coste, Paris: Vrin,
1972.

de *conviction* qui répondent en quelque sorte à cette idée. Mais en plusieurs endroits de ce Chapitre ils ne peuvent qu'exprimer fort imparfaitement la pensée de M. Locke, qui fait absolument dépendre l'*identité personnelle* de cet acte de l'Homme *quo sibi est conscius.* J'ai appréhendé que tous les raisonnements que l'Auteur fait sur cette matière, ne fussent entièrement perdus, si je me servais en certaines rencontres du mot de *sentiment* pour exprimer ce qu'il entend par *consciousness*, et que je viens d'expliquer. Après avoir songé quelque temps aux moyens de remédier à cet inconvénient, je n'en ai point trouvé de meilleur que de me servir du terme de *Conscience* pour exprimer cet acte même. C'est pourquoi j'aurai soin de le faire imprimer en Italique, afin que le Lecteur se souvienne d'y attacher toujours cette idée. Et pour faire qu'on distingue encore mieux cette signification d'avec celle qu'on donne ordinairement à ce mot, il m'est venu dans l'esprit un expédient qui paraîtra d'abord ridicule à bien des gens, mais qui sera au goût de plusieurs autres, si je ne me trompe; c'est d'écrire *conscience* en deux mots joints par un tiret, de cette manière, *con-science*. Mais, dira-t-on, voilà une étrange licence, de détourner un mot de sa signification ordinaire, pour lui en attribuer une qu'on ne lui a jamais donnée en notre Langue. A cela je n'ai rien à répondre. Je suis choqué moi-même de la liberté que je prends, et peut-être serais-je des premiers à condamner un autre Écrivain qui aurait eu recours à un tel expédient. Mais j'aurais tort, ce me semble, si après m'être mis à la place de cet Écrivain, je trouvais enfin qu'il ne pouvait se tirer autrement d'affaire. C'est à quoi je souhaite qu'on fasse réflexion, avant que de décider si j'ai bien ou mal fait. J'avoue que dans un Ouvrage qui ne serait pas, comme celui-ci, de pur raisonnement, une pareille liberté serait tout à fait inexcusable. Mais dans un Discours Philosophique non seulement on peut, mais on doit employer des mots nouveaux, ou hors d'usage, lorsqu'on n'en a point qui expriment l'idée *précise* de l'Auteur. Se faire un scrupule d'user de cette liberté dans un pareil cas, ce serait vouloir perdre ou affaiblir un raisonnement de gaité de cœur; ce qui serait, à mon avis, une délicatesse fort mal placée. J'entends, lorsqu'on y est réduit par une nécessité indispensable, qui est le cas où je me trouve dans cette occasion, si je ne me trompe. – Je vois enfin que j'aurais pu sans tant de façon employer le mot de *conscience* dans le sens que M. Locke l'a employé dans ce Chapitre et ailleurs, puisqu'un de nos meilleurs écrivains, le fameux Père *Malebranche*, n'a pas fait de difficulté de s'en servir dans ce même sens en plusieurs endroits de la *Recherche de la Vérité.* Après avoir remarqué dans le Chap. VII du IIIe Livre qu'il faut distinguer quatre manières de connaître les choses, il dit que *la troisième est de les connaître par conscience ou par sentiment intérieur. Sentiment intérieur* et *conscience* sont donc, selon lui, des termes synonymes. *On connaît par conscience*, dit-il un peu plus bas, *toutes les choses qui ne sont point distinguées de soi . . . Nous ne connaissons point notre Ame*, dit-il encore, *par son idée*, nous *ne la connaissons que par conscience . . . La conscience que nous avons de nous-mêmes ne nous montre que la moindre partie de notre Être.* Voilà qui suffit pour faire voir en quel sens j'ai employé le mot de *conscience*, et pour en autoriser l'usage.

We may translate this second note as follows:

The English word is 'consciousness', which might be expressed in Latin as *conscientia, si sumatur pro actu illo hominis quo sibi est conscius*. The Latins often used the word in this sense, as in the case of Cicero's Epist. Ad Famil. Lib. VI, Epis. 4: *Conscientia rectae voluntatis maxima consolatio est rerum incommodarum*. In French, in my opinion, only the words *sentiment* and *conviction* correspond in some measure to this idea. But in several places in this chapter they can only express M. Locke's thought very imperfectly, insofar as he makes the idea of *personal identity* depend absolutely on the action of Man, *quo sibi est conscius*. I apprehended that the Author's reasonings on this matter would be entirely lost if I made use at certain junctures of the word *sentiment* to express what he means by *Consciousness*, as I have just explained. After having thought for some time about the means of remedying this inconvenience, I could find nothing better than to use the term *conscience* to express the act itself. This is why I will take care to have it printed in italics to remind the reader always to connect it to this idea. And to make sure that this meaning is to an even greater extent distinguished from that ordinarily attached to this word, I thought of an expedient that will at first seem ridiculous to many people, even as it may, if I am not mistaken, gratify the tastes of others: to write *conscience* as two words joined by a dash, in this manner: *con-science*. But, it will be said, this is a strange license you have taken to detach a word from its ordinary signification in order to attribute to it another that has never been given to it in our language. To this, I have nothing to say. I am shocked myself at the liberty I have taken and would perhaps be the first to condemn another writer who had recourse to such an expedient. But I would have been wrong to do so, it seems to me, if, after having put myself in the place of this writer, I concluded that he could not have done otherwise. It is this that I wish others would consider before deciding whether I have done well or badly. I admit that in a work that was not, as this is, one of pure reasoning, such a liberty would be completely inexcusable. But in a philosophical discourse, one is not only permitted, but obliged to employ new words or use words differently than they are customarily used, when there is nothing that will express the author's *precise* idea. To hesitate to take liberties in such a case would be to lose or weaken the reasoning willingly: this would be in my view a scrupulousness put to very bad use. I understand when one is reduced to such expedients by an inescapable necessity – which, if I am not mistaken, is the case in which I find myself on this occasion – I see that I would have been able to use the word *conscience*, as M. Locke uses it in this chapter, without going to such lengths, and even more, because one of our best writers, Father Malebranche, did not find it particularly difficult to use the word in exactly this sense in several places in the *Search After Truth*. After having remarked in chapter 7 of Book III that we must distinguish four ways of knowing things, he says that *the third way is to know them through consciousness or through internal sentiment*. *Internal sentiment* and *consciousness* are thus for him synonymous terms.

One knows through consciousness, he says a little earlier, *all the things that are not distinguished from the self . . . We do not know our Soul through its idea, we know it only through consciousness . . . The consciousness we have of ourselves only shows us a small part of our Being.* This will suffice to make clear the sense in which I have used the word *conscience* and to justify this usage.

Let us pause here for a moment. The preceding passage is that which contemporary readers encounter, and it results from a very instructive transformation: in the first edition of his translation,[9] Coste's second note, identical to the above up to the phrase 'by an inescapable necessity, which, if I am not mistaken, is the case in which I find myself on this occasion', continues in the following way:

Je viens de voir au reste une Bible de la Traduction de *Genève,* où l'on s'est servi du mot de *Conscience* dans le sens que je viens de marquer. C'est dans la première Épître aux Corinthiens, chap. VIII, vers. 7. *Il n'y a pas connaissance en tous, car quelques-uns en mangent* (de ces viandes sacrifiées) *avec* conscience *de l'Idole,* c'est-à-dire, quoiqu'ils sentent, qu'ils croient en eux-mêmes que l'Idole à qui ces viandes sont offertes, est quelque chose, et qu'il leur a communiqué quelque vertu. Je ne rapporte pas cet endroit pour confirmer l'usage du mot de *conscience* en ce sens-là, car je sais que la Version de Genève n'est d'aucune autorité dans notre langue, mais seulement pour faire voir le besoin que nous en avons.

Or, reverting to English:

Further, I have just seen a copy of the Geneva translation of the Bible where the word *conscience* is used in the sense I have just noted. It is in I Corinthians 8:7. *But the knowledge is not in everyone, for some eat of it* (sacrificial food) *with a consciousness [conscience] of the Idol,* that is, although they feel and believe within themselves that the Idol to whom this food is offered is something and that it communicates to them some virtue. I do not relate this passage to verify the use of the term *conscience* in the sense previously noted, for I know that the Geneva edition has no authority in our language, but only to demonstrate the need we have of it.

The term that the pastors in Geneva translated as *conscience* is the Greek *suneidêsis*,[10] about which I will speak later (while *gnôsis* is translated as

---

9   Published in Amsterdam in 1700 by Henri Schelte, publisher of Le Clerc's *Bibliothèque Universelle,* about which I will have more to say.

10   In the École française de Jérusalem's modern version, the translators have used the term 'habitude' (habit) here, which inevitably introduced a discrepancy in relation to the other translations of *suneidêsis* in this context. In the English of the King James version, the word 'conscience' is used throughout (and not 'consciousness').

connaissance). Beginning with the second edition of his translation (1729), Coste suppressed this biblical reference which posed both semantic problems (for we are here at the border between the 'cognitive' and 'moral' uses of *conscience*), as well as problems of theological authority (the book was intended for distribution in France, a Catholic country), and instead introduced the reference to Malebranche that we now know, and which pointed to other problems. We need to account for this rectification.

We may admire the style and the 'conscientiousness' of the author as both translator and philosopher here; nevertheless, it appears that the text – in its two successive versions – contains several difficulties we might profitably seek to clarify. In turn, the inquiry into the elements of this clarification reveals that we are in the presence not only of a crucial account of the formation of the concept of consciousness in modern philosophy – one capable of addressing a number of sources of confusion and myth – but also of a moment in this formation, the neglect or forgetting of which must be remedied if we want to provide a precise account of an invention that continues to determine our thought.

By tracing the history of this invention alongside Locke's treatise, I hope to contribute to the recognition of the philosophical role of the translation of philosophers: for whoever has for nearly three centuries referred in French to *conscience* is governed by the decision made by Pierre Coste, after that of Locke himself. I also intend to underscore – using a privileged example, but one that is undoubtedly not unique – the extent to which the fundamental concepts of our tradition have always emerged out of a certain labour on originally transnational languages.

The first question raised by a reading of Coste's note concerns why it came so late in the *Essay*. And at the same time, why Coste did not translate 'consciousness' by '*conscience*' or '*con-science*' before Chapter XXVII of Book II. His statements seem to suggest that up to that point, partial equivalents (such as 'knowledge', 'sentiment' and 'conviction' – *connaissance, sentiment* and *conviction*) might suffice, but that afterwards they were incompatible with theoretical exactitude (in a work of 'pure reasoning'). They suggest that this is the moment at which certain tensions, arising from the history of Latin and French, must be resolved. But they leave the new element that would intervene shrouded in darkness. And this delay is all the more surprising in that the word 'consciousness' appears in Locke's text *from the first chapter of Book II* (and even, if we take into account the additions to the second edition, in I.xx.4), not in a vague or episodic fashion but in a conceptually systematic way. Indeed, the characterization of consciousness that the Anglo-Saxon tradition generally takes to be definitive of Locke's position appears in II.i.19: 'Consciousness is the perception of what passes in a Man's own mind.' That is: 'consciousness' is the perception of what passes or happens in a man's mind; but also, it is the fact of a man's perceiving what passes or happens in his own mind (in a mind that is his, that properly belongs to him, that is his property).

Coste was clearly aware of the demands of a theoretical translation (and what could we possibly add to what he himself has said of the matter?), and did not retreat from innovation. Why, then, did he render Locke's 'conscious to himself that he thinks' (II.i.1) as *convaincu en lui-même qu'il pense* ('convinced in himself that he thinks')? Similarly, in I.i.2 he translates Locke's 'it being hard to conceive, that anything should think, and not be conscious of it' as *il n'est pas aisé de concevoir qu'une chose puisse penser, et ne point sentir qu'elle pense* ('it is not easy to conceive that a thing can think and not feel that it thinks'); 'without being conscious of it' as *sans en avoir une perception actuelle* ('without having an actual perception of it'); and in II.i.19, the definition of consciousness cited above as *cette conviction n'est autre chose que la perception de ce qui se passe dans l'âme de l'homme* ('this conviction is nothing other than the perception of what happens in a man's soul', etc.), before suddenly, in II.xxvii.9, arriving at *puisque la* con-science *accompagne toujours la pensée, et que c'est là ce qui fait que chacun est ce qu'il nomme* soi-même as the translation of 'since consciousness always accompanies thinking, and 'tis that, that makes everyone to be, what he calls *self*'.

The only basis for a response provided by this precise establishing of context is also crucial – it is the conjunction of the *two* fundamental theoretical terms in a single phrase, not found before this point, but which henceforth become correlatives: the self and consciousness. The question of consciousness comes up before II.xxvii.9, the chapter devoted to the problem of personal identity, but not 'self' as a noun. Coste thus 'invents' *con-science* at the very moment he is constrained by language and by the theoretical material to create not one, but two, neologisms, one pertaining to vocabulary and the other to meaning.[11] We may surmise that these two extraordinary creations are as closely connected for Coste as they are for Locke, but the full significance of this fact will only appear retrospectively.

Before starting down this path, however, it is necessary to try to trace it more clearly through the uses of the terms in question, as much in French as in English and Latin, that is, through the different branches of European co-lingualism.[12] Let us put ourselves in the position of translator and begin with the English. 'The English word is "consciousness" which is expressed in

---

11   Although he invented '*le soi*' to translate 'the self' and '*con-science*' for 'consciousness', Coste was never able, however, to produce a neologism for 'self-consciousness'. It is for this reason that in §16 of Locke's treatise, Coste is content to translate the latter term by using the word '*con-science*' again, adding in a note: 'self-consciousness: an expressive word in English which cannot be rendered into French without losing something of its force. I've included the word here for those who read English'.

12   I have borrowed this concept from Renée Balibar's *Le colinguisme*, Paris: PUF, 1993.

Latin by "*conscientia*"', writes Coste, which proves that he had to resort to Latin to understand what it meant. In effect – and this is a critical element of our problem – 'consciousness' is not only a concept defined by Locke, but is, as an English word, a quasi-neologism, as the most comprehensive of the current lexicographies-dictionaries show.[13] The sole, but crucial, precedent is found in Ralph Cudworth's *True Intellectual System of the Universe* (1678).[14] Locke was clearly conscious of his innovation at the conceptual (if not linguistic) level. The formula always cited as a definition was, in fact, an intervention in the course of his foundational argument against the idea of a 'non-conscious thought', which he believed was implied by the doctrine of innate ideas. It is an *elenchus* which results in an identification of 'thought' and the 'consciousness of thought', since their separation would contradict itself: 'thinking consists in being conscious that one thinks'. (II.i.19) Further, he rigorously distinguished this neologism from the moral concept, 'conscience', which he also thought it necessary to define.[15] What linguistic or conceptual obstacles prevented Coste *here* from making use of the 'expedient' that he would soon employ to express the full significance of Locke's invention?

Let us pursue our inquiry by turning this time to Latin, as Coste himself did. I cannot examine the entire lexicography of the term *conscientia*.[16] It seems clear that the term has always been understood on the basis of 'scientia', that is, knowledge in classical Latin. The prefix 'cum' designates a sharing or a community which gives rise either to the idea of a complicity or connivance with others, or to the idea of an internal tribunal (*for intérieur*), a secret judgment (secret because of the knowledge that one shares only with oneself and to which one answers only in himself). From this follows the classical construction, *sibi*

---

13   Above all the Oxford English Dictionary, which lists as the first uses of 'conscious':
'1625 BACON *Ess., Praise* (Arb.) 353 Wherin a Man is Conscious [MS and ed. 1612 conscient] to himselfe, that he is most Defective. 1690 LOCKE *Hum. Und.* II.i, If they say, That a Man is always conscious to himselfe of thinking.' And for *consciousness*: '1678 CUDWORTH *Intell. Syst.* (1837) I.93 Neither can life and cogitation, sense and consciousness . . . ever result from magnitudes, figures, sites and motions. 1690 LOCKE *Hum. Und.* II.i.§19 Consciousness is the perception of what passes in a Man's own Mind.'

14   Ralph Cudworth, 1617–1688, the importance of whose work is now fully recognized, was a Master of Christ College and the principal exponent of 'Cambridge Platonism'. Locke met him in London in 1681 and became a friend of Cudworth's daughter, Lady Masham (herself the author of philosophical works and a correspondent of Leibniz's), at whose home he spent the last years of his life. Her eulogy to Locke and her account of his life written shortly after his death are found in a letter to Jean Le Clerc, 12 January 1705 (Jean Le Clerc, *Epistolario*, Vol. II (1690–1705), a cura di M. G. e M. Sina, Florence: Leo S. Olschki Editore, 1991, 497–517). On this important figure in the world of European letters, see Sarah Hutton, 'Damaris Cudworth, Lady Masham: Between Platonism and Enlightenment', in *The British Journal for the History of Philosophy* 1: 1, 1993.

15   Locke, *Essay*, I.iii.8: 'nothing else but our own Opinion or Judgment of the Moral Rectitude or Pravity of our own Action'.

16   See Balibar, 'Conscience' in Cassin, *Vocabulaire*. Also, C. S. Lewis, 'Conscience and conscious', *Studies in Words*, Cambridge: Cambridge University Press, 1967.

conscire, sibi conscius esse, rendered in English as 'conscious to (with) oneself (himself)', which does not mean 'being conscious of oneself', but 'being informed, having knowledge' of something (*alicujus rei*) which, further, has a primarily juridical function. In addition, in ancient philosophy, particularly when it is under the influence of Stoicism as in Cicero and Seneca, the privileged domain of application for this knowledge that one shares only with oneself is moral life: the acts, the speech, the intentions whose value is under discussion. *Conscientia* or *conscientia animi* is therefore a synonym for judgment, for one's self-assessment, and for the authority of this evaluation that approves or condemns, testifies for or imposes the penalty of remorse. The game of the duplication of the person (based on the metaphor of the internal 'voice') is set into motion: in *conscientia* am I the one who knows and judges myself, or who is exposed and judged? This game is amplified by the moral casuistry of Christianity: the question then is to know if the 'voice of consciousness' is natural or supernatural, if it emanates from a human capacity, an innate morality, or if it expresses a divine intervention, a warning and the grace that we receive from Heaven.

By translating the Greek *suneidêsis* as *conscientia,* the entire Christian tradition has glossed and changed Saint Paul's statement in Romans 2:15–16:

These men, without having the law, are a law unto themselves [*nomon mè ekhontes heautois eisin nomos*]; they show the work of the law written in their heart, bearing witness with their conscience [*summarturousès autôn tès suneidèséôs*], as well as the internal judgments of condemnation or acquittal which they apply to their own actions. [They will be justified] on the day God judges the secrets of men [*krinei o theos ta krupta tôn anthrôpôn*] according to my gospel.[17]

Augustine identified *conscientia* (a translation of *suneidêsis* as employed by the Greek Fathers) with the internal man (*intus hominis, quod conscientia vocatur,* in Ps. 45, 3), the secret stronghold through which God's gaze will pierce, or better, in which He is already to be found. Jerome will say that the spark of conscience placed in us, *scintilla conscientia,* even burns in criminals and sinners. But the formula employed by Coste (*conscientia, si sumatur pro actu illo hominis quo sibi est conscius*), which logically entails a complement (*alicujus rei*), seems rather to be of scholastic origin.[18] It recalls the definition of *conscientia* in Thomas Aquinas (Sum. Th. Q. 79, art. 13) where the Angelic Doctor

---

17 This passage is closely linked to the formulations on the unveiling of hearts on Judgment Day in 1 Cor. 14:25 and 2 Cor. 5:10. Locke would make it the basis of his discussion in §22 and §26 of his treatise on identity. (See 'Resurrection', in the *Glossary* below.)

18 The *Thesaurus eruditionis scholasticae* by B. Farber published in 1571 and re-issued in 1696 (cited by Diemer, *Hist. Wört. Der Phil. Art. Bewusstsein*) lists as the second meaning of *conscientia* 'is animi status quo quis alicujus rei sibi conscius est'.

establishes that *conscientia* is not itself 'an intellectual power', but the act corresponding to *synderesis*, the power of the knowledge of practical principles – that is, of moral law – when it is applied to particular concrete cases.[19] We constantly find the terms 'act' or 'actual' used by the translators of Descartes and his interlocutors to describe the 'knowledge' (*connaissance*) that corresponds to *conscientia*. It is important to note here the insistence on the intellectualist aspect of moral conscience (against the doctrines of sentiment, spontaneity, enthusiasm and inspiration). Aquinas took care to situate *conscientia* in an etymology *cum alio scientia* to insist that it is by nature an intellectual act. We are here within a rationalist problematic diametrically opposed to the idea of immediacy or of 'divine instinct' in the manner of Rousseau.

Would it therefore be necessary, in order to explain the meaning of *consciousness* as Coste understood it, to see it as the transposition of a scholastic conception of moral judgment? Even if this background remains present, there are several reasons to oppose a genesis of this type. Locke and Coste were Protestants.[20] 'Conscience' in their language and according to their cultural formation is both a personal inspiration and an affirmation of freedom (after Luther, for whom *Gewissen* and *Gewissheit*, 'conscience' and 'certitude', were closely associated, Calvin placed *adhesion de conscience* or 'adherence to the dictates of conscience' at the centre of the confession of faith, while the Anabaptists formulated the idea of 'conscientious objection', *objection de conscience*). Moreover, Coste translated in an atmosphere dominated by Cartesianism and by discussions of Cartesian doctrine. It is impossible not to take into account the French texts that it is certain Locke himself read. It is here that the explanations offered in Coste's note appear, at first, the most muddled: why call the term '*conscience*' a neologism if it already possesses, as one of its meanings, pure consciousness (*connaissance*) of self? Why does he introduce the reference to Malebranche after the fact and pretend not to have initially observed his authority if the neologism he had used suffices to settle the matter?[21] Why doesn't he mention Descartes?

---

19   Its development in Scholasticism proceeded from Jerome, but through the effect of an astonishing misunderstanding. The copyists thought they read the word '*sunteresis*' in his text, which they interpreted first as a derivative of '*térésis*', *conservatio* ('to keep'), then as a derivative of *hairèsis, electio* ('choice'). Thus was forged a fictional Greek word (*sunderesis*), but one which fulfilled the essential function of dividing conscience into a passive faculty (the trace of divine creation) and an active faculty (operating in the condition of sin after the Fall). Thomas Aquinas and Bonaventure then formed the 'practical syllogism' of the process by which revelation illuminates our actions and guides them: 1. *sunderesis*, 2. *conscientia*, 3. *conclusio*. This represents a fundamental intellectualist way of thinking whose domination in no way disappeared with its theological justification (C.f., H. Reiner, *Hist. Wört. Der Phil. Art. Gewissen*).

20   They belonged to the liberal, Arminian wing of European Protestantism. See my discussion below of Jean Le Clerc's circle.

21   Of course, it is possible that Coste did not initially think of citing Malebranche but later found him a better reference than the Geneva Bible. But it seems very unlikely that Coste was not

A solution to these difficulties may be found in the following observations:

1. Descartes, with two possible exceptions, one of which is doubtful and the other a chance remark, never uses the word 'consciousness' (*conscience*) in French, or the adjective 'conscious' (*conscient*) or the expression 'to be conscious' (*être conscient*).[22] Further, he very rarely used the Latin terms *conscientia* and *conscius esse*, the two major exceptions being found in two closely connected texts: Definitions I and II (*Cogitatio, Idea*) in the *Geometrical Exposition of the Responses to the Second Objections*[23] and article 1.9 of the *Principles of Philosophy*. (In neither case did the French translators, Clerselier and Abbé Picot, whose text was reviewed by Descartes, use the term '*conscient*' [conscious] or '*être conscient*' [to be conscious]). *Conscientia* does not appear in the *Meditations*, which would later be considered the foundation of the theory of the subject conscious of itself, notably in the analyses of the 'thing that thinks' in the Second and Third Meditations, any more than it does in the *Discourse on Method or The Passions of the Soul*. Without Descartes there would not have been any invention of *conscience* in French (and before it 'consciousness' in English), not because he invented it, but because it emerged as a response to difficult problems posed by the inter-pretation of his doctrine.

---

familiar with Malebranche's texts, not only because of their notoriety, but also for a more specific reason: in 1696, when he joined Locke to work on the translation, Locke himself had just finished writing a critique of *The Search After Truth* in which, as we shall see, the terminology of self-knowledge played a central role. For a confirmation of the close association of Locke and Coste in the confrontation with Malebranche, see Jean Deprun, *La philosophie de l'inquiétude en France au XVIIIe siècle*, Paris: Vrin, 1979, 193.

22 See Descartes' Letter to Gibieuf, 19 January 1642. 'I derive this only from my own thought or consciousness'. 'Je ne le tire que de ma propre pensée ou conscience'. G. Rodis-Lewis (*L'œuvre de Descartes*, Paris: Vrin 1971, 240) comments in a note: 'According to a manuscript copy, while the édition Clerselier, perhaps out of excessive scrupulousness, omitted the phrase "*ou conscience*" this term was used in this metaphysical sense in French only once, in the Replies to the Third Set of Objections (A.T. IX, 137): he speaks of "intellectual acts that cannot exist without thought, perception or consciousness and knowledge [*actes intellectuels qui ne peuvent être sans pensée, ou perception, ou conscience et connaissance*] (given that the last two terms represent the translation of the single Latin word, *conscientiae*, from A.T. VII, 176, it is possible that Descartes himself added "or consciousness" [*ou conscience*] to Clerselier's French translation).'

23 In an erudite work which appeared after my own (*L'invention du moi*, Paris: Presses Universitaires de France, 2010, 146–9), Professor Vincent Carraud returned to essentially the same set of texts, with the addition of a handful of others, to draw from them a radically opposed conclusion: 'may we from now credit Locke with the "invention of consciousness" according to the expression that serves as the title of Étienne Balibar's work? Obviously not'. It is certainly his right to do so, even if he refrains from any discussion of my arguments (except implicitly to make use of them . . . against me!) and believes himself duty bound to warn the reader that my articles in the *Vocabulaire européen des philosophies* are 'swarming' [*fourmillent*] with errors (without indicating what they are). This really does not seem to me to be the way to conduct the kind of scholarly discussion that is necessary. I am prepared in principle to accept any corrections to what I have written that follow from such a discussion.

2. 'Conscience' was, however, introduced into French by Descartes' closest disciples, who were engaged in the controversies concerning the dualism of the animal body and mind, as well as the foundations of metaphysics; in the first place, it was used by Louis de la Forge, editor of L'homme (Man) (1664) and author of the Traité de l'Esprit de l'Homme (Treatise on the Mind of Man) (1666).[24] It became the object of a nominal definition in the Système de Philosophie of the Cartesian Pierre-Sylvain Régis, which appeared in 1690, the same year as Locke's Essay: 'I am thus assured that I exist every time I know [connais] or that I believe I know something; and I am convinced of the truth of this proposition not through true reasoning, but by the simple and interior knowledge that precedes all acquired knowledges [connaissances] and which I call consciousness [conscience].'[25]

This double fact draws our attention to one of the directions opened by Descartes' influence and to the way it shaped the French language. But until at least the middle of the eighteenth century, the term 'conscience' in any but a moral sense hardly existed and, to the extent it did, called out for clarification.

3. The great exception is Malebranche, for whom the notion of conscience as consciousness is in effect primordial, and we will have occasion to examine this in detail. But its definition as 'internal sentiment' is fundamentally anti-Cartesian: it compels philosophers to take sides. Malebranche's conscience is the imperfect knowledge we have of the soul ('we know of our soul only what we feel passing in us'). This pseudo-knowledge, while undoubtedly 'not false', is nevertheless essentially confused and exposed to all sorts of illusions. Malebranche clearly understands that he has thus destroyed the very core of Cartesianism for apologetic and theological ends (replacing the cogito with the idea of the divine Word in the position of first truth).[26]

Locke's choice on this point is very clear (and he had been perfectly familiar with the thought of the great Oratorian since his youth): to criticize Descartes differently than Malebranche. His 'consciousness' is not a confused idea that marks the limit of self-knowledge and self-mastery. It is, on the contrary, the

---

24   Louis de La Forge, Treatise on the Human Mind (1664), Trans. Desmond M. Clark, Dordrecht: Kluwer, 1997. See also Geneviève Lewis, Le problème de l'inconscient et le cartésianisme, Paris: PUF, 1950. For complete quotations from Descartes, La Forge, etc. see the dossier in the French edition of my book.

25   Pierre-Sylvain Régis, Système de philosophie, contenant la Logique, la Métaphysique et la Morale (Paris: 1690) T. I, 63. Régis' work was written some years before its publication. (I am grateful to Dr Monette Martinet for this information.)

26   See Jean-Pierre Osier, 'Presentation', Nicolas Malebranche, Traité de Morale (1684), Paris: Garnier-Flammarion, 1995. At the same time that he transfers to the 'internal sentiment' of the soul the functions Descartes attributes to the confused idea of the union of soul and body, Malebranche restores to God the clarity of the cogito and the ontological sufficiency (suffisance) of which it is the sign.

mind's immediate recognition of its operations on its internal stage, an indefinitely open field in which it is both actor and spectator. Locke's 'consciousness' is not 'less conscious', as we would say today, than the Cartesian *cogito* but 'more'. This is undoubtedly why Coste could turn to this important precedent only after long hesitation and, even then, continue to inscribe this difference within the word itself by means of a graphic 'expedient' that served as the mute trace of the latent conflict.

4. Another approach to this situation may be found in an examination of the texts of Leibniz. Against the Cartesian conception of knowledge, Leibniz takes a position opposed to that of Locke: *for innate ideas* and against the notion that the mind can inspect or know itself solely through its own reflection. *The Discourse on Metaphysics* (1686) does not employ the term, but the correspondence with Arnauld contains a number of references to consciousness (associated with 'internal experience', 'thought' and 'reminiscence').[27] In every case, this concept refers to a notion far better integrated into the economy of the system and more decisive for its future development: that of *apperception*, which finally becomes the fundamental notion (see *Monadology*, §14, 1714). It appears that the reading of Locke played a role in this decantation. In Chapter II.xxvii.9 of the *New Essays*, Leibniz, who in general was using Coste's translation of Locke's *Essay*, retranslated 'consciousness' as *conscienciosité*. Thus, he refused Coste's neologism in order to situate consciousness in the system of the categories of perception.[28] The conceptual opposition of Leibniz and Locke, as well as the terminological opposition of Leibniz and Coste, demonstrate that the two sides of the Cartesian metaphysics of the 'thing that thinks' have from this point on become incompatible.

5. It was necessary to wait until Condillac for the term *conscience*, once again presented as an innovation, to be definitively naturalized in French. But this usage was derived from Locke, and consequently from Coste. In explaining the 'analysis and generation of the operations of the soul' in the *Essay on the*

---

27   Leibniz, *Discourse on Metaphysics* and *Correspondence with Arnauld* (Letter 26 from 9 Oct. 1687, available online at archive.org. See also, Martine de Gaudemar, *Leibniz: De la puissance au sujet*, Paris: Vrin, 1994.

28   Leibniz, *New Essays Concerning Human Understanding*, eds P. Remnant and J. Bennett, Cambridge: Cambridge University Press, 1996. Le Clerc's letter to Locke (9 April, 1697) shows that Leibniz had already read the *Essay* in English and had written some remarks for the benefit of his friends. However, the labour that led to the composition of the 'dialogue' (in which Locke's point of view is represented by citations or summaries placed in the mouth of 'Philalethe') in 1702–1703 was based on Coste's translation. Extremely sensitive to the question of philosophical idiom, Leibniz discusses translations by confronting French, English and even German etymologies (for example, in the case of 'uneasiness' in the *New Essays*, where he calls Coste the 'French interpreter') (II.xx.6). The *New Essays* remained unpublished during Leibniz's lifetime (Locke's death in 1704 dissuaded him from pursuing the debate) and were finally published in 1765. The suggestion of retranslating consciousness as *conscienciosité* remained a dead letter, supposing it ever had a chance of being considered.

Origin of Human Knowledge (1746), Condillac begins by examining 'percep-tion, consciousness, attention and reminisicence' (I, 2, 1). In §4:

> It is universally agreed that the mind has perceptions of which it cannot take notice . . .
> The sentiment that produces this knowledge . . . I call 'consciousness'. If, as Locke says,
> the mind has no perception of which it does not take notice, seeing that it would be a
> contradiction for a perception not to be noticed, then perception and consciousness
> must be taken for the same operation. But if on the contrary the opposite sentiment was
> the true one, they would be two distinct operations; and it would be with consciousness
> and not perception, as I have supposed, that our knowledge properly begins.[29]

Condillac, who makes no reference to Descartes, will introduce the concept of *attention* (§5) alongside that of consciousness, as a surplus of consciousness (*un plus de conscience*) distinguishing certain perceptions from others. He declares his opposition to Leibniz's position (even if he borrows his description of 'small perceptions' in part from him) and draws, though with reservations, from Locke's, but only by first modifying it through the study of threshold phenomena, of more or less focused attention, of memory and of forgetting. Following Locke, and, so to speak, in the margins of his text, there finally emerges 'the sentiment of my being', the recognition of the permanence of a 'being which is constantly the same we [*nous*]', the identity of 'the I [*moi*] of today' and 'the I [*moi*] of yesterday' being tied to the idea of time arising from the succession of our thoughts. Eight years later, in the *Treatise on the Sensations*, Condillac again delays the entrance of 'consciousness' onto the scene. It does not appear until Chapter 6 of Book I, following his account of the genesis of the faculties conceived as transformations of pure sensation. Citing Pascal in a note ('where then is the "I" [*le moi*], if it is neither in the body nor the mind?'), he writes in the course of his famous allegory of the animated statue which is used as a model for the reconstruction of the development of the understanding: 'The smells the statue does not remember thus do not enter into its idea of its person . . . Its "I" is only the collection of sensations it experiences, and of those that its memory recalls. In short, it is at once the consciousness of what it is and the memory of what it was' (*Treatise on the Sensations*, I.vi.3).

Conscience had thus finally become in French as well as English the unitary concept designating the perception of things, including the self (*le soi*), under-stood as an internal multiplicity of representations and the temporal continuity

---

29   Condillac, *Essay on the Origins of Human Knowledge*, Cambridge: Cambridge University Press, 2001. The paragraph was copied by de Jaucourt in the article *Conscience* (Phil. Log. Métaph.) in the *Encyclopédie*, which offered the following 'definition': 'the opinion or internal sentiment that we ourselves have of what we do', adding 'it is what the English express with the word *consciousness*, that can only be rendered in French by means of periphrase.' See Glyn Davies, *Conscience as Consciousness.*

of its existence. Condillac's formulations were taken up by the Ideologues and criticized, from one side by Maine de Biran, and from another by Victor Cousin. The dialectic of the 'materialist' and 'spiritualist' (or, from another perspective, the 'psychological' and 'transcendental') conceptions of consciousness could then be put into play. It will persist up to our own time.

But before returning to Locke's *Essay* to examine the theoretical operations which provoked this remarkable translation, we must first seek to clarify the invention itself – whose preliminary results on the double plane of words and ideas we have just observed – in a broader context.

2. THE EUROPEAN INVENTION OF CONSCIOUSNESS

The invention of consciousness has its roots in the concatenation of intellectual events that inaugurate modernity. It concerns the entire field of theology, of politics, of moral and philosophical thought, as well as literature.[30] We may imagine it as a drama consisting of several episodes whose protagonists belong both to an Insular and a Continental culture on both sides of the Channel. They speak Latin (also reading and sometimes reconstructing Greek, but not Arabic), Italian, Dutch, French (the language of the 'Republic of Letters'), English and, beginning in the eighteenth century, German.

The first episode, whose heritage is quite visible in Locke's personalization of consciousness and his identification of its continuity with the autonomy of the 'self', corresponds to the debates initiated by the Reformation around the notion of *freedom of conscience*. One of its most striking results was the possibility of using the word 'conscience' not to designate a faculty of the soul, or the internal testimony of the subject's double, but as another name for the singular individual. This metonymical personification permitted the discrimination of 'consciences' according to their actions and their experiences: 'a noble conscience', 'an enlightened conscience', 'a firm conscience', 'a conscience divided against itself', etc.[31]

Another decisive episode opened in the epoch of the Enlightenment, with the radicalization of sensualism in the theory of the genesis of the intellectual faculties

---

30   The very unity of these different planes can be retroactively understood as the field of a collective consciousness, composed of a multiplicity of individual 'consciousnesses' concerned with their place in the world and in history. Hence, the wordplay in the title of Paul Hazard's *La crise de la conscience européenne* [*The Crisis of the European Conscience/Consciousness*] (1680–1715), Paris: 1935, part of whose conditions of possibility I have attempted to reconstitute. Useful analyses may also be found in R. Ellrodt, *Genèse de la conscience moderne: Études sur le développement de la conscience de soi dans les littératures du monde occidental*, Paris: PUF, 1983.

31   The metonymy was already operative in Calvin: 'I say that these remedies and palliatives are too weak and superficial for troubled and dejected consciences afflicted and struck down by the horror of their own sin'. *Institutes of the Christian Religion* (IV, 41). At the same time, it was political struggle that inscribed the play of meanings at the core of the uses of the word 'conscience', making the interior scene (*for intérieur*) also a 'fortress' and a 'force', a concept that would compete with 'mind/spirit' (*esprit*) and 'genius' (*génie*) to signify the new principle of individuality.

(Condillac), the competing analyses of the natural and the institutional self in the work of Hume and Diderot, and the Rousseauist recasting of the relation between public man and private man. In the epoch of European revolutions and wars, it would lead to the psychologies of internal sense (*sens intime*) (Maine de Biran) and the dialectical divisions of self-consciousness (Kant, Fichte and Hegel).

The interval, however, saw a long moment of speculative construction. In one essential sense, it proceeded from the paradoxical way in which Descartes 'settled' the question of scepticism. The affirmation of *certitude* inscribed the guarantee of truth at the core of individual thought, but in the form of an identification of immediacy and reflexivity, or of the identification of 'presence to self' and 'knowledge (savoir) of self' for thought, in which the 'substantial' distinctions between the finite and the infinite, the soul and the body – which were in fact always merely the other side of existentially indissoluble unities – were enigmatically implicated. This paradox soon led to the emergence of conflict, in which consciousness became *both* the concept of 'self-knowledge' (*connaissance de soi*) and that of 'self-misrecognition' (*méconnaissance de soi*). Locke's work and the translation of his concepts on the continent were situated at the heart of this metaphysical tension, to which no resolution would be found until Kant's transcendental dialectic (in the 'Paralogisms of Pure Reason'). To understand this fully will require us to take a fairly long detour.

After re-reading Descartes' essential texts, I will, for the sake of clarity, present the conflict in the following way: on the one side, the partisans of an *affirmative* conception of consciousness, for whom the concept, understood as the soul's recognition (*reconnaissance*) of itself, takes on a foundational role; one the other, the partisans of a *negative* conception, for whom the concept of consciousness is also identified, but who see its function as essentially one of misrecognition (*méconnaissance*) or misunderstanding (*méprise*). These are the two fundamental, and for a long time distinct, pathways along which the philosophy of subjectivity developed. The first camp consists of the French 'Augustino-Cartesians' who, it must be said, are no more faithful to Augustine's question (how can God, 'higher than what is the highest in me', make himself felt in 'the most intimate interiority' of my soul?) than to Descartes' ('who therefore am I, I who am certain of my existence as a thinking thing?'). They are in this sense, before Locke, the inventors of what Wolff and Kant would call rational psychology. In the second camp we find Malebranche, as well as Spinoza,[32] whose philosophies, absolutely opposed on the questions of creation and of nature, nevertheless have in common the fact that, for them, 'consciousness' (or *conscientia*) constitutes the soul's

---

32   To attempt an examination of the developments specific to Spinoza here would lead us too far from our objective: to illuminate the content and conditions of the composition of Locke's treatise. See Etienne Balibar, 'A Note on *Consciousness/Conscience* in the Ethics', *Studia na* 8, 1994; reprinted and expanded in the Postscript to this edition.

misrecognition (méconnaissance) of itself. Separate from this antinomy, but no less decisive for what followed (not only because of Locke's debt to them, but also for the ideas and words that they transmitted to Leibniz), is the position of the Cambridge Platonists, who made consciousness the 'express' or 'explicit' form of the perception of oneself present to some extent in any individuality.

2.1. Cogito and Cogitatio: The ethics and metaphysics of the certitude of oneself in Descartes

Historians of philosophy tell us that the moment in which consciousness came to signify *the essence* of subjectivity coincided with a return to the foundation of thought through the metaphysical experience of doubt. They thus fundamentally identified consciousness with the *cogito*, or made the latter the philosophical prototype of the former (obviously greatly aided by the way in which Kant, referring to Descartes in the *Critique of Pure Reason*, identified the problems of self-consciousness [*Selbstbewusstsein*] with the interpretations of 'the I think' [*das Ich denke*]), 'the sole text of rational psychology, from which it is to develop its entire wisdom'.[33] The reality is more complex. The philosophy of the *Meditations* is not that of consciousness (*Bewusstsein*), but of certitude (*Gewissheit*) and the conditions of achieving it. In the original Latin text, the word *conscius* occurs only once, in an important passage in which the French translator (reviewed by Descartes himself) nevertheless did not render the word as 'conscious' (*conscient*):

> I must therefore now ask myself whether I possess some power enabling me to bring it about that I who now exist will still exist a little while from now. For since I am nothing but a thinking thing . . . if there were such a power in me, I should undoubtedly be aware of it [*si quae talis vis in me esset, ejus procul dubio conscius essem*]' (Third Meditation).

Taking it as a given that 'the soul always thinks', this philosophy did not open the way to a programme of knowledge for which consciousness would be the organ and medium, but to a metaphysical conflict that divided the post-Cartesians. By participating in this conflict in an original way, Locke proposed a philosophy of mind that, while supplanting Cartesianism, prescribed in advance the paths to its rediscovery and even to its reinterpretation.

It is known that the text of the *Meditations* does not contain the canonical formula '*cogito*' or '*cogito (ergo) sum*'. However, it is there we discover the most subtle version of the argument that establishes the truth ('every time I say it or conceive it in my mind') of the proposition of existence, 'I am, I exist' (*ego sum,*

---

33   Kant, *Critique of Pure Reason*, trans. Paul Guyer and Allen W. Wood, Cambridge: Cambridge University Press, 1998, The Transcendental Dialectic, 'Paralogisms of Pure Reason', A 343/B401, 413.

ego existo). It is this formulation that tradition has registered under the name 'Cogito'. Is it another name for consciousness? Why would it imply such a notion?

The certitude of my existence is immediately understood as the certitude of the existence of the 'thing that thinks' that I am: 'But what is it that I am? A thing that thinks. What is a thing that thinks? It is a thing that doubts, conceives, affirms, denies, wants, doesn't want, a thing which also imagines, feels.' It is certainly an *experience* of understanding. At the same time, the proposition 'I am a thing that thinks', despite its syntactical complexity, expresses a simple idea grasped in what Descartes calls elsewhere an *intuition*. After leaving doubt behind, the certitude 'I am' becomes equivalent to the certitude 'I think'; that is, it no longer concerns anything external to thought in the process of its own execution and expression (or of its own execution *in* its expression, albeit only tacitly). It is thus a matter of pure self-reference. But 'I think', in its turn, regresses to infinity, for it is an idea that envelops all the modalities of thought, the thoughts of all possible objects and finally all my actions insofar as I think them. To the initial enumeration of terms (I doubt, I conceive, etc.), Descartes adds other modalities which concern corporeal actions present to thought: I walk, I breathe, etc. We may represent this in the following schema:

I am = I think =	I doubt I conceive I affirm I deny I (do not) want I imagine I feel (*Je sens*) I walk I breathe etc.

But there is also a reciprocal movement, in which all of the modalities of my thought are brought together in one simple idea:

I doubt I conceive I affirm I deny I (do not) want I imagine I feel I walk I breathe etc.	= I think= I am

The expression 'I am thinking' (*je suis pensant*) or 'I am a thing that thinks' is, in sum, a *general equivalent* of all the infinitely diverse modalities of thought, with their own objects and references. Let us note that the term 'thing' here is in no sense a way of denaturing subjectivity: it is rather, for Descartes, a nominalization of the question 'what?', hence the way of making us understand that *it is from the point of view of a subject, in the 'first person', that 'thought' and 'existence' can be immediately identified.*[34] In this meditation, the subject (*ego*) recognizes itself as the author of all its thoughts.[35] Thus the certitude discovered here is at once the certitude that *it is I who thinks in me* (no one thinks in my place, not even God – perhaps especially not God) and the certitude that *I truly think 'what I think'* (there is an intrinsic truth to my thoughts: even if they are false, fictional, etc. they are my thoughts and as such 'belong to me', (*m'appartiennent, pertinere*).

This being the movement of the *Meditations*, it might seem that the emphasis would shift if we were to examine other texts, particularly the *Responses to the Second Objections* and the *Principles of Philosophy*.[36] The problem, as indicated in the French translation of *Principles*, I, §9, is knowing 'what it is to think': a problem of defining a category rather than interpreting an experience. Here once again, however, we are confronted with a relation between 'substance' and 'modes', or between the principal attribute of this substance (which in practice becomes confused with it), that is, thought (*cogitatio*) and its modes, all of which derive from *cogitare* or are *cogitationes*:

To understand To imagine To feel To see To walk etc.	= to think (thoughts)

34   Before being supplanted by 'substance' (the use of which by Descartes profoundly deviates from its traditional usage) 'thing' is here an oxymoronic term denoting at once the question that the experience of its coincidence with thought poses to the subject, and the supplement of singularity that *ego cogito* or *ego sum cogitans* contains in relation to the essence of the *cogitatio*. One might speak of a *haecceity* of thought that is properly the Cartesian subject.

35   Which does not necessarily mean that it recognizes itself as their *cause*: in the Third Meditation, Descartes will employ this distinction by showing that among all my 'ideas' there is at least one (the idea of God) of which I could not have been the cause because it infinitely surpasses me in perfection. I am no less, 'formally', its author in the sense that it is truly I who think it. Hence the creation of an acute tension between *Ego* and *Ille*, between Man and God, between first and third person and the risk it poses to my *identity*. See Etienne Balibar, "'Ego sum, ego existo', Descartes au point d'hérésie', *Bulletin de la société française de la philsophie*, 3, 1992 (reprinted in *Citoyen Sujet*, 87–119).

36   A different interpretation may be in found in Vincent Descombes, *La denrée mentale*, Paris: Éditions de Minuit, 1995. Although he describes philosophy of mind (*philosophie mentale*) as 'post-Cartesian rather than Cartesian', Descombes persists in attributing to Descartes what was in fact only articulated by Locke.

Let us note here that it is not a question of being or existing. We are exploring the attribute of thought in its entirety.[37] Nevertheless, we now see the intervention of the term *conscientia* ('*Cogitationis nomine intelligo illa omnia quae nobis consciis in nobis fiunt, quatenus eorum in nobis conscientia est*'), an occurrence perhaps unique in Descartes. What does it mean exactly? It seems to me that it is necessary to follow the guiding thread furnished by the translations reviewed and approved by Descartes, which, though they certainly confront the contemporary reader with an obsolete language, have the immense advantage of dispelling any illusion concerning the transparency of words. What do these translations say? Quite simply that *we know* or that *we possess a knowledge* of what thought is: 'By the word "thinking" I understand everything that occurs in us such that we immediately perceive (*apercevons*) it through ourselves etc.'[38] What is this apperception or this immediate knowledge? Here we might make a few simple remarks:

– First, *conscientia* is itself one 'thought' among others. *Descartes nowhere says that thought in general is consciousness (conscience)*; but he does say that there is no thought without this other thought – or this 'idea of the idea', as Spinoza would later say – that is consciousness.

– Second, he makes use of this thesis, which he posits as an axiom, to add a comprehensiveness clause: we can exhaustively account for the modes of thought for, just as nothing pertains to thought without our knowing it, so there are thoughts corresponding to all of our actions. There are thus neither unconscious thoughts nor unthought actions.

---

37   We will see how Locke modifies the function of this enumeration from the perspective of his own articulation of 'reflection' and 'consciousness'.

38   Compare the Latin text of the 'Arguments proving the existence of God and the distinction between the soul and the body arranged in geometrical fashion', appended to the Second Set of Replies ('*Cogitationis nomine complector omne id, quod sic in nobis est, ut ejus immediate conscii sumus . . . Ideae nomine intelligo cujuslibet cogitationis formam illam, per cujus immediatam perceptionem ipsius ejusdem cogitationis conscius sum*') with Clerselier's French translation: '*Par le nom de pensée, je comprends tout ce qui est tellement en nous, que nous en sommes immédiatement connaissants . . . Par le nom d'idée j'entends cette forme de chacune de nos pensées, par la perception immédiate de laquelle nous avons connaissance de ces mêmes pensées*'. (A.T. IX, 124). In English: '*Thought*: I use this term to include everything that is within us in such a way that we are immediately aware of it . . . *Idea*: I understand this term to mean the form of any given thought, immediate perception of which makes me aware of the thought.' Alquié (*Œuvres philosophiques de Descartes*, Paris: Garnier, 1967, 586) provided the following annotation: 'Au lieu de *connaissants*, nous dirions mieux: *conscients*. Car le latin est: *ut ejus immediate conscii sumus*. La pensée (*cogitatio*) est donc, pour Descartes, synonyme de conscience . . . cf. *Principes*, I, 9 [Instead of 'knowing' (*connaissants*) it would be better for us to say 'conscious', for the Latin is '*ut ejus immediate conscii sumus*'. Thought (*cogitatio*) is therefore for Descartes synonymous with consciousness, see *Principles*, I, 9]. For his part, Martial Gueroult, in *Descartes selon l'orare des raisons* (Paris: Aubier, 1953) persists in equating the essence of thought and that of consciousness in order to to show, above all, that there is no real difference between thought and the thought of thought.

– Third, this means that *conscientia* is an operator that will always relate every thought to an ego that can think it and that reciprocally inscribes the subject among other thoughts (determining that there is, among other things, a thought of myself). We are tempted to say: the 'I' or *ego*, this self that thinks, walks, sees, etc. is also 'objectively' inscribed (that is, as *idea*) in the world of thought. It is not *external* to it.

– Finally, this knowledge is *immediate*, that is, it is not the result of a relation or of an act of reasoning. This point is decisive: in the history of philosophy, what will come to be called 'consciousness' will no longer always be a clear or rational knowledge but will always be immediate, or originally grounded in immediacy.

The fact that Descartes establishes this knowledge as immediate is precisely what troubled his readers insofar as it led to a mutation in the notion of 'reflection'. Until then, reflection signified a mediate operation: in particular, when the Aristotelians said that the soul and its operations are known though reflection, they meant that they are not known directly but only through their effects and their differences. In contrast, reflection in Descartes means that the soul or thought recognizes itself in each of its modalities, because it is present there each time (and other texts add that it is *identically* present, that is, that certain modes, such as intelligence, have no privilege in this respect; as can be seen in §9 of the *Principles*, reflection is equally present in feeling and willing).[39]

We must ask, however, *of what* exactly we have *knowledge* here, and what is its domain or object? In a certain sense, this domain extends to infinity, since all *cogitationes* belong to it in principle. But in another sense, it is infinitely impoverished given that, every time, it is a matter of one and the same thing: the fact that we think in a given modality or that conceiving, willing, feeling, etc. are thoughts that an *ego* may relate to itself. It is therefore not a question of establishing a program of reflexive inquiry within this 'consciousness' in order to discover the faculties of the soul or to analyze its logical operations, etc. – despite what some of Descartes' successors thought, and quite different from Locke's own theory and practice in regard to the mind. This is why the famous formula in the *Meditations*, stating 'that the soul is easier to know than the body', in no way leads to a rational psychology or a metaphysics of the soul. If the soul is 'easier to know', it is above all because it finds itself present everywhere, even in the perception of the smallest 'piece of wax', but also because, unlike the knowledge of the body, which is complex and difficult, knowledge of the soul is simple and always identical to itself. It is for this reason that Descartes says that such knowledge should not detain us for very long and that the matter

---

39 On the paradoxes of reflection in Descartes, see Jean-Marie Beyssade: *La philosophie première de Descartes (Le temps et la cohérence de la métaphysique)*, Paris: Flammarion, 1979, and his edition of the *Entretien de Descartes avec Burman*, Paris: PUF, 1981.

may be settled quickly. It will suffice to grasp its principle. At the limit, if there is in fact a metaphysics of the soul in Descartes, this metaphysics is a science of a single point (*une science ponctuelle*).

The formula which states that we cannot think without knowing that we think and that we know ourselves thinking is, however, no less important. It is this that, through Locke's discussion of innate ideas, leads to his making 'consciousness' the very subject of thought, while also raising the problem of the unconscious. It is useful to recall here certain of Descartes' formulae.[40] In his response to the fourth set of Objections (those of Arnauld), he writes:

> We cannot have any thought of which we are not aware at the very moment it is in us (*nec ulla potest in nobis esse cogitatio, cujus eodem illo momento, quo in nobis est, conscii non simus*). In view of this I do not doubt that the mind begins to think as soon as it is implanted in the body of an infant, and that it is immediately aware of its thoughts, even though it does not remember this afterwards because the impressions of these thoughts do not remain in the memory. (A.T., IX, 190)

And in the Responses to the Sixth Objections:

> We cannot fail constantly to experience within ourselves that we think (*non potest non esse sibi conscius*) . . . therefore no one can reasonably infer that he does not himself think. Such an inference would be made only by someone who has previously been convinced that he operates in exactly the same way as the brutes, simply because he has attributed thought to them; he then remains so stubbornly attached to the sentence, 'Men and the brutes operate in the same way', that when it is pointed out to him that the brutes do not think, he actually prefers to deny his own thought, of which he cannot fail to be aware (*Nam sane fieri non potest quin semper apud nosmet ipsos experiamur nos cogitare*). (A.T., IX, 229)

For his part, Bourdin would write in the Seventh Objection:

> If one who employs this method says that he thinks . . . and that he thinks in such a way that by a reflexive act he contemplates and considers it, what brings it about that he thinks, or even that he knows and considers that he thinks (what is properly called 'being conscious of' [*apercevoir*] or to have internal knowledge [*connaissance intérieure*] (*et consideret se cogitare (quod vere est esse conscium, et actus alicujus habere conscientiam*), and if he says that this capacity belongs to a faculty . . . that is spiritual [*spirituelle*], and on the basis of the fact that he is a mind [*esprit*], he

---

40 See the dossier in the French edition of this book for the most complete list of these formulae, together with detailed references.

says that he has not yet said what he must say, what I expect him to say and what I have precisely wanted often to suggest to him, when I have seen him vainly attempt to tell us what he is . . . he will say nothing new.

It is this adversary of Descartes who introduces the term *reflection* in its Scholastic sense as a synonym of *conscientia*: the soul does not know itself directly, but only through reflection. Descartes responds:

> When our author says that it is not sufficient that a thing is a substance that thinks for it to be completely spiritual and above matter, by which alone it may properly be said to deserve the name of spirit, and beyond, that it is required that, by a reflexive action on its thought, it thinks that it thinks, or that it has an internal knowledge of its thought (*ut actu reflexo cogitet se cogitare, sive habeat cogitationis suae conscientiam*) he is mistaken . . . For the first thought, whatever it is, by which we perceive [*apercevons*] that we have already perceived [*aperçue*], does no more differ from the second, by which we perceive that we had already perceived it, than this second differs from the third thought by which we perceive that we have already perceived having earlier perceived a given thing; and there is no reason whatsoever why the second of these thoughts will not come from a corporeal subject, if it is agreed that the first come from this subject as well.[41]

It seems possible to interpret these texts (which have provoked much discussion) by suggesting that Descartes here defends four successive theses that, from his point of view, form a single doctrine:

1. The soul or mind (*mens*) *cannot not think* because such is its essence. In other words (and this doubly negative formulation confers the value of a principle on his thesis), it would be contradictory to postulate simultaneously that the essence of the soul is to think and that it is capable of not thinking.[42]

2. The thesis concerning essence can also be transposed to the plane of existence: as long as a soul exists, it does not stop thinking. In other words, the soul *always* thinks. But this fact in no way implies that the soul *remembers* having earlier thought when it thinks (or having existed when and by the fact that it exists!), whether this thinking was in a dream, in the time of the gestation of its body, in childhood, or simply one second ago. This reciprocity figures in the *Entretien avec Burman*: for the soul to be 'conscious' (have knowledge) of its

---

41 *Œuvres philosophiques de Descartes*, Vol. II; for Bourdin's objections see 1041; Descartes' reply: 1070-1. See the commentary by J.L. Marion in his *Questions Cartésiennes. Méthode et métaphysique*, Paris: PUF, 1991, 166.

42 As we shall see, it is the constraint of this thesis which leads Locke, finally, to refrain from identifying the faculty of thinking (and of thinking oneself) that he calls 'mind' with the substantial soul [*âme substantielle*] for which he reserves the terms 'soul' and 'spirit'.

thought it is in no way necessary for this thought to have already taken place. In other words, in a radical (and psychologically troubling) thesis: *the thought that is the essence of the soul has nothing essentially to do with memory*, it exists and must be thought outside of any consideration of past time, only ever 'in actuality', that is, *in the very act* of thinking (with its own duration).

3. Descartes maintains, in one and the same movement, that the soul *cannot think without knowing that it thinks* or without 'knowing itself thinking' with certitude. But it is necessary to make some subtle distinctions here. Descartes means above all that *every thought* 'knows itself as a thought' (for example, it is impossible 'to want a thing without our perceiving through the very same means that we want it'). It is a question of *thought's presence to itself*, which is identical throughout all its modalities and which does not depend on the exercise of any particular faculty. At this point, the negative formulation becomes clearer: the soul, insofar as it thinks in one way or another, cannot misrecognize itself (that is, take itself for another kind of 'thing'). It is thus always possible for the soul to know itself as a 'thinking thing' *in general* in one or another of its modalities, or of grasping its own essence in the 'actions' in which it expresses itself.

It is this with which the cogito is essentially concerned, especially when it is articulated, as I have just done, as 'a general equivalent' of the different modalities of thought, immanent in their variation. For the soul or thought never grasps its own generic essence, present in each of its particular modalities in an impersonal way, but through an experience that only has meaning *in the first person* (as 'my experience here alone', *hoc pronuntiatum* as the *Meditations* puts it) even if takes place in a rigorously identical manner in each of us. We are here very close to what constitutes at once the originality and the difficulty of Cartesianism: the knowledge of thought truly grasps a rational, communicable essence, but on the basis of an absolutely singular experience. Cartesianism is that short-circuit, that almost unbearable tension, between the universality of essence and the immediacy of singular existence united in a single statement. If the concept of 'consciousness', as it would take shape soon afterwards according to the modality of Malebranche or of Locke, cannot really be found here, is it not because this concept tends precisely to distend this unity of contraries by introducing a *mediation* (and soon, as we shall see, a whole series of mediations)? Let us reserve judgment for the moment.

4. We thus arrive at the fourth and final thesis: the soul knows (*sait ou connaît*) *what it thinks*, that is, it knows (*connaît*) its own thoughts *for what they are*. Initially, it seems simply to be a matter of applying at the level of detail what has just been proposed for thought in general. But we see almost immediately that the details may pose a problem as soon as the question of the 'union of soul and body' is raised in relation to the sensations, sentiments, passions and even

the imagination.[43] In a certain sense, there exists a whole series of thoughts whose *nature we misrecognize* because we attribute them to the body, as if at the limit it was *the body that thought in us* (when we feel, etc.). In the Sixth Meditation, Descartes explains that this mistake fulfils a vital function: if we do not locate our sensations in the body, we will take them as conclusions of the soul based on information received from the body, and then, putting them into doubt, fail to react spontaneously to the pain and danger as our survival demands. Such a finalist argument compels us to ask if the thesis that the soul knows itself (*se sait ou se connait*) can be upheld *in general*.

Again, it appears that it is possible to distinguish here between two stages. First, it can be said that, even in error, every thought grasps itself in its truth: precisely *as* sensation, will, imagination, judgment and so on. No thought is confused with another. Those that imply the influence of the body or an influence on the body are really thought as 'united' with it or 'confused' with its actions and passions. The contrary, we remember, would imply a mystification. Next, however – and this is a more delicate point – it can be said that it is always possible for us to direct our attention exclusively to *what makes an idea an idea, or to what makes a thought an action of the soul*. Descartes does not say that this possibility is realized in all circumstances or that it is easy to realize; but it is always possible *in principle* and the methods for doing so can be learned through meditation. We thus arrive at a *priority* or 'precedence' that is inherent in the nature of the soul and that manifests itself clearly there. In every case what we think is not confusion but the distinction within thought, a distinction that can only be grasped by thought itself.

What, therefore, does Descartes mean when he repeats that 'the soul is easier to know than the body' and that we have a *better* knowledge of the first than of the second – a phrase certainly not without apologetic intentions, but which must also be reconcilable with his theoretical practice. I do not believe that his intention here is to elaborate a theory of the faculties or the operations of thought.[44] On the contrary, for him it was a matter of providing the same demonstration every time: thought can only be referred to the 'thing that thinks' whose action it is, even if it is affected by external objects, and above all by the body. In the last analysis, the knowledge that I have of myself as thought (the 'something', or this 'thing' that *I* am) has as its objective the reconstruction of the experience of primary certitude and the postulation in every case of the distinction of the soul. This is why the soul can be both infinitely rich (multiple) in objects, encountered in all the occasions presented by everyday life, and

---

43   D. Kambouchner (*L'homme des passions. Commentaires sur Descartes*, Paris: Albin Michel, 1995) offers a discussion of these difficulties, leading to the idea of a 'developed Cogito' distinct from 'pure reflection' (335 ff.).

44   He renounced such a project after the *Rules for the Direction of the Mind*, which remained unfinished.

infinitely poor (simple) in results or conclusions: for *the conclusion is always the same.*

This is to suggest that what the soul knows of itself in its relation to the world is only ever its freedom or power, which consists in its own capacity to think things (and therefore itself) clearly and distinctly – and, by default, to suspend judgment. We see on this point that the objective of self-knowledge is not a speculative matter, but that its metaphysical orientation is fundamentally 'practical' or, if one prefers, *ethical*. But this ethics of intellectual autonomy is as inconvenient as it is risky insofar as it combines both precariousness and a sense of self-sufficiency.[45] It can guarantee the anchoring of its self-certainty in exist-ence only at the price of the greatest insecurity concerning the identity or essence of its 'subject', which at each moment must reconquer its internal alter-ity: *I am not* this God, the perfect idea of whom is inscribed at the heart of my reason as its infinite model or 'eminent' cause, just as *I am not* this body to which my perceptions are so united that I experience my own existence in it, with the result that I am just 'me'.

It is this that his unfaithful disciples, the Cartesians, will soon try to pass off as *science*. But this science will also be named consciousness (*conscience*): *cum scientia.*

2.2. *The idea of a metaphysics of the soul in the French 'Cartesians'*

Although the noun *conscience* as 'consciousness' in French (or *conscientia* in Latin) does not appear in his corpus, it is important to begin by examining Arnauld, in that he contributed to the emergence of the concept by means of two powerful suggestions.[46]

The first is contained in the *Logic or the Art of Thinking* (1662), the work known as the 'Port-Royal Logic', written in collaboration with Pierre Nicole, and which is sometimes seen as one of the sources of the psychologism that dominated logic until the arrival of modern formalism. It was a reorganization of the classical theory of judgments, reasoning and method based on an analysis of the elements of thought. This analysis was a *theory of 'ideas'* in the new sense that the term was beginning to acquire: signs or images of things originating in

---

45   Canguilhem characterized this ethics as a 'claim' (and not a representation) of a 'surveil-lance of the world of things and men'. Georges Canguilhem, 'Le cerveau et la pensée', *Georges Canguilhem: Philosophe, historien des sciences*, Paris: Albin Michel, 1993, 29–30.

46   Antoine Arnauld, known as 'le grand Arnauld', was a theologian and philosopher whose exceptional longevity (1612–1694) allowed him to be the principal 'intellectual' of Jansenism, Descartes' interlocutor during the debate over the *Meditations*, later Malebranche's adversary on the questions of grace and vision in God, and finally Leibniz's correspondent concerning *The Discourse on Metaphysics*. He was the advocate of an attempt to fuse Cartesianism and Augustinianism which may be considered the primary source of *spiritualism* in French philoso-phy. It was he who attempted to show that the *cogito ergo sum* contains antecedents from Augustine that Descartes could only have rediscovered.

the mind itself. From that point on, logical forms would be understood as translating, though the medium of language, the 'mental operations' whose nature was in the last instance independent of this verbal covering. This suggestion would be considerably developed by Locke.[47]

The second was explained in a much later work directed against Malebranche, *Of True and False Ideas* (1683). It was here that Arnauld introduced the notion of the '*cogito*' (later, the 'I think'), understood as a noun, as the basic argument and model of self-knowledge on which a rational metaphysics must rest. This emphasis was associated with a discussion concerning the nature of ideas as 'representations'. Arnauld considered this term to be dangerously equivocal, and preferred that of 'perception', applicable to any situation in which a thing 'is objectively in my mind'. It was thus a matter of finding a middle way between two equally unacceptable extremes: on the one side, the idea that ideas are autonomous 'representative beings' (which leads to the Malebranchian thesis according to which the soul perceives not the objects themselves, but their ideas, that is, their representations or models); on the other, the idea that the 'things themselves' are in some sense sought out by the soul (according to the medieval doctrine of intentionality, later taken up in a modified form by phenomenology). According to Arnauld, ideas should be understood as the means of a '*double relation*': a relation to the soul that thinks (of which they are a modification) and to the object that they represent, according to a specific mode which could not in general be reducible to the notion of a picture or an image. At the limit, ideas are nothing more than the name given to this relation.[48]

The presence of the soul as one of the terms of the double relation that constitutes the idea allows Arnauld to propose a definition of thought (based on the authority of Descartes and his definition of the *cogitatio*) which increasingly identifies thought with *reflection* and then, implicitly, with 'consciousness':

> Our *thought* or *perception* essentially reflects on itself; or as it is more happily said in Latin, *est sui conscia*. For I do not think without knowing that I think. I do not even have knowledge of a square without knowing that I know it . . . Beyond this reflection which might be called *virtual*, that is found in all our perceptions, there is another, more *explicit* through which we examine our perception with another

---

47   In 1675–1676, Locke translated three of Pierre Nicole's *Essais de Morale*, in which the latter argued, among other things, that it is necessary to go beyond words to the things themselves. See Yves Michaud, *Locke*, Paris: Bordas, 1986; John Marshall, *John Locke: Resistance, Religion and Responsibility*, Cambridge: Cambridge University Press, 1994.

48   On Arnauld's conception of the 'idea' and his critique of the thesis of the obscurity of the soul to itself, see J.-M. Beyssade, 'Sensation et idée: le patron rude', and D. Kambouchner, 'Des vrais et des fausses ténèbres: La connaissance de l'âme d'après la controverse avec Malebranche' in Jean-Claude Pariente, ed., *Antoine Arnauld. Philosophe du langage et de la connaissance*, Paris: Vrin, 1995.

perception, as each of us experiences effortlessly . . . It follows that every perception being essentially representative of something, and for that reason called an *idea*, it cannot essentially reflect on itself, unless its immediate object is that *idea*, that is, *the objective reality* of the thing that my mind is said to perceive [*apercevoir*].[49]

We must not forget that in the seventeenth century, 'objective reality' meant the representation of an object in opposition to the 'formal reality' of the thing that is its being in itself (*qui est son être en soi*). We can see, then, that the double relation constitutive of the idea is itself reduplicated through an operation that arises from the soul itself. From this reflection, which always exists, if only virtually, Arnauld derives the subjective principle of any science, beginning with the very science of the soul and of God, the entities of which we have the clearest ideas of all.

We find analogous conceptions among the 'orthodox' Cartesians in the last third of the seventeenth century. As early as 1666, Louis de la Forge, physician and philosopher, who had just published Descartes' posthumous *Treatise on Man*, provided a 'sequel' of his own under the title *Traité de l'esprit de l'homme*, in which he declares that his 'design is merely to explain at greater length than he [Descartes] had done the Faculties of the Soul'. In so doing La Forge straight-away claims a double patronage: that of the author of the *Meditations* and that of the author of the *Confessions*. Following Descartes, La Forge understands 'idea' to mean 'nothing other than the forms of the Mind's thoughts', represent-ing to us 'two kinds of Beings . . . that which is extended, called Body, and that which thinks, called Mind (*Esprit*)'. The mind, 'that is, the thing that thinks', therefore thinks itself. The knowledge of thought through itself, which the Cartesian word 'cogitare' served to designate, is essentially identical to Augustine's *intelligere*, addressed to the *interior man* (*homo interior*, while the body is *homo exterior*).[50]

Later, La Forge will describe this self-knowledge as a retreat and an askesis, a way for the mind to 'withdraw into itself to see itself without being seen', and finally as a *consciousness* (for which he will also use the name 'internal senti-ment'): 'I understand by Thought here that perception, consciousness (*conscience*) or internal knowledge (*connaissance intérieure*) that each of us feels immediately by himself when he perceives what he does or what passes in him (*ce qui se passe en lui*).' And again:

What is this admirable function whose essence seems so hidden? . . . If all the func-tions of knowledge are operations that contain nothing of matter and do not leave the soul, it is a gross abuse to look elsewhere than in the Mind itself to discover its

---

49   Antoine Arnauld, *Des vraies et des fausses idées*, Paris: Fayard, 1986, 2.
50   La Forge, *Traité de l'esprit de l'homme*, 82.

workings . . . We have already proven that it is the nature of the mind to be a thing that thinks and we have said that the essence of thought consists in that consciousness (*conscience*) and that perception (*perception*) that the mind has of all that passes in it.[51]

Here, La Forge carries out three fundamental operations at once: he introduces the neologism consciousness (*conscience*); he makes it the very essence of thought, the modality according to which 'the soul always thinks'; and he identifies it with *interiority*, or with the movement by which 'internal man' retreats into himself, that is, contemplates himself as 'pure mind' (*pur esprit*). La Forge's contributions here are closely tied to the demonstration of the *immateriality* and the *immortality* of the soul, which for their part precede and govern the analysis of its 'faculties'.[52]

His apologetic concerns are plainly expressed in his treatment of the question of the unity of soul and body, which signals a new departure from Descartes. For not only did La Forge introduce, in his interpretation of Descartes, the fundamentally anti-Cartesian concept of an Alliance or Treaty between Body and Soul based on the model of the 'government of the world', whose provisions La Forge does not hesitate to enumerate, and which, like it, is concluded under the guidance of God. He also deduced from this (although not without difficulty, for how can he reconcile this thesis with the fundamental *monism* of the Cartesian conception of thought?) the idea that the Soul or the Mind of Man contains a 'superior part' (the only part that is truly immortal or immaterial) and an 'inferior part' (capable of union with the body and subject to its influence) which are at war with each other, particularly in the passions.[53]

But what is perhaps most noteworthy is the way in which La Forge's recourse to the idea of *interiority* contributes to the suppression of the question of the 'I' and of the *first person* once he has dutifully paid his respects to the 'cogito'. On this point, La Forge, wanting to be both Augustinian and Cartesian, is in fact neither: the concept of consciousness or internal sentiment that he introduces is impersonal (it is an essence or a faculty), as distant from the *ego* of the *Confessions* in the throws of internal combat ('I was myself one who wanted and

---

51   Ibid., 100, 112, 156.

52   Although La Forge invokes Augustine, there is considerable difference between the way he treats the question of the interiority or intimacy of the soul and the way this question appears in the *Confessions* and *On the Trinity*. For Augustine, what we discover 'in the deepest part of ourselves' is, on the one hand, a permanent struggle between the hope of salvation and the inclination to sin, and, on the other, the call of God himself, the 'internal master' who transcends our nature and places it, as it were, 'outside of itself'. This reference plays no role in La Forge, who is much more of a naturalist.

53   Descartes (in *Passions of the Soul*, Art. 47) explicitly demarcated himself from the 'imagination' that there exist 'struggles between superior and inferior parts of the soul'. The soul for him had no parts because its entire essence was thought alone under a multiplicity of modalities.

did not want', *ego eram, ego, qui volebam, ego, qui nolebam*) (VIII.x.22), as from that of the *Meditations* in the grip of the question, 'who am I?' and 'who (or what) thinks in me?'

The movement was completed and codified, as I said, in a third author, Pierre-Sylvain Régis (1632–1737), who in his *Système de philosophie, contenant la Logique, la Métaphysique at la Morale* offered two definitions of consciousness. The first – formal and fairly general – appeared in the glossary of unfamiliar terms found at the end of the work: 'consciousness' (*conscience*) is one's own internal testimony to oneself concerning something. The second was specifically linked to a summary of the Cartesian texts: 'I am therefore assured that I exist every time I believe I know something; and I am convinced of the truth of this proposition not by true reasoning but by a simple and internal knowledge that precedes all acquired knowledge and which I call *consciousness* [*conscience*].'

Above all, however (given that physics is the science of bodies), he identifies metaphysics with the science of the truths pertaining to souls, that is, the 'knowledge of intelligent substances' understood either 'in themselves', or as Minds (*Esprits*), or 'in relation to the body' to which the mind is united or 'which pertains to it more than others'. Régis's system thus converts the Cartesian 'I' into 'a conscious self (*moi*)', which in turn becomes the subject–object of a metaphysics of the soul that is simultaneously intellectualist and spiritualist, or of a rational psychology. We should ask ourselves to what extent Lockean 'empiricism' differs from this point of view. For if it does differ, it is less because of its practical reorientation to the things themselves than because of its direct confrontation with other theoretical discourses, profoundly but differently influenced by a theological perspective: that of Malebranche, who denied that the human soul was capable of knowing itself clearly; and of the Cambridge Platonist Ralph Cudworth, who coined the neologism 'consciousness' in English on the basis of a fictional Greek etymology and sought by this means to oppose the materialism that threatened a teleology of the progressive emergence of spirit (*esprit*) in nature. Let us examine them one after the other.

2.3. *Consciousness as misrecognition (méconnaissance): Malebranche*

The Cartesians were the theoreticians of transparent consciousness as self-knowledge; Malebranche and Spinoza, each in his own way, called consciousness a state of darkness or necessary misrecognition.[54] But unlike Spinoza, who characterized consciousness as misrecognition insofar as it was incapable of forming an adequate idea of corporeal individuality, the multiplicity of which always exceeded its power of perception (*Ethics* II, p. 27), Malebranche made

---

54 The connection with Spinoza, asserted by his adversaries and even by certain of his partisans, was the cross that Malebranche had to bear for much of his life. He was never spared having to defend his theories of 'occasional cause' and 'vision in God' against the charge of 'Spinozism'.

misrecognition a characteristic of the relation that the soul maintains *with itself*. Surprisingly, he describes this relation in the very language that Descartes used to characterize the 'confusion' of the union of the soul and the body. This is undoubtedly why he uses the terms 'consciousness' (*conscience*) and 'internal sentiment' (*sentiment intérieur*) indifferently, or uses the one to clarify the other. At the same time, he explains that the human soul's confused representation of itself is linked (not causally, but symbolically) to the influence acquired by the body on the soul or, more precisely, a soul 'complacent' to the body that, in man, is a result of the Fall. It is thus a matter of a conception strictly governed by the dogma of the initial perversion of human nature. Malebranchian consciousness is intrinsically linked to the fallen *love of oneself* that must be converted in order to be transformed into a *love of God*.

We must, however, be careful not to twist Malebranche's thought, whose radical finalism also contains a constructive dimension. For he explains that without this love of the body – if the soul were capable of thinking itself and knowing itself in a pure way – it would turn away from the needs and tasks of earthly life and aspire to nothing more than to know God and to unite immediately with him, which would be opposed to man's earthly destiny. Misrecognition is therefore *useful* and has a *practical* end. It inscribes the supernatural economy of salvation in the natural requirements of health and *vice versa*.

In *The Search After Truth* (1674) Malebranche explains his theory of consciousness as confused knowledge of the soul and his opposition to Cartesianism on this point at length.[55] He distinguishes four 'modes of knowledge' (*manières de connaître*) (to which correspond four different objects of knowledge):

1. Only God is known to us 'through himself', that is, he is knowable in himself or, more precisely, *he makes himself known in us*, as our 'internal master' or the 'light of our own spirit'. This supremely adequate knowledge, *illuminating* rather than *illuminated*, begins with what Malebranche calls *general idea of being* and leads to the idea of *the infinite* or *perfect being* which is also the idea of *order* (such that there are few classical authors who better fit the term 'ontotheology').[56] They reveal to us that our essence is united with the divine essence and is not separable from love: but this refers to intellectual love and not to a sentiment.[57]

---

55   Malebranche, *The Search After Truth*, Book III: Part 2, chapters 6–7.

56   See in particular the *Entretiens sur la métaphysique et la religion* (1688), Tome XIV, *Œuvres complètes de Malebranche*, A. Robinet, ed., Paris: CNRS/Librairie Vrin.

57   'Because *Truth* and *Order* are relations of greatness and of real perfection, immutable, necessary relations contained in the Divine Word, he who sees these relations, sees what God sees; he who bases his love on these relations, follows a law that God loves invincibly. There is thus between him and God a perfect conformity of mind and will. In a word, because he knows and loves what God knows and loves, he is as similar to God as he is capable of being' (*Traité de morale*, J.-P. Osier, ed., I, 1, 14 [p. 62]).

2. The question of what knowledge 'through ideas' is remains the essential (and most contested point) in Malebranche's theory. Ideas are considered both as *archetypes* (an inspiration derived from Platonism) and as *representations* of things which are substituted for things for the understanding. And, according to Malebranche, the 'site' of these archetypes is God himself, which means that *we see in God*, as if on a transcendental screen, the geometrical ideas of bodies, and more generally the 'eternal truths' of reason and science. Note that the properties referred to here are the geometrical and mechanical qualities of bodies which correspond to clear and distinct ideas (for which Locke would invent the expression 'primary qualities').

3. Knowledge by *consciousness* or *internal sentiment* is knowledge that we have of our own mind or soul; it is immediate but obscure or confused (as we experience it and as may be further explained from the theology of the Fall). The 'self' (*soi*) that it delivers to us is an alienated, ambivalent self both present to and escaping us at the same time.[58]

4. Finally, 'conjecture' is the way we know 'the souls of other men and therefore the very essence of the *other*, namely, his thought which is similar to ours, his sentiments which, like ours, arise from the unity of soul and body, his "instituted" language . . . It is thus conjecture that makes communication or society possible'.

The identification of consciousness with internal sentiment gives rise in Malebranche to a very beautiful phenomenology that extends throughout his moral doctrine. As he is the first great philosopher to use the term 'consciousness' in a metaphysical and psychological sense, this equation will have serious consequences for the French philosophical tradition (for example, in Rousseau). In a certain sense, it introduces a *third term* between the idea of knowledge and that of judgment. In relation to true knowledge, consciousness obviously has a *restrictive* impact which opposes the Cartesian illusion of the soul's perfect knowledge of itself (and consequently also opposes the notion of the *self-sufficiency* of the knowing soul in which Malebranche, along with every 'antihumanism' of that century, saw heresy and perhaps even blasphemy). But in another sense, through the confused sentiments that we have of ourselves, we grasp something essential, that is, *the presentiment of our freedom*, inseparable from a supernatural destination.[59]

---

58   'I am nothing but darkness to myself' (*Méditations chrétiennes et métaphysiques*, IX, 15). Cited by Michel Henry (*Généalogie de la psychanalyse*, Paris: PUF, 1985), who offers an interpretation of Malebranche as presenting a contradictory doctrine: on the one hand, a radically phenomenological 'repetition' of the Cartesian cogito within the element of *affectivity*, and on the other an ontological devaluation of this same cogito as deprived of, or alienated from, the light.

59   See Elucidation I, 'Elucidations of the Search After Truth', in which the scheme of alienation cannot end but instead can only continue to reproduce itself: 'Our senses then are not as corrupt as might be imagined; rather, it is the most inward part of our soul, our freedom, that has been corrupted' (*The Search After the Truth*, Book I, Chapter 5). It is striking to observe that this

Finally, in relation to Descartes and in a vocabulary directly inspired by him, the situation is reversed: confusion does not proceed from the 'union of the soul and the body', but from 'the union of the soul with God' lived (because of sin) in the alienated mode of separation. And this reversal results in an astonishing proposition, unacceptable to a Cartesian: if we are capable of clearly distinguishing the soul from the body, it is not so positively, because we always already have a clear idea of the soul, but negatively, because the only clear idea we have is that of the body!

> We only know of our soul what we feel [*sentons*] passing in us . . . It is true that we know enough through our consciousness or by the internal sentiment that we have of ourselves that our soul is something great but it may be that what we know of it has little to do with what it is in itself.[60]

A few years later (1678), in the *Elucidations* to the *Search after Truth*, Malebranche underscored this point:

> When M. Descartes or the Cartesians with whom I speak assure us that we know that soul better than the body, they understand by body nothing more than extension. How can they maintain that we know the nature of the soul better than that of the body, when the idea of the body or of extension is so clear . . . and that of the soul so confused that even the Cartesians argue daily about whether the modifications of colour belong to it . . . It may be said that we have a clear idea of a being and that we know its nature when we can compare it with other beings of which we also have a clear idea . . . But we cannot compare our mind with other minds in order to recognize some relation; we cannot even compare the modes of our mind, its own perceptions, to each other.

The conception of consciousness developed by Malebranche deserves, for a number of reasons, to be called *existential*.[61] There is no doubt that in Descartes

---

anti-Cartesian theorization of the obscurity of consciousness has as its counterpart not only a theocentric ontology and morality, but on another plane, one of the first occurrences of the idea of a 'science of man' (in the objective genitive), making man the object of an anthropological discipline. (See the Preface to *The Search After Truth*: 'Of all the human sciences, the science of Man is the most worthy'.)

60   Malebranche, *Search After Truth*, Book 3, Part 2, chapter 7.

61   It would prove of great interest to Merleau-Ponty, who devoted a course to it: *L'union de l'âme et du corps chez Malebranche, Biran et Bergson*, [*The Union of Soul and Body in Malebranche, Biran and Bergson*] (Paris: Vrin, 1978): 'We see that in Malebranche today's problems are already there' (29). The Malebranchian themes never ceased to recur in the problematics of consciousness between the eighteenth and twentieth centuries (notably in the work of French authors), but on the basis of an a priori position, which might well be called Lockean, of the subject as 'self-consciousness' which is then completed, rectified, even subverted, from the side of affectivity and of 'the flesh'.

the point of the 'Cogito' already consisted in the certitude of an existence (*ego sum, ego existo*). But this became more powerful to the extent that the corresponding experience was intellectual. It is the inverse in Malebranche. Returning to the famous analysis of the 'piece of wax' from the Second Meditation, Malebranche opposed the geometrical or intelligible qualities of bodies to their sensible qualities (colours, tastes, odours, etc.), which are indissociable from the sensations (*sentiments*) of pleasure and pain. For it is these sensations that reveal to us something of our soul of which, in precisely a 'confused' way, they are 'modifications'. Inscribing *sensation, sentiment* and *consciousness* in a continuity that is ontological as well as semantic, Malebranche thus opens the way to a description of subjectivity as a set of qualitative lived experiences (*vécus*) inseparable from an individual particularity which remains incommunicable. And even, strictly speaking, unanalyzable. Locke, for whom the distinction between 'primary' and 'secondary' qualities plays a fundamental role, will be compelled, in opposition, to show its compatibility with the thesis of the total access to analysis of the operations of the mind (*esprit*) (which he distinguishes from the soul [*âme*]).[62]

Locke's counter-argument concerning this opposition appears in a text that is noteworthy in a number of ways, not least because it points us to the interpenetration of theoretical problems and questions of language: it appears in the critical notes on Malebranche's theory of 'ideas', written in 1696 (at the very moment Coste was translating the *Essay*) and published after his death in 1706 in the *Posthumous Works*.[63] Locke absolutely rejected the distinction operative in the *Search After Truth* between knowledge 'through ideas' – pertaining to the objective essences that we see 'in God' (that is, exactly as they exist in the divine understanding) – and knowledge through sensation (*sentiment*), bearing on the sensible qualities of which we perceive only the modifications of the mind that they produce in us (or as our own affections). For him, all ideas or perceptions proceed from sensation, reflection or their combination, whatever their degree of clarity or confusion (*Essay* II.i) The side of objectivity (the representation of things) and that of subjectivity (the modification of the mind) cannot therefore be divided among the different modes of knowledge, but are present in *every* case. On this occasion, Locke turns to Malebranche's use of the term '*sentiment*' (in French) to declare the

62   See the discussion of the problem of primary and secondary qualities in Emmanuel Picavet, *Approches du concret. Une introduction à l'épistémologie*, Paris: Ellipses, 1995. This terminology of antithetical qualities plays no part in Descartes and the Cartesians. It is often thought that Locke developed them on the basis of Boyle's formulations.

63   'Examination of P. Malebranche's Opinion of our "Seeing all things in God" ', *The Works of John Locke*, London: New Edition, 1823, Vol. IX, 211–55. See Charlotte Johnson, 'Locke's Examination of Malebranche and Norris', *Journal of the History of Ideas*, 1958, 551–8. Locke's journal shows that he made a detailed study of Malebranche's theses in *The Search After Truth*, as well as Arnauld's critique of Malebranche in *Of True and False Ideas*.

impossibility of translating it for want of first being able to comprehend it (*Examination*, §42). This difficulty reaches its most extreme point when Malebranche declares that 'consciousness or internal sentiment' is the mode of the soul's knowledge of itself. In that case, Locke asks,

> Is not the idea of a human soul as much a real being in God as the idea of a triangle? And if so, why does not my soul, being intimately united with God, not see its own proper idea that is in it as well as it does the idea of a triangle which is there as well? And how may we justify the fact that God has given us the idea of a triangle and not that of our soul, by saying that God has given us an external sensation for the one, but none for the other, when it is an internal sensation that perceives the operation of the external? (§ 46)

Locke has no difficulty in rendering the French *conscience* as the English 'consciousness', putting into practice the inverse operation that Coste at the very same moment – perhaps with his help – sought to accomplish in his translation of the *Essay*. At the same time, he found it utterly impossible to find an English equivalent for that *sentiment intérieur* which, for Malebranche, is another name for *conscience* as consciousness and, above all, for the very idea of 'sentiment' (which corresponds neither to the Lockean idea of sensation nor to that of reflection, and which for that reason is not a *perception*).[64]

We can only be struck by the way in which the incompatibility of the problematics of consciousness, or of the relation of the mind to itself, was thus materialized through the untranslatability of words at the very moment theoretical interests had never been closer. Two pathways were thus prefigured which might either confront each other or form the terms of an antithesis (as in the Kantian Transcendental Dialectic), but which would never be reconciled. And this incompatibility will be communicated to a great extent through national traditions that will interpret *conscience*/consciousness either as internal sense (*sens interne*), which is essentially a perception and hence a representation, or internal sentiment (*sentiment intérieur*), which is essentially an affect or a feeling of immediate 'presence'.

2.4. '*Sunaisthêsis, Con-sense and Consciousness*': The Cambridge neologism

Ralph Cudworth (1617–1688), who, along with Henry More, was one of the the the principal representatives of the Cambridge Platonists, was an adherent of moderate Protestantism (Latitudinarianism) and a partisan of freedom of conscience in relation to both Church and State, given that according to his conception of morality, Good and Evil were the result of a natural sentiment

---

64   See below (Section 3.3) my discussion of 'the origin of ideas and internal sense'.

rather than commandment and constraint.[65] His monumental work, directed against the materialists (from Democritus to Hobbes),[66] *The True Intellectual System of the Universe: the First Part: Wherein All the Reason and Philosophy of Atheism is Confuted and Its Impossibility Demonstrated*, although finished in 1671, was only published in 1678.[67] It was shaped by his reading of Plotinus and by neo-Platonist interpretations of Aristotle (cited in Greek in his text). He defended the thesis that atomism, the basis of all atheisms from the time of antiquity, in reality constituted a late, reductive and distorted interpretation of a vanished 'true philosophy', which he sought to recover (an idea close to the Hermetic theme of the *prisca philosophia*):[68] its foundation would be a conception of the universe as an animated whole composed of monads, or spiritual atoms.

Cudworth's philosophy represents a generalized vitalism that is both monist and hierarchical. Monist, because the entirety of nature is intelligible on the basis of a single principle by which individuals are formed, which he calls 'plastick nature', which is both form and force. Hierarchical, because along the entire scale or ladder of nature – from material or inanimate individuals to spirits, passing through vegetable and animal life – this principle of activity and self-formation is manifested in ever purer and ever freer forms. Cudworth's system (of which it would not be difficult to find modern and contemporary versions from Bonnet and Maupertuis to Bergson and Teilhard de Chardin) is thus a vast teleology, *simultaneously naturalist and spiritualist*, in which nature progresses towards its own perfection. All the forms and degrees of being are immanent in

---

65   On Cudworth and Cambridge Platonism, in addition to the classic works of Cassirer and Colie, see J.L. Berteau's introduction to Cudworth's *Traité de morale et Traité du libre arbitre* (Paris: PUF, 1995), as well as his 'La conscience de soi chez les Platoniciens de Cambridge', in E. Ellrodt, *Genèse de la conscience moderne*. See also. J.A. Passmore, Ralph Cudworth, Cambridge: Cambridge University Press, 1953; Samuel S. Mintz, *The Hunting of the Leviathan: Seventeenth Century Reactions to the Materialism and Moral Philosophy of Thomas Hobbes*, Cambridge: Cambridge University Press, 1969; C.A. Patrides, *The Cambridge Platonists*, Cambridge: Cambridge University Press, 1969; R. Popkin, 'Cudworth', in *The Third Force in Seventeenth Century Thought*, Leiden: Brill, 1992.

66   He was one of the first to use the term 'materialism'. See O. Bloch, *Le Materialisme*, Paris: PUF, 1985, 6. He proposed a classification of the four classical forms of materialism (Democritean or atomist, Stratonian, Stoic and hylozoic).

67   An envisioned second part was never completed. Cudworth's book was never translated into French but was summarized at great length in several instalments of Jean Le Clerc's *Bibliothèque choisie*, published in Amsterdam between 1703 and 1706 (see Vols I, II, and V – the latter containing a response to Bayle's critiques of the doctrine of plastic natures). This publication played an important role in the renaissance of vitalist conceptions in the face of the mechanism inspired by Harvey and Descartes. See Jacques Roger, *Les sciences de la vie dans la pensée française au XVIIIe siècle*, 1963, rééd. Paris: Albin Michel, 1993, 418 ff.

68   See Frances Yates's discussion of Cudworth's positions on this point in *Giordano Bruno and the Hermetic Tradition*, Chicago: Chicago University Press, 1964; also Martin Bernal, *Black Athena: the Afroasiatic Roots of Classical Civilization*, Rutgers: Rutgers University Press, 1987; and Alfred Rupert Hall, *Henry More: Magic, Religion and Experiment*, London: Blackwell, 1990.

the same process (which could not fail to create theological difficulties for Cudworth, who was accused of pantheism and of reducing God to the world). But this entire progression is oriented to its end, and the perfection of the divine soul simultaneously represents the organizing force and archetype of the universe, whose constituent individualities resemble it more or less completely.

In this context, Cudworth fabricates, among other abstract terms ending in 'ness', 'consciousness', from the adjective 'conscious', itself only recently naturalized. He made it the equivalent of 'Con-sense', which he refers to the Greek terms *sunaisthêsis* and *sunesis* found in Plato and Aristotle, thus fabricating a fictional etymology (for the Latins never considered the word *conscientia* as a 'translation' of such terms, relating it instead to the Stoic and Christian terms *suneidos* and *suneidêsis*).[69] This neologism intervenes in the continuous process in which the doctrine of 'plastic natures' is recapitulated when Cudworth seeks to distinguish a vital force, ignorant of its own ends (that which forms simple organisms), from the force that directs animal actions. On this occasion Cudworth also inserts a critical reference to Cartesianism: the dualism of two substances, extension and thought, is no more capable of accounting for the production of life and for finality in general in nature than materialism.

The concept of consciousness in Cudworth, endowed with a significance at once ethical, ontological and cosmological, thus crystallizes the conjunction of naturalism and spiritualism that I have already noted. It might seem sufficient to say that *consciousness* is the mark of certain kinds of natural beings, namely, those situated near the top of the scale of beings. But it is more interesting to note that *consciousness* in this sense is not a uniquely human trait, even if it above all characterizes human actions: it 'begins' with the vital sentiment or self-sensation of beings inferior to man and extends to the superior intelligences, in particular to God, who is eminently 'conscious'. In this case, consciousness is not limited to the role of informing action or behaviour, but becomes the very principle of creation in that the Superior Intelligence (*Noûs*) is not content to pursue external ends, however rational they may be, but 'thinks itself', 'desires itself' and 'enjoys itself'.

Its extensive role results in the fact that consciousness is a matter of degree (which differs essentially from the reflexive definition introduced at the same time by the French Cartesians, from whom Cudworth thus sought to demarcate himself: for him, reflection is a superior degree of consciousness among other possible degrees). Even more interestingly, this leads him to use the term 'inconscious', which generally appears in the pair *senseless and inconscious*,

---

69   See the discussion of the usage of Greek terms *suneidos, sunesis, suneidos,* and *sunaisthê-sis* in A. Cancrini: *SUNEIDESIS. Il tema semantico della 'con-scientia' nella Grecia antica,* Lessico Intellettuale Europeo, VI, Edizioni dell'Ateneo Roma, 1970, as well as H.-R. Schwyzer, *'Bewusst' und 'Unbewusst' bei Plotin,* Entretiens de la Fondation Hardt sur l'Antiquité classique, Tome V, *Les sources de Plotin,* Vandœuvres-Genève, 1957.

which characterizes 'matter'.[70] Inconsciousness and consciousness are contraries; however, by virtue of the principle of hierarchical continuity that organizes the entire system, this contrariety only has a relative meaning: it reproduces itself fundamentally at each level of the scale, which can always be compared to the more primitive which precedes it, or the more perfect that follows it. Only God is perfectly 'conscious', without a trace of inconsciousness, his intelligence perfectly perceiving itself, his mind moving itself (the 'self-active Mind'). Inversely, Cudworth says explicitly that the inconscious mind is a 'thought asleep' (or lethargic, in a stupor: *drowsy, unawakened* or *astonished cogitation*). Thus he opens the possibility of maintaining that consciousness emerges from life, or that life, and even simple matter, are *inconscious energies* or inconscious forms of intelligence, blind to their own ends.[71]

We can thus see that the reference to consciousness plays a decisive role in the economy of Cudworth's system and in the strategy he directs against materialism as he goes after it on its own naturalist terrain. It is this that prevents the hierarchy from being reversible. To attribute 'thought' to the most elementary forms of nature on the grounds that they are endowed with the capacity of development or individuation is possible only if thought may be 'conscious' or 'inconscious' of itself. Nature is the ascent from matter to thought because it is the ascent of inconscious energy to conscious energy (or of the latent forms of consciousness towards its actual and reflected forms). This is precisely the point of departure of the Leibnizian doctrine of perception and more generally of all the attempts to assemble life, sentiment and consciousness into a progression which would then be inscribed in an evolution that expresses the order of nature itself insofar as it has mind or spirit (*esprit*) as its end.

Finally, we should note that with this expansion of the idea of consciousness comes a total abandonment of any direct reference to the formula and the question of the 'I'. At the same time, the theme of '*sunaisthèsis*, Con-sense and consciousness' is closely associated with a group of terms connoting reflection, autonomy and self-reference. This displacement is decisive for the formation of the notion of self-consciousness which must – through an explicit conceptualization of the 'self' (*soi*) – be differentiated from mere redundancy. Cudworth, it appears, did not invent the term self-consciousness (which the Oxford English

---

70   'The hylozists never able, neither, to produce *Animal Sense* and *Conciousness* out of what *Senseless* and *Inconscious*'. Cudworth, *True Intellectual System*, 666–7.

71   The difference with Malebranche is thus total, insofar as it is a general difference between theories of *self-misrecognition* and theories of *the unconscious* whose encounter will come only with contemporary developments in psychoanalysis. Far from, for Malebranche, misrecognition characterizing beings inferior to man, as well as man's own animality, it represents the alienated form of what is most elevated with him: the soul, the image of his Creator from which the Fall has turned him away. In opposition, Cudworth's pantheistic optimism leaves little room for the moral and theological consequences of original sin. He was also a partisan of 'free will' and in general an adversary of predestination and Augustinianism.

Dictionary attributes, before Locke, to the Cambridge Platonist John Smith, who in 1675 used it in a sense close to 'egoism'), but he employed *self-conscious* along with other terms of the same facture. His insistence (and that of the Cambridge Platonists in general) on the prefix 'self', according to the real or fictional model of Greek terms beginning with 'auto', is not without interest for those who would explain the way Locke isolated the idea of *the self*.[72] It might also be acknowledged that the thesis according to which 'consciousness' and 'self' are not tied to the substantial difference between soul and body, but instead to their plastic integration into a unique form explicitly directed against Cartesian dualism, made it possible for Locke to neutralize the question of substance and render the functions of the mind autonomous in relation to 'the soul' and 'the body'.

It is striking to see that the drafts of Locke's *Essay*, which date back to the beginning of the 1670s, contain not a single occurrence of the word 'consciousness', which occupies, in contrast, a central place in the final version, from the first edition of 1690 to the second edition of 1694 (where it is even more prominent). But the word appeared under his own pen in a note in his Journal, dated 20 February 1682, where, discussing precisely Cudworth's book and his positions concerning the immortality of the souls of beasts, Locke anticipates the conception of personal identity that he would not fully develop until 1694. In a certain sense everything is already there:

> Identity of persons lies not in having the same numerical body made up of the same particles, nor if the mind consists of incorporeal spirits in their being the same. But in the memory of one's past self and actions continued on under the consciousness of being the same person, whereby every man owns himself.[73]

3. MIND, CONSCIOUSNESS, IDENTITY: THE ISOLATION OF THE 'MENTAL' IN *AN ESSAY CONCERNING HUMAN UNDERSTANDING*

The composition of the *Essay* took place over a long period and in several European cities of scientific, religious and political significance. The first manuscripts date from 1671, when Locke had just been elected to the Royal Society on Boyle's recommendation, and had begun his service as physician, advisor

---

72   See J. L. Breteau. The Cambridge Platonists' predilection for the idea of reflexivity, as well as for neologisms derived from Greek and Latin that allow it to be expressed, appears clearly in Henry More's *Immortality of the Soul* (1659). We will have occasion to stress its importance for the genesis of Locke's formulations concerning personality and the self. See 'Personality' and 'Self' in the Glossary.

73   See G. A. J. Rodgers, 'Zue Entstehungsgeschichte des *Essay Concerning Human Understanding*' in Udo Thiel, Hrsg, *John Locke. Essay über den menschlichen Verstand*, Berlin: Akademie Verlag, 1997; Michel Ayers, *Locke: Epistemology and Ontology*, London: Routledge, 1991, Vol. II, 254–5; and particularly Marshall, *John Locke*, 153, who specifies the context.

and secretary to the Earl of Shaftesbury, a leader of the Whig Party. In the years that followed, he travelled extensively in France (notably Montpellier and Paris), where he frequented both Cartesians (Arnauld and Nicole) and the Epicurean disciples of Gassendi, reading and translating certain of their texts and reacting to the ideas of Malebranche. In 1683, his freedom, if not his life, was under threat because of his participation in a conspiracy against Charles II. He was forced to seek refuge in Holland, where he completed both the *Two Treatises of Government* and the *Essay*.[74] He established close relations with humanist theologians (Arminians or Remonstrants) such as Phillip Van Limborch, who were adversaries of Calvinist predestination and partisans of a rational interpretation of the Scriptures, and with exiled French Protestants who were the founders of the Republic of Letters.[75] In 1688, after the Glorious Revolution, he returned to

---

74   Robert Ashcraft, *Revolutionary Politics and Locke's Two Treatises of Government*, Princeton, NJ: Princeton University Press, 1986; Marshall, *John Locke*, 1994.

75   One of Locke's close friends in Amsterdam was Jean Le Clerc, who was born in Geneva in 1657 and died in 1736, a philosopher and philologist linked to the Arminian Church and very active in the debates of the time. From 1686 he was editor of the *Bibliothèque Universelle et Historique*, succeeded after 1703 by the *Bibliothèque choisie* (see. A. Barnes, *Jean Le Clerc (1657–1736) et la République des Lettres*, Paris : Droz, 1938). In Vol. VIII (1688) of the *Bibliothèque*, there appeared a French translation of a summary in manuscript form of an *Essai Philosophique concernant l'Entendement [Humain]*, written by Locke himself, and which concluded with the following statement: 'This is an extract from an English work that the author wanted to publish to satisfy some of his closest friends and to give them a summary of his sentiments. If any of them who takes the trouble to examine them, believes himself to have found a place where the author is mistaken, or where there is something obscure and defective in this system, he need only send his doubts or objections to Amsterdam to the bookstore where the *Bibliothèque Universelle* is published. Although the author has no great desire to see his work published and believes that one should have more respect for the public than to offer it what one believes to be true before knowing if others agree or judge it useful; nevertheless, he is not so reserved that it may not be hoped that he will be disposed to give his entire treatise to the public if the manner in which this summary is received gives him occasion to hope that he would not do badly in publishing his work. The reader may note that in this version certain terms are used in a new sense or perhaps have never before appeared in any French book. It would take too long to express them through paraphrase and it is thought that in philosophy it is permitted to take the same liberty in our own language that is on occasion taken in others, that is, of forming analogical words when common usage does not furnish those that are needed. The author did it in his English and it may be done in this language, without it being necessary to ask the reader's permission. It may well be desired that one might do as much in French and that we might equal in the abundance of terms a language that ours surpasses in the exactitude of expression' (140–2).

It may be seen through this text, intended to entice the scholars of Europe, that Locke's philosophy was presented in a French summary before it was published in its original language (but not without some confusion concerning the author: see *Bibliothèque choisie*, Année 1705, Tome VI, 'Eloge de feu M. Locke'). It was Le Clerc who proposed Pierre Coste (1668-1747), a young Protestant from Languedoc who was his protégé and collaborator, as translator of the whole *Essay*. In 1696 Coste moved to England to be able to work with the author and was hired to be the tutor of the son of Lady Masham, Francis Cudworth Masham (Cf. *The Correspondence of John Locke*, Edited by E.S. de Beer in Eight Volumes, Oxford 1978, Vol. III ff., as well as Jean Le Clerc, *Epistolario*, cit., Vol. II). Later, he translated Newton's *Optics* (1720). In contrast, Locke does not appear to have associated with Bayle, whose conceptions were far from his own, even if posterity has linked them as advocates of tolerance.

England and published three works simultaneously: the *Essay* (in English, under his own name), *The Two Treatises* (in English, anonymously) and *A Letter Concerning Toleration* (in Latin, anonymously). These remain his most famous books.

Several editions of the *Essay* appeared during Locke's lifetime, each containing certain modifications. The most important modifications were the changes to the discussion of freedom and the will in Chapter XXI ('Of Power') of Book II, the addition of Chapter XXVII ('Of Identity and Diversity'), the concluding Chapter XXXIII ('Of the Association of Ideas') to the same Book, and finally the addition of Chapter XIX ('Of Enthusiasm') to Book IV, a critique of illuminationist and mystical conceptions of religion in the name of a 'reasonable Christianity' that prohibited anyone from exercising 'tyranny' over his own mind or the minds of others.[76]

The *Essay* is the first of the great modern treatises on the theory of knowledge. Its objective, explained in the preface (I.i), is to proceed to a critical examination of the different *faculties of knowledge* that form *human understanding* from the double point of view of their 'agreement' with or 'proportion' to their objects (in order to derive criteria of certitude and truth) and of the limits of their validity (so as to establish the limits of their exercise, above all, the border between reason and faith). The essential propositions concerning consciousness are contained in four groups that mark its progression:

1. The refutation of the theory of 'innate ideas', developed in the Book I. Locke demonstrates the possibility of *dissociating the 'Cartesian' principle according to which the mind cannot think without knowing that it thinks* from the representation of a 'thinking substance' and, a fortiori, from the thesis that 'the soul always thinks'.

2. The description of 'the original' of ideas in sensation and in reflection as the perception of 'external sense' and the perception of 'internal sense' (II, i). By introducing this latter notion, Locke opens the possibility of an analysis by the mind of its own functioning. *Consciousness* is thus defined as 'the perception of what passes in a man's own mind' (II.i.19).

3. The definition of a criterion for *personal identity* that is nothing other than consciousness itself (II.xxvii). This chapter was added in 1694, as much to complete his argument as to counter the objections of the theologians concerned

---

76 Locke devoted an entire work to this topic, which, although published once again anonymously, drew from the positions he took in his debate with Stillingfleet. It concluded with a magnificent profession of faith in favour of freedom of conscience: 'I shall think it according to my master's rule, not to be called nor to call any man on earth Master. No man, I think, has a right to prescribe to me my faith, or magisterially to impose his interpretations or opinions on me: nor is it material to anyone what mine are any further than they carry their own evidence with them.' *A Second Vindication of the Reasonableness of Christianity*, in *The Works of John Locke*, London, 1823, Vol. VII, 359.

about the dissolution of the substantiality of the soul (which offered proof of the immortality of the soul).[77] Locke responded by showing that the person, with its moral, juridical and religious attributions (we are responsible for our actions and will have to account for them on the day of 'judgment'), is more accurately identified by a theory of consciousness than by a metaphysics of substance. Having thus recast his theory, Locke proceeded to introduce references to consciousness in the second edition that had not appeared in the first.

4. Finally, the analysis of the relation between the 'internal operations of the mind' and their 'expression' by means of the signs of language (III.i–ii), which leads to a distinction between 'mental truths' and 'verbal truths' (IV.v). There emerges at this point a bifurcation that is fundamental for the entire history of philosophy, marking the triumph of the point of view of conception or representation over that of enunciation. While Locke discusses this only at the end of his work, it is possible to see that it governs the forms of his argumentation from the beginning. I will therefore proceed according to the following order: first, I will show how Locke *isolated the mental (Mind, Thought) from the verbal (Language, Words)* and how this separation allowed him to reformulate the principle of identity within the element of consciousness; I will then show that this separation coincided with a recasting of the traditional notion of 'internal sense'. To conclude, I will attempt to establish the unity of the concepts of *consciousness, self (soi)* and *identity* in a theory of the 'Person', which is the first great modern doctrine of the individual subject, and I will combine the characteristics of the interiority and exteriority of the mind into a 'topography' that could be compared to other examples in philosophy of a construction of the 'subject' as a complex set of relations.

3.1. The mental and the verbal

In Chapter I of Book III, Locke takes a position against the notion that words in language are *signs of things* in favour of the notion that words are *signs of the ideas of things*. The idea that words are names of things is absurd, for words also denote *relations* and thus intellectual operations. They must be able to signify 'a multitude of particular existences' (or generality, which is the case with common nouns),[78] presence or absence (or affirmation or negation), and finally notions of 'things that fall not under our senses' (even if they have their origin in experience). This means that only ideas present in the mind can confer a meaning on language.

---

77   See Ayers, *Locke*, II, 'Personal Identity Before the *Essay*', 254–9.

78   Primary ideas (genetically as well as logically) being sensible, we are led back not to 'the things themselves', but to their impressions or representations in the mind. The word or name is thus the general term that designates a class of objects of sensible experience. See Geneviève Brykman, 'Philosophie des ressemblances contre philosophie des universaux chez Locke', *Revue de Métaphysique et de Morale*, Oct.–Dec. 1995, 439–54.

Does this mean that, according to Locke, words are not related to things? Absolutely not, but it must be admitted that this relation is the result of a 'supposition' of the mind. The relation established between ideas and their verbal and written sign is first strictly individual: 'Words in their primary or immediate Signification, stand for nothing but the Ideas in the mind of him that uses them' (III.ii.2). Words are for each individual 'signs of internal conceptions' and 'marks for the Ideas within his own Mind' (III.i.2): 'That then which Words are the Marks of, are the *Ideas* of the Speaker: Nor can any one apply them, as Marks, immediately to any thing else, but the *Ideas*, that he himself hath' (III.i.2). It follows from this that every individual must have *acquired ideas* to be able to make use of the corresponding words, and that individuals attribute to words a univocal relation to things in consequence of their intention of establishing a 'secret reference' to other men: 'they suppose their Words to be the Marks of the Ideas in the Minds also of other Men, with whom they communicate' (III.ii.4).

In IV.v ('Of Truth in General'), Locke extends the correspondence between words and ideas to that between *verbal propositions* and *mental propositions*. This in turn makes possible a distinction between the 'Truth of Thought' or 'Mental Truth' and the 'Truth of Words' or 'Verbal Truth': here the French translation (as *vérité mentale* vs *vérité verbale*) allows a unification of the terminology and underscores the new conception of thought as 'mental activity' (*activité mentale*). Speaking of 'mental propositions' allows Locke formally to preserve the classical thesis which says that 'Truth properly belongs only to Propositions' (IV.v.2), given that mental propositions are nothing more than operations of thought. It is necessary to return to these operations to establish whether the statements constitute 'real truth' or 'nominal truths', that is, presumed truths that may be mistaken. We see here *the birth of psychologism* in philosophy, which is less the result of a critique of the idea of a necessary truth existing in itself than a disqualification of language as the originary element of thought (an 'anti-linguistic turn' as it were).[79] We can also see that psychologism is not the effect of the birth of a psychology: rather, it is the condition of psychology, the programme that psychologists will seek to carry out:

---

79   Of course, this disqualification would be immediately followed by a requalification that aimed to provide the indispensable instrument of the progress of knowledge. But it is the question of the semantic foundation that is important here. It is not so much a question of chronological anteriority as of a logical priority, even if it contains a genetic dimension. Locke did not mean that we could know the world without the use of language; on the contrary, Book III of the *Essay* is entirely devoted to explaining its necessary function, which is the feedback effect of social communication on the constitution of the understanding. But he wanted to show that the use of words and their relation to ideas are always, in the last analysis, based on a norm of signification that belongs exclusively to the interiority of consciousness, or to the way consciousness perceives its own operations. It is – to take up only one reference – exactly what Frege sought to avoid by opposing the subjective questions of 'representation' (*Vorstellung*), that referred in his eyes to psychology, to the objective questions of 'sense' (*Sinn*) and 'denotation' (*Bedeutung*) that arise from logic (see the *Ecrits logiques et philosophiques*, trad. et introduction de Claude Imbert, Paris, Seuil, 1971, 102 ff.).

But to return to the consideration of Truth. We must, I say, observe two sorts of Propositions, that we are capable of making.

First, *Mental* wherein the *Ideas* in our Understandings *are* without the use of Words *put together, or separated*, by the Mind, perceiving, or judging of their Agreement, or Disagreement.

Secondly, Verbal Propositions, which *are Words*, the signs of our *Ideas*, put *together or separated in affirmative or negative Sentences*. By which way of affirming or denying, these Signs, made by Sounds, are as it were, put together or separated one from another. (IV.v.5)

Locke thus shows how the operations of the mind (that is, consciousness) 'tacitly' duplicate those of language and constitute its norm of truth:

Every one's Experience will satisfie him, that the Mind, either by perceiving, or supposing the Agreement or Disagreement of any of its *Ideas*, does tacitly within it self put them into a kind of Proposition affirmative or negative, which I have endeavoured to express by the terms *Putting together* and *Separating*. But this Action of the Mind, which is so familiar to every thinking and reasoning Man, is easier to be conceived by reflecting on what passes in us, when we affirm or we deny, than to be explained by Words. When a Man has in his Mind the *Idea* of two Lines . . . he, as it were, *joins* or *separates* those two *Ideas*, viz. the *Idea* of that line and the idea of the kind of Divisibility, and so makes a mental Proposition, which is true or false, according as such a kind of divisibility, Divisibility into such *aliquot* parts, does really agree to that Line or no. When *Ideas* are so put together, or separated in the Mind, as they, or the Things they stand for do agree, or not, that is, as I may call it, *mental Truth*. But the *Truth of Words* is something more, and that is the affirming or denying of Words one of another, as the *Ideas* they stand for agree or disagree. (IV.v.6)

Later, Locke notes that the passage from mental propositions to verbal propositions carries the specific risk of losing any relation to reality:

Though our Words signifie nothing but our *Ideas*, yet being designed by them to signifie *Things*, the Truth they contain, when put into Propositions, will be only *Verbal*, when they stand for *Ideas* in the Mind, that have not an agreement with the reality of Things. And therefore Truth, as well as Knowledge, may well come under the distinction of *Verbal* and *Real*; that being only *verbal* Truth, wherein Terms are joined according to the agreement or disagreement of the *Ideas* they stand for, without regarding whether our *Ideas* are such, as really have, or are capable of having an Existence in Nature. But then it is they contain *real* Truth, when these signs are joined, as our *Ideas* agree; and when our *Ideas* are such, as we know are capable of having an Existence in Nature: which in Substances we cannot know, but by knowing that such have existed. (IV.v.8)

Language is thus, at once, more (a garment) and less (a presumption) than thought. The initial situation (in which we needed words to express complex ideas) is thus reversed. It is necessary to return to pure thought to establish what in it is 'really' truth according to its two aspects: internal coherence and correspondence with things. But this assumes that thought contains within itself a criterion of certitude, and that it is capable of comparing itself both with itself and with its exterior.

3.2. The principle of identity

Even before arriving at the statement of a criterion of identity for the human *person,* Locke inscribed a statement in the constitution of consciousness that renders this consciousness the 'identity to itself' (*une identité à soi*). Without this preliminary moment, there could be no question of *founding* anything at all. Consciousness could not guarantee the identity of the person if it did not contain the principle of identity in itself. Let us observe that in this way Locke rediscovers the functions of the *certitude* that characterized the Cartesian 'cogito', but by distributing them throughout a theoretical constitution of the subject, instead of concentrating them in the pure statement of the 'I', that is, in the paradox of self-reference. At the same time, it is possible to grant his analysis a general character. The singularity of the subject (which Locke calls *the self*) can be described without it being necessary for this subject to *state itself immediately* in the first person, as in the Cartesian meditation. In compensation, according to a classical dialectical schema, the statement of the self-identity with which this constitution begins coincides with the refutation of the error that is the 'doctrine of innate ideas'. In this way, we witness the production of a necessary truth on the basis of its contrary, which confirms that it is truly a matter of a foundation.[80]

Most of Book I is occupied with the refutation of the doctrine of innate ideas. I will set aside for the moment the unceasing discussion of exactly at whom, among the ancients and the moderns, Locke's arguments are aimed.[81] It will suffice to admit that, even if Descartes cannot be recognized in all the formulations Locke criticizes, the argument the latter develops finally results in a dissociation of the two parts of the Cartesian heritage. On the one hand, the 'false' idea that certain notions may owe their universality to a divine insemination in the human mind. On the other, the 'true' idea that thought is immediately present to itself, or that it is intrinsically reflexive. Between these two, the proposition that 'the soul always thinks', interpreted as the idea of a substantial

---

80   I will not discuss the 'empiricism' attributed to Locke by the philosophical tradition. For what concerns us here, it is rather his *rationalism* that is striking.

81   On this point, see John Yolton, *Locke and the Way of Ideas*, Oxford: Oxford University Press, 1968; and Jean-Michel Vienne, *Expérience et raison. Les fondements de morale selon Locke*, Paris: Vrin, 1991.

permanence, is set in contradiction with experience. But its refutation opens the way to another thesis, essential to the theory of consciousness: *the mind always remembers having thought.*

The first moment of the critique of the doctrine of innate ideas consists in showing that the general principles of logic and of morality (what are traditionally called 'common notions') are neither original nor universal:

> this Argument of Universal Consent, which is made use of, to prove innate Principles, seems to me a Demonstration that there are none such: Because there are none to which all Mankind give a Universal Assent. I shall begin with the Speculative, and instance in those magnified Principles of Demonstration, *Whatsoever is, is*; and *'Tis impossible for the same thing to be and not to be* . . . these Propositions are so far from having an universal Assent, that there are a great part of Mankind, to whom they are not so much as known.
>
> For, first 'tis evident, that all *Children* and *Ideots*, have not the least Apprehension or Thought of them. (I.ii.4–5)

The second moment emerges from the objection that innate truths can be found *imprinted on the soul without its knowing it*, or without the soul having this knowledge 'actually' at its disposal. It is this objection – by means of which Leibniz, for example, attempts to salvage the notion of innate ideas – that Locke declares absurd:

> it seeming to me near a Contradiction, to say, that there are Truths imprinted on the Soul, which it perceives or understands not; imprinting, if it signify any thing, being nothing else, but the making certain Truths to be perceived. For to imprint any thing on the Mind without the Mind's perceiving it, seems to me hardly intelligible . . . To say a notion is imprinted *on the Mind*, and yet at the same time to say, that the mind is ignorant of it, *and never yet took notice of it*, is to make this Impression nothing. No Proposition can be said to be in the Mind, which it never yet knew, which it was never yet conscious of . . . For if these Words (to be in the Understanding) have any Propriety, they signify to be understood. So that, to be in the Understanding, and, not to be understood; to be in the Mind, and, never to be perceived, is all one, as to say, any thing is, and is not, in the Mind or Understanding. If therefore these two Propositions, *Whatsoever is, is*; and *It is impossible for the same thing to be, and not to be*, are by Nature imprinted . . . all that have Souls must necessarily have them in their Understandings, know the Truth of them, and assent to it. (I.ii.5)[82]

---

82   Note that Coste is not rigorous in his translations of the words 'Soul' and 'Mind', which proves that this distinction is new or unworkable for him. See the entry 'Mind' in the Glossary. Coste's translation: 'Car de dire qu'il y a des vérités imprimées dans l'Âme que l'Âme n'aperçoit

Locke continues to repeat this formulation, not only in the same chapter (§9), but throughout the work, every time he must return to the foundation of his theory. Thus, in II.ii.10 and above all in II.ii.19:

Can the Soul think, and not the Man? Or a Man think, and not be conscious of it? . . . If they say, The Man thinks always, but is not always conscious of it; they may as well say, His Body is extended, without having parts. For 'tis altogether as intelligible to say, that a body is extended without parts, as that anything *thinks without being conscious of it*, or perceiving, that it is does so. They who talk thus, may, with as much reason, if it be necessary to their Hypothesis, say, That a Man is always hungry, but does not always feel it: Whereas hunger consists in that very sensation, as thinking consists in being conscious that one thinks. If they say, That a Man is always conscious to himself of thinking; I ask, How they know it? Consciousness is the perception of what passes in a Man's own mind. Can another Man perceive, that I am conscious of any thing, when I perceive it not myself? No Man's Knowledge here, can go beyond his Experience.[83]

---

ou n'entend point, c'est, ce me semble, une espèce de contradiction, l'action d'*imprimer* ne pouvant marquer autre chose (supposé qu'elle signifie quelque chose de réel en cette rencontre) que *faire apercevoir* certaines vérités. Car imprimer quoi que ce soit dans l'Âme, sans que l'Âme l'aperçoive (*without the Mind's perceiving it*), c'est, à mon sens, une chose à peine intelligible . . . Dire qu'une Notion est gravée dans l'âme (*imprinted on the Mind*), et soutenir en même temps que l'âme ne la connaît point (*that the mind is ignorant of it*), et qu'elle n'en a eu encore aucune connaissance (*and never yet took notice of it*), c'est faire de cette impression un pur néant. On ne peut point assurer qu'une certaine proposition soit dans l'Esprit, lorsque l'Esprit ne l'a point encore aperçue, et qu'il n'en a découvert aucune idée en lui-même (*which it never yet knew, which it was never conscious of*) . . . Car si ces mots, *être dans l'Entendement*, emportent quelque chose de positif, ils signifient *être aperçu et compris par l'Entendement*. De sorte que soutenir qu'une chose est dans l'Entendement, et qu'elle n'est pas conçue par l'Entendement (*to be in the Understanding, and, not to be understood*), qu'elle est dans l'Esprit sans que l'Esprit l'aperçoive, c'est autant que si on disait qu'une chose est et n'est pas dans l'Esprit ou dans l'Entendement. Si donc ces deux Propositions: *Ce qui est, est*, et, *Il est impossible qu'une chose soit et ne soit pas en même temps*, étaient gravées dans l'âme des Hommes par la Nature . . . tous ceux qui ont une Âme devraient les avoir nécessairement dans l'esprit, en reconnaître la vérité et y donner leur consentement' (I.i.5).

83 Coste's translation: 'Or l'Âme peut-elle penser, sans que l'Homme pense? Ou bien, l'Homme peut-il penser, sans en être convaincu en lui-même? . . . ils peuvent tout aussi bien dire, que le Corps est étendu, sans avoir des parties. Car dire que le Corps est étendu, sans avoir des parties, et qu'une Chose pense, sans connaître et sans apercevoir qu'elle pense, ce sont deux assertions également inintelligibles. Et ceux qui parlent ainsi seront tout aussi bien fondés à soutenir . . . que l'Homme a toujours faim, mais qu'il n'a pas toujours un sentiment de faim; puisque la Faim ne saurait être sans ce sentiment-là, non plus que la Pensée sans une conviction qui nous assure intérieurement que nous pensons. S'ils disent, que l'Homme a toujours cette conviction, je demande d'où ils le savent, puisque cette conviction n'est autre chose que la perception de ce qui se passe dans l'âme de l'Homme. Or un autre Homme peut-il s'assurer que je sens en moi ce que je n'aperçois pas moi-même? C'est ici que la connaissance de l'Homme ne saurait s'étendre au delà de sa propre expérience'.

We may clearly see the theoretical inversion Locke carries out here. The principle of identity and the principle of contradiction are relativized as acquired beliefs or knowledge, that is, he has posited their de facto non-universality (not all men – a category which includes children, savages and idiots – have knowledge of these principles as *statements*). But this is in order to discover them inscribed in the very structure of the mind in the form of the thesis: *it is impossible that man does not think that he thinks, or that he thinks without thinking.* And through a sudden counter-attack, this contradiction is imputed to those (Cartesians, or at least those reputed to be Cartesians) who postulate that the soul always thinks, that is, continuously. It is not the statements or even the corresponding 'mental propositions' which are universal, but the *non-contradiction of the mind* and, in consequence, the *mind's identity to itself* as an activity or operation of thought. Finally, Locke refers this affirmation to the *experience of each person*, which does not mean that it is relativized, but on the contrary that at the heart of every experience we feel the same collision with the impossible and in consequence the same point of universal certitude. The name of this necessity in which thought finds itself not thinking without thinking is precisely *consciousness*.

Obviously, this name by itself produces an effect. We might thus summarize this effect by reformulating the 'double negation' inherent in the articulation of the logical and the psychological: *thought is consciousness because a nonconscious thought is a contradiction in terms*, a non-thought. But this new formulation, equivalent in Locke's eyes, also reveals the postulate underlying the entire argument: *that to think and to know are two fundamentally identical notions*. This is the case because both are identical to a third term: *perception*. It is equivalent to saying: it would be contradictory for the mind to *think without knowing* that it thinks, or it would be contradictory for the mind to *think without thinking* that it thinks, or think and not think at the same time.

In what preceded (the refutation of the doctrine of innate ideas), we saw the direct application of this equivalence; in what follows, the reverse: as soon as thought knows or thinks (i.e. perceives) that it thinks, it by definition can itself undertake to know all its modes, all its operations. Locke, more than the Cartesians, would thus have a better claim to being the *true* founder of rational psychology which, nominally grounded in experience, is in fact composed of all the mind's reflections on itself. And which precedes in this sense, both in principle and in fact, any constitution of 'science'.[84]

---

84   Let me suggest that the one who introduced the term into philosophy, Christian Wolff, as a good Leibnizian, called Locke's rational psychology *psychologia empirica* in order to reserve for his school the 'true' *psychologia rationalis*. This point of view was still alive and well in the twentieth century, for example in the commentaries of Cassirer (*The Philosophy of the Enlightenment* [1932], Princeton, NJ: Princeton University Press, 2009).

3.3. The origin of ideas and internal sense

When (in the first edition of the *Essay*) Locke introduced the noun *consciousness* (II.i.19), he had already moved to a positive construction. We are no longer concerned with the soul (*l'âme*) (despite some terminological inconsistency) but with the structure of the mind (*l'esprit*).[85] It is a question of showing from what the material of all thought – that is, ideas – arises, as well as why it is possible for the mind to analyze the logic of mental operations. In fact, these two explanations are one and the same, which means that the possibility of self-knowledge is *originarily* inscribed in the structure of the mind.

His thesis is that *ideas have a double origin:* they arise either from the sensation of the qualities of objects in the external world or from the reflection of the mind or the understanding on its own operations. Locke specifies (II.i.3–5) that the two 'Fountains' can both be considered kinds of perception, insofar as both *receive* ideas; in the one case, they are received through the channel of the sense organs, while in the other they are formed through an analogous faculty 'which might properly enough be call'd internal Sense' (II.i.4). At the same time, he directs our attention to the fact that ideas derived from reflection are not merely ideas to the second degree or 'ideas of ideas', as if the mind would in some sense observe primary ideas that came to it through sensation, but are perceptions of the *operations or actions of the mind*, or of the way that mind *operates on (and with)* the primary ideas that come to it from sensation.

Is consciousness then purely and simply identical to *internal or interior sense*? Here again there are nuances that compel us to take into account the historical uses of the same terms. The paradox is that that the expression 'internal sense', destined for so important a future,[86] would appear only once in Locke's text. I would explain this fact in the following way: the expression 'internal sense' was not invented by Locke, but has an Aristotelian and Medieval origin designating the soul's perception of phenomena localized in the interior of the organism.[87] At the same time, Descartes spoke of 'the interior senses' through which I experience internal sensations (hunger and thirst) and the sentiments of pleasure, pain, joy, sadness and so on.[88] In sum, Locke tells us that

---

85   On the translation or non-translation of mind by *esprit*, see the entry 'Mind' in the Glossary and my article 'Âme/Esprit' in Cassin, ed., *Vocabulaire*.

86   In particular in Kant (via Tetens). On Kant's 'debt' to Locke, see Beatrice Longuenesse, *Kant et le pouvoir de juger: Sensibilité et discursivité dans l'analytique transcendentale de La critique de la raison pur*, Paris: PUF, 1993; and Jocelyn Benoist, *Kant et les limites de la synthèse*, Paris: PUF, 1996.

87   See Ruth Harvey, *The Inward Wits: Psychological Theory in the Middle Ages and the Renaissance*, London: The Warburg Institute, 1975, and H.A. Wolfson, 'The Internal Senses in Latin, Arabic and Hebrew Philosophical Tetxs', *Harvard Theological Review* XXVIII (1935), 69–133.

88   Descartes, *Principles of Philosophy*, IV, §190. Also, see Kambouchner, *L'homme des passions*, I, 269 ff.

if there is an internal sense, this sense can be nothing other than *the reflection* through which the mind perceives its own operations. In a certain sense, then, the term is useless. But in another, it has the advantage of underscoring the parallelism of 'interior perception' and 'exterior perception', that is, of showing that *a reflection is as immediate as a sensation,* and that it engenders ideas as 'simple' as those engendered by sensation, beginning with the idea of thought itself, which is the original characterization of consciousness. From this, another consequence follows: by remaining implicitly an 'interior sense', reflection appears not only as a becoming conscious of experience, but also as *being itself an experience,* precisely an experience of 'interior' phenomena, an experience of *interiority.*

But this experience, even if it is immediate, is nevertheless not simple. This fact pertains to the structure of what Locke calls *perception.* Descartes, in the Third Meditation, began by distinguishing two genres of thought: on the one hand, acts of will *(les volontés),* affections and judgments, and, on the other, ideas that are 'like images of things'. He followed by classifying ideas into three categories according to their origin: innate, or contemporaneous with the very formation of my mind; adventitious, or ideas received from the exterior (whether from sensible objects, other men or from God); and finally, factitious, that is, ideas forged by my own mind. As soon as the category of innate ideas, as in Locke's case, is eliminated (which comes down to saying that the universality of reason cannot be *given* but must be a *constructed* universality, in science as well as in morality), there remain adventitious and factitious ideas: those I receive and those I form. But their very correlation suffices for a reconstitution of the entire field of the understanding, effectively rendering *analyzable* all that Descartes had declared unanalyzable, including the clarity and distinctness of certain 'simple natures'. What is more, it permits the reintegration of the *operations* that Descartes had set aside (in particular, judgment, which is again analyzed according to the modalities of 'reunion' and 'separation') into the field of ideas.

The Lockean conception itself undoubtedly presents a number of enigmas. First, concerning the relation of sensation and reflection. If we re-read II.i.3 and the sections that follow, we see that there is an anteriority of the ideas from sensation, which means that the primary material of all knowledge and thought is produced by the external world, or rather, by its representation, the elements of which are ideas of 'qualities'. But this necessary, primary matter is clearly insufficient: no thought would be possible if there were not also ideas afforded by reflection, if therefore a primary reflection did not, alongside the ideas of a sensible origin, constitute other, equally elementary ideas of an intellectual or internal origin that were in fact just as originary as the others. This primary reflection is thus the prototype of a gap or discrepancy *(décalage)* in the origin itself that persists through the entire process of the constitution of the understanding (or of experience).[89]

As has been seen, Locke insists on the fact that the ideas produced by reflection are not *perceptions of other ideas* (which would originate in ideas from sensation), but *perceptions of mental operations* ('Operations of our own Minds') referring to other ideas. This means that it is not a matter of a superposition of formally identical levels of representation, each of which would form an 'object' for the next one, going *ad infinitum,* as in the Spinozistic conception (deriving from Descartes) of the *idea of the idea* (*idea ideae*). But neither are we concerned with a means of returning or reducing, little by little, all the ideas or intellectual representations to a *sensible* prototype from which they would only extract general characteristics. For, between the first perception (sensation) and the second perception (reflection), there must always already be interposed the third term of an 'operation', however elementary it may be. This is why what the mind perceives through reflection are not ideas that would simply be deposited in it, but rather its own operations, and in a sense *itself, insofar as it essentially 'operates' or is an activity.* Paradoxically, what Lockean 'reflection' perceives is *more immediate*, or more originary, although more differentiated, than if it were an 'idea of the idea'.[90]

Locke nonetheless proposes an enumeration in many ways similar to that of Descartes when he describes the modes of *cogitatio*, but this time it is a question of the primary elements of the understanding furnished by reflection:

> which Operations, when the Soul comes to reflect on, and consider, do furnish the Understanding with another set of *Ideas*, which could not be had from things without; and such are, *Perception, Thinking, Doubting, Believing, Reasoning, Knowing, Willing* and all the different actings of our own Minds; which we being conscious of, and observing in our selves, do from these receive into our Understandings, as distinct *Ideas*, as we do from Bodies affecting our Senses. (II.i.4)

The difficulty is finally concentrated in the notion of perception, the linchpin of every one of Locke's classifications: not only because of the broad significance he confers upon it, rendering it practically synonymous with sensible or intellectual representation,[91] but by reason of the meaning, as often *passive* as

---

89 On the way that Condillac rethought this dislocation so as to be able to read in it the production of the understanding itself (still presupposed by Locke to be a set of given 'faculties'), see Jean Mosconi, 'Sur la théorie du devenir de l'entendement', *Cahiers pour l'Analyse* 4, Sept.–Oct. 1966 (see the online edition curated by Peter Hallward et al. at http://cahiers.kingston.ac.uk/names/mosconi.html).

90 The distinction would appear sufficient to invalidate the idea of an essential continuity between Locke and Descartes in the invention of the mind, suggested by Richard Rorty at the beginning of *Philosophy and the Mirror of Nature*, Princeton, NJ: Princeton University Press, 1981.

91 Coste sought to render this breadth by translating the English *perception* with the French *aperception* (apperception), which made it possible to say that the mind 'takes notice of what passes within itself' ('s'aperçoit de ce qui se passe en lui-même').

active, with which he endows it. Thus, sensation is fundamentally passive, in that it transmits to us the qualities of external objects, but it can also be designated as the first and primary level of the mind's activity. In the same way, reflection is first the simple perception of the internal operations of the mind, but this perception in its turn is described as an 'operation' (and Locke says that the *first* of the 'ideas from reflection' is precisely *the idea of perception* which is practically the elementary idea of the mind) (II.ix.2).

It almost seems as if the Lockean conception were founded on a fundamental dualism: *a dualism of representations and operations* which would be the two faces of perception, or which would play alternating roles in its genesis. This explains the fact that the mind can sometimes be described as a blank slate (a tabula rasa) without any prior inscription and sometimes as a dynamism characterized by its powers or faculties ('the powers of the Mind'), constantly animated by what Locke will later call its 'uneasiness'.[92] The mind of which Locke speaks is in this sense a logico-psychological machine which permanently engenders new representations by 'operating' on the material composed of the simple ideas from sensation and reflection (or, to put it another way, on the basis of the initial difference between the ideas from sensation and the ideas from reflection). The mind continuously works in this way to extend and increase the diversity of its perception of the world.

In a sense, what founds Locke's analyses is a *double dualism* whose terms are perpetually superimposed: on the one hand, the distinction between sensation and reflection that refers to the heterogeneity of exterior and interior, of sensible elements and elements having their origin in the understanding itself; and on the other, the distinction between the passive side (perception proper) and the active side (the operations that both make perception possible and take it as their object). Moreover, these distinctions are not synonymous. It is perfectly possible to conceive of a totally passive understanding, and an entire philosophical tradition sees a kind of perfection in such a conception (for example, under the name of 'intellectual intuition'). Conversely, it is not necessary to consider sensation purely passive, as a 'reception' of the qualities of objects without the intervention of the power or energy of the mind: on the contrary, some of Locke's successors in psychology would increasingly emphasize this power. In fact, is it not the case that empiricism, or what bears the

---

92 In the great chapter 'Of Power' (II.xxi). But the essential phrase appears even earlier (II.i.4): 'The term *Operations* here, I use in a large sense, as comprehending not barely the Actions of the Mind about its *Ideas,* but some sort of Passions arising sometimes from them, such as the satisfaction or uneasiness arising from any thought'. I will return to the relations between the problem of *consciousness* and that of *uneasiness* (for which, as I have noted, Coste was compelled to devise a neologism). On the formation of the notion and on the history of its translation, see Deprun, *La philosophie de l'inquiétude,* 192ff. Deprun once again underscores the importance of the confrontation with Malebranche.

name, is permanently afflicted with this superposition? This is certainly true of Locke. But it also bears directly on the definition of *consciousness*: for it is essentially first and foremost *the very moment of the difference* between sensation and reflection, or between the mind's activity and its passivity.

Is consciousness therefore reflection in 'internal sense'? It seems that Locke aims at a more complex conception: *consciousness is already present in the first reflection*, since it is 'the perception of what passes in our own mind', that is, the perception of the sensations that introduce ideas into the mind and of the operations to which they give rise. It might be said that the concept of consciousness duplicates (*double*) that of reflection, including under a single name that which makes it possible (the initial difference between sensation and intellectual operation, between passivity and activity) and that which it will make possible: the work or development of the understanding in which the reciprocity of the point of view of 'ideas' and that of 'operations' never ceases to function. From this point on, it is also necessary to say that *consciousness is always present in the course of the progress of the understanding*: to the extent that experience develops, consciousness reflects its actions or its successive forms. It is therefore the instance of the totalization of knowledge in the form of the mind's self-knowledge, which is in turn coextensive with experience itself. It is here that we again find the principle of identity at work. *Consciousness is a self-identity that is maintained*, or better, *reiterated through difference*: the difference or inequality of the first reflection, and the progressive differentiation of experience of the mind that is formed by it.

Such an identity, at once differential and totalizing, must always be thought as an *interiority*. In II.i.8, Locke writes in a remarkable way:

And hence we see the Reason why 'tis pretty late, before most Children get *Ideas* of the Operations of their own Minds; and some have not any very clear, or perfect *Ideas* of the greatest part of them all their Lives. Because, though they pass there continually; yet like floating Visions, they make not deep Impressions enough, to leave in the Mind clear distinct lasting *Ideas*, till the Understanding turns inwards upon it self, *reflects* on its own Operations, and makes them the Object of its own Contemplation.[93]

Up to this point the interiority of the mind was only posed in a negative way: in opposition to the exteriority of sensation, or more precisely, to the exteriority that *sensation denotes*, since it places the qualities that it registers outside of itself (in 'objects' or 'bodies') and, in opposition, places itself on the inside. It might also be supposed that the interiority of mental operations is conceived by

---

93   Coste found the metaphor audacious, but translated it nevertheless: 'vienne à se replier pour ainsi dire sur soi-même'.

means of the distinction from their *verbal expression,* and from the 'exit' from the interior that the translation of ideas into words and the communication of thoughts to others represents. But we now have, if it can be said this way, an internal mark of interiority that, again, is united with consciousness. The latter is, at every moment, the means of access to the interiority that has already constituted it. Or *could* be the means of access (witness children and unreflective adults), because with reflection the folding (*le pli*) is virtually there, and one can fold it (*replier*) at will as many times as necessary.

Like the imprint on a tablet, reflection is of course already a metaphor, as old as the comparisons between thought and vision (or the idea of 'the mind's eye', found in Plato). Reflection (*réflexion*) and *repli* (fold/folding) have a common semantic root, but are not strictly equivalent notions. It might even be suggested that they derive opposing meanings from it: while the fold interiorizes an initial exteriority, reflection permits the deployment of a quasi-exteriority at the heart of interiority. The metaphorical representation of the mind as a 'stage' (*scène*) on which the thoughts that the mind itself observes 'pass' and on which intellectual or affective events 'take place' (*se passent*) is also obviously present in Locke. It was traditionally the target of objections concerning the duplication of the mind into observer and observed and the ghostly nature of the internal scene (or stage). Locke minimizes or circumvents these objections by recourse to the metaphor of the fold, which will be found frequently in the history of the debates on consciousness and the subject.

4. THE SUBJECT CONSCIOUSNESS: THE SELF, OR RESPONSIBILITY

As I have noted, the expression 'self-consciousness' does not appear before II.xxvii, the chapter only added in 1694. It figures only one other time in the entire *Essay.* But the term is essentially linked to the idea that the continuity of consciousness is the criterion of personal identity, for which Locke invents or systematizes the nominal expression 'the Self'. The Lockean subject, to which the functions of intellectual vigilance as well as those of responsibility and of 'property in oneself' will be attached, is thus essentially a self-consciousness, or more precisely a consciousness *of 'the Self'*.[94]

---

94   In the last analysis, what is surprising is not the presence of the quasi-neologism 'self-consciousness' in Locke's text (even if it represents an insurmountable obstacle for Coste) but its rarity (one single occurrence, in § 16: *hapax legomenon* as it were!), even as the entire linguistic organization of the treatise tends to place the reflexivity of the *self* at the core of the phenomenology of consciousness and, reciprocally, to make the continuous presence of consciousness the very essence of the 'self' that recognizes itself as such. Rather than invoke here the slowness of the acclimatization or backwardness of language in relation to thought, it seems preferable to invoke a *conflict of inspirations*: if it is true that *self-consciousness,* at the moment the *Essay* was written, was appropriated by Trinitarian theologians to whom Locke sought, in part, to respond, it is easier to understand why his own use of the term was so limited (and perhaps polemical). The general

For Locke the notion of identity is not univocal: it must be differentiated according to the domains to which it is applied.[95] The first domain is that of 'substances', above all the body, that are identical or different according to whether they preserve the same 'material', that is, corpuscular composition. The second is that of living organisms that preserve their typical form despite the transformations they undergo, which Locke calls 'individual identity'. This especially applies to human individuals who can be *named* (Adam, Socrates, Peter, Paul). But Locke seeks to distinguish this individual identity (which might also be called *invariance*) from *personal* identity, which rests solely on the continuity of consciousness in time. He is not afraid to confront the paradoxes (or so they seem) that may result from a strict application of this criterion, such as fusions and duplications of personality: if two individuals (Socrates and Plato) have or had the same thoughts, the same memories, the same consciousness, they are, or would be, a single person; conversely, if the same individual has or had two distinct consciousnesses, like the 'Day-Man' and the 'Night-Man' evoked in such a striking way in II.xxvii.23, they are, or would be, two persons (and two distinct subjects of imputation).

It is thus a matter of the same logico-psychological 'principle of identity' that is extracted from the critique of innate ideas:

> to find wherein *personal Identity* consists, we must consider what *Person* stands for; which, I think, is a thinking intelligent Being that . . . can consider it self as it self, the same thinking thing in different times and places; which it does only by that consciousness, which is inseparable from thinking, and as it seems to me essential to it: It being impossible for any one to perceive, without perceiving, that he does perceive . . . Thus it is always as to our present Sensations and Perceptions: And by this every one is to himself, that which he calls *self*: It not being considered in this case, whether the same *self* be continued in the same or divers Substances. (II. xxvii.9)

---

meaning of the treatise's argumentation would thus be not to promote the idea of self-consciousness by rationalist means, but to conquer the problematics of the self and of consciousness for rationalism, against the mystical discourses of self-consciousness. As a partial confirmation, we might cite the following passage from *Mr. Locke's Second Reply to the Bishop of Worcester*: 'The remainder of your lordship's period is: "and that without any respect to the principle of self-consciousness". Answer. These words, I doubt not, have some meaning, but I must own, I know not what; either towards the proof of the resurrection of the same body, or to show that any thing I have said concerning self-consciousness is inconsistent: for I do not remember that I have any where said, that the identity of body consisted in self-consciousness' (325). It was only after Locke (and owing to him, to a large extent) that *self-consciousness*, hence *Selbst-bewusstsein* and *conscience de soi* in their turn, were repatriated to the realm of metaphysics and transcendental philosophy, but this is another problem that exceeds the limits of this inquiry.

95   On the question of analogy and equivocity in the Lockean conception of identity, see the Glossary entries 'Diverse, Diversity', 'Identity' and 'Sameness'.

Such a criterion, however, is liable to the objection that we *forget* a signifi-cant part of our actions without believing that we have changed our identity. To this, Locke responds with a more fundamental articulation of consciousness and memory, which renders forgetfulness a mark of imperfection and finitude on the basis of an *internal temporality* essential to the subjectivity of thought:

consciousness, as far as ever it can be extended, should it be to Ages past, unites Existences, and Actions, very remote in time, into the same Person, as well as it does the Existence and Actions of the immediately preceding moment: So that whatever has the consciousness of present and past Actions, is the same Person to whom they both belong. Had I the same consciousness, that I saw the Ark and *Noah's* Flood, as that I saw an overflowing of the *Thames* last Winter, or as that I write now, I could no more doubt that I, that write this now, that saw the *Thames* overflow'd last Winter, and that view'd the Flood at the general Deluge, was the same *self*. . . that I that write this am the same *my self* now whilst I write (whether I consist of all the same Substance, material or immaterial, or no that I was Yesterday). For as to the point of being the same *self*, it matters not whether this present *self* be made up of the same or other Substances, I being as much concern'd, and as justly accountable for any Action was done a thousand Years since, appropriated to me now by this self-consciousness, as I am, for what I did the last moment. (II.xxvii.16)

Such in fact is the Lockean 'Cogito', similar to that of Descartes in that it combines in a single certitude both the fact of existence and the experience of thought, but at the same time fundamentally different to it in that it situates the entirety of this experience in the 'historical' element of memory. *Ego sum quis sum*: I am that I am, insofar as I possess the certitude of always being the one I have been because I am conscious of thinking what I have thought (and doubt-less also because I am at each instant conscious that *I will have thought* what I am at present thinking). As modern phenomenologists – themselves drawing on two centuries of post-Lockean psychology – will say later, with more technical terms: consciousness involves a 'retention' as well as a 'protention'. It is perhaps not exactly *historical*, but it is always already, intrinsically, *temporal* or *temporal-ized* in a 'nascent' or 'virtual' form. We will see more of this in a moment.

Thus, the objections Descartes ignored – above all the idea that *reflection requires time* and that there cannot be a 'consciousness', an idea of the idea or a thought of what I think, in the absence of a duration of time, about which it might be asked whether this duration does or does not change the initial repre-sentation – become, for Locke, positive theses incorporated into the very concept of consciousness and the means of reformulating the *cogito*.[96]

---

96   We may note the persistence of a close relation to the theme of scepticism that recurs in the problem of consciousness in Hume and Hegel. Locke literally reverses Montaigne's

We thus see that memory is entirely situated in the realm of *responsibility*, which means that it does not refer to the past without perpetually anticipating the future, without, in a certain sense, 'arriving' *from the future*: which is fundamentally a way to totalize time subjectively, in the present of consciousness. It is thus closely linked to the notion of thought's *appropriation* of itself.

If we consider these observations together, we might add the following. For Locke, thought as consciousness, and self-consciousness as the activity of thought – in short, the *subject* – are essentially related to the fact that ideas alternate between two modes of being: not the possible and the real, but rather *virtual existence and actual existence*. Either ideas are present to me as perceptions or they are absent, not in the sense of an annihilation, but in the sense of being held in reserve in a temporal 'place' that links the past and the future in the very possibility of the present.[97] And each of these two modes of existence *is presupposed by the other*, which means that consciousness is in memory and memory in consciousness. This is precisely the full meaning of *Mind*, which indeed is in complete accordance with its etymology. But this means that we once again encounter the figure of *identity in difference*, in the form of an identity that 'passes' from virtual to actual existence, or from the virtuality to the actuality of thought. Is this not finally very close to the dualisms that we have already encountered? If this could be demonstrated, we might gain an important insight into the way that Locke tied the problematic of consciousness to that of internal time and therefore into his role as founder of modern philosophy, qua philosophy of 'the subject'.

The differences that constitute the very structure of consciousness (sensation and reflection, passivity and activity, actual presence and virtual presence) must always be thought in the modality of a *passage*, and in consequence of a *duration*, however brief, of a 'moment of time' (which I am tempted to call, with Locke's contemporary and friend, Isaac Newton, a *fluxion*). Reciprocally, every passage or movement of thought has as its essence a play of differences that increase over time and that is preserved throughout the experience of consciousness. Not only does consciousness always already contain a temporal differential (which the formula 'the perception of what passes in a man's own mind' admirably expresses: consciousness is the presence to itself, as 'perception', of an action that happens, that is therefore in the process of happening),[98] but it

---

formulations: 'I now and I earlier are two' (but 'my book is always one'). See Jean Starobinski, *Montaigne en mouvement*, Paris: Folio Gallimard, 1993.

97 This notion might be developed through an examination of II.x, 'Of Retention', in which Locke sketches out a phenomenology of memory. See 'Memory' in the Glossary.

98 The counterpart of this proposition may be found in the chapter devoted to Duration as 'a mode of thought', which, however, does not contain the word *consciousness* even though it reproduces its definition exactly (II.xiv.3). This will later be the basis for the theoreticians who preserve the 'flux of consciousness' *without consciousness*, which is henceforth designated as a hypostasis. See William James, 'Does Consciousness Really Exist?', (1905) in *Essays in Radical Empiricism*, Cambridge, MA: Harvard University Press, 1976. This flight forward is typical of the entire philosophical history of the theme of subjectivity.

contains a *nexus* of three temporal instances. I will have to answer in the future (whether the ultimate future of the Last Judgment, or the immediate future for which I have provided with the vigilance I exercise over my thoughts) for this 'action', already happening, of which I am conscious at this moment. And what Locke finally shows is that the retention of the past is united with present consciousness by virtue of the horizon of the Judgment to come in which it is always already inscribed. It might be said that in the constitution of Locke's 'Mind', the three instances of the past, present and future are other names for *memory, consciousness and judgment*, whose interdependence, whose coexistence in interiority, must be thought by referring them to a common term, which is precisely action.

But this also means that the form of self-identity (*identité à soi*) indicated by 'self-consciousness' (*conscience de soi*) (that *I am I* or *I=I* whose 'formalism' Hegel would later criticize by attributing it to a metaphysical tradition continuing from Descartes to Kant and Fichte) is in reality an *equalization* rather than an equality given in advance: it is a movement of a return to self that takes place through the (more or less complete) retention of the past by virtue of the future that has always already judged it and awaits it. And in consequence, it is the very movement of a self-appropriation enacted in the field of the experience of consciousness:

> *Person*, as I take it, is the name for this *self*. Where-ever a Man finds, what he calls *himself*, there I think another may say is the same *Person*. It is a Forensick Term appropriating Actions and their Merit; and so it belongs only to intelligent Agents capable of a Law, and Happiness and Misery . . . And therefore whatever past Actions it cannot reconcile or appropriate to that present *self* by consciousness, it can no more be concerned in, than if they had never been done: And to receive Pleasure or Pain, *i.e.*, Reward or Punishment, on the account of such Action, is all one, as to be made happy or miserable in its first being, without any demerit at all . . . And therefore conformable to this, the Apostle tells us, that at the Great Day, when every one shall *receive according to his doings, the secrets of all Hearts shall be laid open* (I Cor. 14:25 and 2 Cor. 5:10). The Sentence shall be justified by the consciousness all Persons shall have, that they *themselves* in what Bodies soever they appear, or what Substances soever that consciousness adheres to, are the *same*, that committed these Actions, and deserve that Punishment for them. (II.xxvii.26).[99]

---

99   The corresponding passage in Paul is 1. Cor. 14: 24–5: 'But if all prophesy, and there come in one that believeth not, or *one* unlearned, he is convinced of all, he is judged of all: And thus are the secrets of his heart made manifest [*ta krupta tês kardias autou phanera ginetai*]; and so falling down on *his* face he will worship God, and report that God is in you of a truth'. It is interesting to note here that the context of Paul's letter evokes *the disappearance of the veil from words (tongues) at the moment of the clarity of the 'face to face'*. We thus return, but along a theological path, to the idea that the 'truth of thought' and the essence of the mind are revealed by being abstracted from language. See 'Resurrection' in the Glossary.

And it is undoubtedly through the unity of reflection, memory, responsibility and appropriation, united in a single phenomenology of 'internal perception', that Lockean consciousness remains, at least in its formal structure, a *moral* consciousness. Consequently, the fact that it constitutes the criterion of personal identity, itself required by legal responsibility, can only ever be the reverse side of its own constitution. This unity that we have called (since Kant) the subject, and that Locke – the first to do so – calls self-consciousness, is indissolubly logical (self-identical), moral and legal (responsibility, appropriation) and psychological (interiority and temporality). It secretly calls itself *My Self*. And even if it properly belongs to the rational, quasi-experimental discipline devoted to constructing what Locke calls its 'history',[100] it nevertheless has the constitution of an Idea of reason. This Idea, far from resting on a metaphysical substantialism, is entirely the result of its deconstruction. It is true that this deconstruction is carried out in the name of *another* metaphysical conception, perhaps more originary than that of substance: the conception of the *proper* and of *appropriation*.

By inscribing the time of memory and judgment in the interiority of consciousness, Locke carries out a return to the Augustinian conception of 'internal man', incomparably more profound than what we observed among the 'Cartesians' (Arnauld, La Forge). But he does so only to subvert it: for *memory*, constitutive of the subject and of its mode of access to truth in Augustine, is not *subjective* in this sense. Rather, memory in Augustine represented the trace in the very depths of each human soul (*interior intimo meo, in interiore homine*) of an absent transcendence (*superior summo meo*) and an eternity (*veritas*). This is why memory was tied, not to an experience of 'property in oneself' and of appropriation (even if limited by the empirical possibilities of the mind), but on the contrary to an experience of my ontological insufficiency and to my desire to reunite with God in the beyond.

The Lockean invention of consciousness – and it is this that will constitute its power, even as it does not cease to provoke criticism – does not sacrifice any of the symbolic significations traditionally associated with the interrogation of the individual concerning the origins and ends of his own thoughts, and therefore 'Man's destination'. But by formulating consciousness in a way that, according to its own terms, comprehensively historicizes the marks of transcendence or inscribes them as so many regulative representations in its relation to itself and in the mind's immanence – so many ways to perceive itself at work, that is, to see itself 'operating', 'acquiring',

---

100   The term is used by Locke, who in his introductory chapter (§ 2) speaks of the *Essay's* 'Historical, plain Method'. This will be taken up by Voltaire in the *Philosophical Letters* of 1734 to oppose Locke's empirical method to the 'romance of the soul' written by Descartes and Malebranche. On the rarity of the term *conscience* as 'consciousness' in Voltaire outside of this passage (where it is in fact an Anglicism), see Glyn Davies, *'Conscience' as Consciousness*, 68–9.

'inquiring', 'progressing' and 'passing' – it carried out a secularization of these metaphysical questions as well.

5. INTERIOR/EXTERIOR: THE LOCKEAN TOPOGRAPHY OF CONSCIOUSNESS

To conclude, let me try to localize in a single topography the relations of interiority and exteriority that have so far appeared as characteristics of the operation of Lockean *consciousness*, and in this sense are constitutive of the new conception of the 'mental' reality of which it is the determinant aspect. These relations permit us to understand at the same time its extraordinary impact, connecting the 'psychological', 'physiological' and 'transcendental' problematics of the subject, and its constant exposure to critical questioning.

We have seen that Locke, at the beginning of Book II of the *Essay*, calls 'reflection' a *second perception* (but *originarily* possible, as indicated by the expression 'internal sense') by which the *mind* perceives its own operations, beginning with sensation, which is the source of all our information about the world. The structure of internal space is determined in an immanent way by this originary duplication or fold that determines the superposition of 'ideas from sensation' and 'ideas from reflection'. Or rather, the ontological difference between the exterior (the world and its objects, the facts of qualities, modes, substances, relations, etc.) and the interior (ideas, the operations on these ideas and subsequently their concatenation into increasingly complex thoughts) is reproduced or projected in the midst of the mind itself, and therefore in interiority as the fold of sensation and reflection, or an idea of exteriority and an idea of interiority. The interior thus ideally contains both itself and its other. This might be interpreted – and these interpretations have alternately dominated Locke's posterity – either as the indelible trace of exteriority (of matter) at the heart of the interiority (of the mind), or as the anticipation and condition of possibility of a relation to the exteriority of the world within the very structure of interiority: either Condillac or Kant.

I hope, however, to have shown that the structure of folding back or of a return of exteriority within interiority itself can only be theoretically sustained if it is correlated with a series of other demarcations that themselves immediately become so many problematic articulations. The *topography* of the relations between the interior and the exterior, in the double sense of an imaginary disposition of theoretical 'spaces' and the reciprocal localization of problems, thus acquires a complexity that the philosophical tradition continually tried to untangle, either by taking over its terms as they are, or by proceeding through their reversal, subtraction and addition. It will be recalled that the first and most important of these articulations is the separation of ideas and words, or *thought* and *language*.

Words also constitute *an exteriority* in relation to ideas and their 'interiority', although certainly not exactly in the same sense as objects of experience in general: the fact that they are perceptible as sensible objects, modes or qualities is a necessary condition of the functioning of language, but does not suffice to characterize it. At the very least, it is necessary to add that words as *signs* pertain to the world of social communication (which Locke in another context, that of the *Second Treatise of Government*, would call *civil society*).[101] It is at this new limit (or, if you prefer, front) between the mental interior and the social and verbal exterior that the Lockean subject (or 'person') discovers the possibility of observing in himself the conditions of the first *truth* of his knowledge (which reside in the nature of his mental operations) and of the working for their *progress* (which resides in the acquisition of new ideas, the development of the correspondence between ideas and things by means of the signs of the language common to all and finally the passage from *mental propositions to verbal propositions* with the corresponding forms of truth).

The position regarding the nature of the sign which Locke defends rests on a strict hierarchization of thought and language, for words can only acquire a univocal meaning in a public space of communication on the condition that they are first 'signs of ideas', later to become 'signs of things' in a movement that goes from the interior to the exterior but remains anchored in interiority – the very condition of *meaning* (*sens*). In order for the separation of the mental and the verbal not to be transformed into a solipsistic barrier (hardly a Lockean idea), the passage to exteriority – like communication itself and therefore civil society – must in a certain way be anticipated within the mind. This would be at least in the form of that 'responsibility' or ability to answer (and to answer for oneself) which, as we have seen, constitutes an originary dimension of consciousness, inseparable from its own temporality.

We see here the point of departure for modern 'puzzles' concerning the relation between language and subjectivity which arise from the recurring confrontation between the hypothesis of a pure thought which would *precede* the transindividual dimension of communication, and that of a linguistic or quasi-linguistic (semiotic) structure governing the operations of thought. Of course, by dissociating the mental and the verbal, Locke has provided the means of resolving the questions that encumbered his predecessor Hobbes: how, if language is the element of truth, and if what characterizes it is an infinite power of metaphor or fiction, is it possible to guarantee a *true*, purely referential usage of words?[102] But in another way, Locke must now show that the conditions of

---

101   The articulation is explained in finalist terms from the first lines of Book III: 'God having designed Man for a sociable Creature, made him not only with an inclination, and under a necessity to have fellowship with those of his own kind; but furnished him also with Language, which was to be the great Instrument and common Tye of society' (III.i.1).

102   Etienne Balibar, 'L'institution de la vérité. Hobbes et Spinoza', in *Lieux et noms de la vérité*, Paris: Éditions de l'Aube, 1994.

the translation of thoughts into words, which constitutes an anticipation of society within individual thought itself (a 'secret relation' between the *mind* and other *minds)*, reside in consciousness itself. This consists in the fact that each responsible individual or person imagines a consciousness analogous to his own in the minds of others (III.ii.4); in other words, consciousness is already the form of a *virtual* relation to others at the same time that it is *actually* the form of the relation to oneself. Of course, such a conception can easily lead to an aporia. When he abandons the terrain of a phenomenology of consciousness to take up the question of the truth of mental propositions as adequation to a certain reality, Locke is tempted to argue that *ideas themselves are signs* in a more general sense and, in consequence, that words are the signs of signs. He will go so far as to evoke in the concluding lines of the book a *semeiôtikè* or science (doctrine) of signs which would include the knowledge both of ideas and of language (logic, properly speaking).[103]

The definition of language thus tendentially presupposes a representation of thought as an internal language or a language of ideas.[104] Further, the reasoning by which we secretly establish the objective reference of words cannot, in its intention, anticipate the result of their communication without raising the difficult question of a 'private language', a near contradiction in terms. *Language of Thought* and *Private Language* are problems for analytic philosophy and cognitive science today. Wittgenstein called their relevance into question by grouping their presuppositions together in his critique of 'the myth of interiority'.[105] But this critique only confirms the importance of the new point of view of interiority inaugurated by Locke in philosophy: without a preliminary isolation of consciousness with respect to the transindividual moment of communication (even if this moment is *retroactively* reinscribed in the interiority of the person), the subject could not be identified with consciousness and there would be no psychology.

But this theoretical structure calls for still another remark. It is easy to see that Lockean interiority (the interiority of the mental, folded back upon itself as

---

103 'So that Truth properly belongs only to Propositions: whereof there are two sorts, *viz.* Mental and Verbal; as there are two sorts of Signs commonly made use of, *viz. Ideas* and *Words*' (IV.v.2); 'For since the Things, the Mind contemplates, are none of them, besides it self, present to the Understanding, 'tis necessary that something else, as a Sign or Representation of the thing it considers, should be present to it: And these are *Ideas*'. See Ayers, *Locke*, I, 60 ff., 'Ideas as Natural Signs'.

104 A notion defended today once again by certain philosophers working towards a *Philosophy of Mind*: Cf. Jerry Fodor, *The Language of Thought*, Cambridge, MA: MIT Press, 1975.

105 See Jacques Bouveresse, *Le mythe de l'intériorité. Expérience, signification et langage privé chez Wittgenstein*, Nouvelle édition, Paris: Éditions de Minuit, 1987; Geneviève Brykman, 'Le mythe de l'intériorité chez Locke', *Archives de Philosophie* 55, 1992, 575–86. Descombes (*La denrée mentale*, 186 ff.) rightly suggests that the amphibology of the interior and exterior is dissolved in the perspective of a *modern* concept of organism, as it took on its definitive form in Claude Bernard. This is precisely what is bracketed *in* the Lockean point of view. However, the self-reference implied in such a concept of the organism does not necessarily refer either to *consciousness* or to *self*.

consciousness and, in this way, by its own means, discovering the criterion of its 'identity') is profoundly different from a spiritual interiority endlessly opening onto transcendence, as in Augustine, as well as from an organic interiority (founded on the hierarchization and integration of 'souls' or principles of life, as in Aristotle), to say nothing of attempts at compromise between the different traditions (as in Cudworth and the Cambridge Platonists, and later Leibniz). It is not as easy – although it is perhaps more decisive – to see the element of intrinsic *equivocity* that Lockean interiority contains. This equivocity is the consequence of the very topography I have just indicated. In effect, the immanence of the field of consciousness forms the object of two competing modes of exposition that, however, are never completely separate in the passages I have analyzed. On the one hand, *positively*, it is presented as the mind's identity to itself, or, as the lived experience corresponding in each subject to the fact that 'I am My self' or 'I am my own self', throughout the flow (*train, succession, continuation*) of the states of consciousness (apart from problems of troubled memory and personality).[106] Consciousness is thus the perception that perceives itself or which immediately becomes for itself an object of reflection. On the other hand, however, immanence never ceases to be explained *negatively* (even, as we have seen, as the negation of the negation according to the classic form of *elenchus*): it is thus the other of the outside, or its reverse side (*envers*). In fact, this exteriority is understood in different ways and according to different logics which never totally coincide.

It is the exteriority of the sensible world, the object of perception (which was privileged by the classical 'empiricist' reading of Locke), but also of the world of signs, and through it the totality of the ties and bonds that constitute the 'common' or the human 'community'. It is at the point of proximity or at the diverse borders of these different exteriorities that they, while continuing to mark an opening and an alterity (even if under the form of the pure differential of activity and passivity), are transposed to the heart of interiority itself, allowing it to be defined or recognized as such. Interiority is thus a paradox (Kant will later say an amphibology) of an immanence or an autonomy that can only be determined by being thought as negation, or as the 'place' that is originally, always already, subtracted from exteriority. And it is conceived as this paradoxical univocity (based on the principle of identity) that perpetually remains overdetermined by the multiple figures of its other (or, to put it another way, by the equivocity of the world).[107] Perhaps the multiplicity of names it gives itself and

---

106   See 'Memory' and 'Personality' in the Glossary.

107   I will not explore here the reciprocal hypothesis that the 'equivocity of the world' as it appears in Locke's cosmology – the perceived *natural* world and the meaningful (*signifiant*) *social* world (while Spinoza and Leibniz always sought to think them in the same categories as moments of a single nature or a single whole) – would itself be the correlate of the emergence of the subject as 'self-consciousness'.

that it inscribes in an open series (*mind, consciousness, self, person* and, before long, 'the subject') functions to control and perhaps exorcise this strange (and in fact equivocal) way in which exteriority returns to and permeates the very idea of interiority. From this it will be asked by Locke's successors what flows from this overdetermination when, in a later stage, the interiority and identity of the subject are called into question by the emergence of 'critical' questions: Is there a non-subjective consciousness which can exist without the I (*Je*) 'accompanying' it? Is there a non-conscious subjectivity? Does 'I' designate a self, a sameness (*mêmeté*) or ipseity (*ipséité*), or is it nothing more than the mirage of a reflection, an artifice of grammar or, conversely, the surface effect of a more original alterity?

Rather than take up these questions, however – all of which, if only in the form of antithesis, have inherited the Lockean reference to the interiority of the self and of consciousness and in consequence the equivocities it conceals – we must, one last time, complicate our topological representation. For the exteriority of perception and of nomination are not sufficient to exhaust the field of what is for consciousness its 'exterior'. Perhaps there remains a third type of exteriority (and thus a supplementary degree of equivocity proper to the interior/exterior relation) connected to the way Locke poses the problem of *affect*.

The difficulty, which is hardly insignificant, arises from the fact that when Locke undertakes what he himself called an outline of a 'treatise on the passions',[108] whose axis is constituted by the analysis of the relation between *Desire* and *Uneasiness,* the exposition alternates between an implicit reference to the individual's 'own body' – the affections of which make possible an explanation of the association of the sensations, on the one hand with ideas, and on the other with the feelings (*sentiments*) of pleasure and pain – and a phenomenological neutrality in which the affects are merely described as modes of experience or 'ideas' of the mind (without reference to the body or the external world). It is the second point of view that incontestably dominates, and this theoretical choice must be understood in the light of the sceptical attitude Locke maintained regarding any notion of substantial relations underlying the operations of the mind and its relations with the body in the unity of an individual.[109] It must certainly be understood in relation to the emergence in the analysis of power – on the horizon of Locke's critique of theories of the Good as the 'final

---

108   Locke, *Essay,* II.xx–xxi.

109   On the possibility of considering the correspondences between the problematic of consciousness and that of uneasiness in Locke's text as the effect of the 'retreat' of the soul, see 'Concern' in the Glossary, as well as my more detailed essay (revising some formulations of this book) 'My Self and My Own: One and the Same?', in Bill Maurer and Gabrielle Schwab, eds, *Accelerating Possession: Global Futures and Personhood,* New York: Columbia University Press, 2006, 21–44.

cause' of desire and the will (II.xxi.38) – of a concept of an object or cause of desire that, however necessarily external to the mind it appears to be, is nevertheless as irreducible to the object of perception as to the communicative sign and which must include in its generality *all* the 'goods' of corporeal, spiritual or social nature that we imagine (of which we have an idea) and whose absence we feel as an 'uneasy desire' (*désir inquiet* – Coste's felicitous rendering of *the successive uneasiness of our desires*) (II.xxi.31–4).

All of these concepts, each of which deserves a long discussion, are in reality *limit concepts* and concepts of a limit between what is called today the *cognitive* (what Locke calls 'perception' in the broadest sense) and the *affective* (which he derives from uneasiness or malaise, another way of understanding *uneasiness*), but especially between *passivity and activity*, of which the combination of uneasiness and desire precisely explains the shifting equilibrium. Uneasiness is defined as the immediate expression of desire, or the difference between pleasure and pain insofar as it sets the will into motion or 'emotion'. There is therefore no action exempt from uneasiness, for all action is an emotion of an individual and contains an irreducible affective dimension. But uneasiness is more generally the motive of mental activity or of the succession of the mind's operations, so that the mind is sometimes passive (sensation), sometimes active (reflection), but never remains 'at rest' in the contemplation of an idea, ever fluctuating from one perception to another depending on the objects encountered.[110]

Leibniz, who approved the translation of uneasiness into French as '*inquiétude*', proposed to render the notion in German as *Unruhe* on the basis of an analogy with the pendulum of a clock in 'perpetual' movement.[111] This amounted to saying that the concatenation of ideas was linked to their affective quality and to the affects of emotion, or affects which they could not but produce, even if, as such, they are no more than representations or percepts. *Uneasiness* works like the dynamic motor of the process whose cognitive form is *consciousness*. But to what 'place', simultaneously exterior to consciousness and therefore to the mind properly speaking (since there is no operation of thought that is not perceived as such) and immediately revealing their unity, should we try to locate the source of this energy? Locke is here in the grip of his own critique of the idea of substance and leaves us between several incompatible suppositions: that uneasiness is the trace in the midst of the mind itself of

---

110   See II.xiv.13 on the impossibility of the mind's having the 'self-same single idea' indefinitely or even for some time. Deprun (*La philosophie de l'inquiétude en France*, 192–5), while qualifying this judgment by showing its difficulties, describes Lockean uneasiness as essentially passive, which permits him to see it as the point-by-point reversal of Malebranche's conception. It seems to me, in contrast, that every phenomenology of 'uneasy desire' or 'the uneasiness of desire' in Locke, where the unity of contraries abounds, points to the meaning of a thought of the differential of passivity and activity or of the continuous transition from one to the other.

111   Leibniz, *New Essays*, 164–6.

the latent relation that the mind maintains with the individual's 'own body', or that it is, like Malebranche's 'depths of the soul' (*fond de l'âme*), an essentially hidden relation of the mind to itself from which proceeds the movement of its perpetual flight forward (*fuite en avant*).

Like that of the 'sign', these limit-notions of affectivity probably lead to aporiae: because uneasiness, which is a malaise of consciousness, just as consciousness is essentially uneasy, is both indissociable and theoretically distinct from consciousness, it seems that the limit of the perceptive and the affective, representing or symbolizing in the mind its passive relation to its own body, as well as its dynamic relation to itself, can never be fixed at a precise point. This limit regresses indefinitely towards a unity of contraries enigmatically indicated by Locke with the term 'power'. But it may also be said that the ever-renewed question of this unity is nothing more than the shadow cast by the initial theoretical distinction.[112] We might even go so far as to suggest that it is by *separating* the two fundamental discussions devoted respectively to uneasiness (and thus to the perpetual differentiation of the mind) and to self-consciousness (and therefore to personal identity) *in theoretical discourse* (*le théorique*) that Locke symbolized the enigma of an interiority that poses within itself the problem of exteriority: the word *consciousness* never appears in II.xxi, just as II.xxvii does not contain the word *uneasiness*, even though their analyses are rigorously correlated.[113]

In the final analysis, each of the characteristics of interiority that for Locke form the essence of consciousness (or mind as a system of conscious operations) thus appears as the reverse side of a specific exteriority whose assignment to its proper place is as problematic as the unity it must forge with the others: it is a question of the articulation of sensation and reflection, of word and idea or

---

112   It would be worth the trouble (but forming the object of another inquiry) to ask if such a difficulty is not more present than ever in Freud's definition of 'unconscious drives', with their double status as psychic traces of somatic excitation and as the fixation of a repressed link between 'representations' (*Vorstellungen*) and 'affects' (*Affekte*) – although of course he has shifted from 'consciousness' to 'the unconscious' as the essential characteristic of the mind. Sigmund Freud, *Das Unbewusste. Schriften zur Psychoanalyse*, Frankfurt a. M: S. Fischer Verlag, 1960.

113   This 'inseparable interior' that affect represents in relation to a consciousness essentially defined in terms of (self) perception is all the more troubling and enigmatic in that it is equally possible to represent it as a second degree of interiority, an 'interior of the interior', that is, an *intimacy* whose source is hidden within it (by analogy with the Augustinian formula: *interior intimo meo*). It is thus inevitable – the concept of amphibology again – that the interiority of consciousness, as a 'scene' in which ideas 'pass' and the operations of the mind, *partes extra partes*, are carried out, is presented for its part as a kind of exteriority, or at least a metaphorical exteriority. Accordingly, pure interiority regresses to infinity and contrary 'places' are converted into each other. But may we not pose an analogous question regarding the other 'exteriorities' we have situated in relation to the mental? The most elementary topography already leads the interrogation in this direction, which I think makes its interest. In the history of the 'science of the mind' these three instances – *affect, pure sensation* and *sign* (or signifier) – all represented abysses of interiority that virtually converted it in its opposite.

of affect and percept. It may thus be explained that Locke, by constructing this topography, prescribed in advance the theoretical emplacements where all the problems characteristic of a discipline centred on the phenomena of 'consciousness' – whether it is conceived as an exercise in introspection, as a critical and transcendental analysis, or as an experimental science articulated with physiology – appear. A phenomenology of consciousness must always reconstitute or reconquer itself by establishing and conceptualizing its limits. But Locke also prescribes in advance the modalities according to which, against the 'primacy of consciousness' (and more fundamentally against the organization of the field of subjectivity on the basis of the notion of consciousness), the hypothesis of an 'unconscious' thought or psychism appears. In a number of contemporary developments to which we might refer, it is thus, again and always, Lockean conceptuality that is at work, even when it is a matter of overturning itself. It is in this way that the invention of consciousness remains interminable.

CHAPTER TWO

Lockean Concepts: A Philosophical and Philological Glossary[1]

TO APPROPRIATE: §§ 16, 26

Although the term is employed only three times in Locke's treatise on identity and difference, it nevertheless occupies a strategic position there. It is this term that most closely approximates the Stoic notion of *oikeiôsis*, whose importance Locke re-established through totally unprecedented means (precisely by introducing the mediation of consciousness).[2] Around it is arrayed a constellation of terms indicating interest (*concern, desire, happiness*), responsibility (*account, accountable, answer, answerable, impute, attribute, reward*) and participation (*to belong, [to be a] part [of], to partake*). In accordance with Stoic ontology, which does not separate the subject and the object, but instead privileges the perspective of the agent and its functions, Locke only applies the term *appropriate* to *actions*: it is the play of consciousness and memory that allows these actions to be claimed as one's own and thus to be 'reconciled with' or 'conferred upon' the subject, which is to say, the 'self'.[3]

But at the same time, the notion of appropriation is identical to that which, in his political works – notably the *Second Treatise of Government* – allows Locke to define civil personality as that of an individual 'proprietor of himself', gathering to himself the goods and rights necessary to his independence through the intermediary of labour (and more generally of effort):[4]

Though the Earth, and all inferior Creatures be common to all Men, yet every Man has a *Property* in his own *Person*. This no Body has any Right to but himself. The *Labour* of his Body, and the *Work* of his Hands, we may say, are properly his. Whatsoever then he removes out of the State that Nature has provided, and left it in, he has mixed his *Labour* with, and joined to it something that is his own, and thereby makes it his *Property*. (§ 27)

---

1 After each term, the number of the paragraph in Locke's *Essay* (Book II, Chapter XXVII, which I called Locke's "treatise") where it appears will be indicated.

2 See V. Goldschmidt, *Le système stoïcien et l'idée de temps*, Paris: Vrin, 1953, 125 ff.

3 § 26: 'reconcile or appropriate', a formula borrowed directly from Cicero's Latin explanation of *oikeiôsis*: *ipsum sibi conciliatur* (*De Fin.*, III, V, 16). [Trans. note: '*Simul atque natum, sit animal . . . ipsum sibi conciliatur et commendari ad se conservandum*: 'from birth every animal is reconciled with itself and recommended to its own care'.]

4 Locke, *The Second Treatise of Government*, Laslett, ed., Cambridge: Cambridge University Press, 1960 (reprinted 1965 Mentor Books), 328, 340, 442.

Man (by being Master of himself, and *Proprietor of his own Person*, and the actions or *Labour* of it) had still in himself *the great Foundation of Property*; and that which made up the great part of what he applied to the Support or Comfort of his being . . . was perfectly his own, and did not belong in common to others. (§ 44)

The nature whereof is, that *without a Man's own consent* [his Property] *cannot be taken from him* . . . Their *Persons* are *free* by a Native Right, and their *properties*, be they more or less, are *their own, and at their own dispose* . . . or else it is no property. (§§ 193–4)

In order for the terminology of these texts to be made consistent with that of the *Essay*, it is necessary to assume that there exists a reciprocal presupposition between the theory of personal identity, based on the internal continuity of consciousness, and the theory of the proprietorship of oneself, based on the material autonomy acquired through labour. It is precisely this complementarity that is missing from the theory of 'possessive individualism' made famous by C.B. Macpherson in his book *The Political Theory of Possessive Individualism*. Macpherson subordinates anthropology to positive law, rendering private property the exclusive *external condition* of personal freedom instead of seeing it as an expression of the property in one's own person that is essentially identical to freedom. Neither is this point completely understood by Tully,[5] who starts from 'an enlarged conception of property' (the sphere of the *suum* [his or its] or the *dominium sui* [absolute ownership of oneself]) to establish the foundation of natural law, or Ayers[6] (who emphasizes the function of the possessive 'own' in the theorization of identity, but regards its economico-juridical connotation as nothing more than an unfortunate ambiguity). It seems necessary here to proceed to the idea of an 'anthropological doublet' of *consciousness* and *labour* that renders any reference to a substantial union of the body and mind irrelevant, in that this doublet is immanent in the sphere of *action* and not attached to the representation of a substrate.

Within the framework of the tradition of natural right – which, perhaps for the first time in the modern era, was founded on a positive, egalitarian anthropology – appropriation thus embodied the meaning of the revolutionary demands for freedom. The general scheme of this anthropology served the movement of thought as much as that of material labour: it made individuality a process of generalized *acquisition* of ideas (knowledge) and objects (properties) (from which, in part, the refutation of the doctrine of innate ideas followed),

---

5   James Tully, *A Discourse on Property: John Locke and His Adversaries*, Cambridge: Cambridge University Press, 1980.
6   Ayers, *Locke*, II, 266.

the 'experience' of a subject rather than a spiritual form destined for some preexisting 'matter'.

CONCERN, TO BE CONCERNED: §§ 11, 13, 14, 16, 17, 18, 25, 26

Concern is *care* (*le souci*) (the Latin *cura*); *to be concerned* is to care or worry about ('*se soucier de*', '*être soucieux*') in the sense of a particular interest that each person has in certain things, particularly himself. The essential mediations of this 'care of the self' (*souci de soi*) are acts (and their consequences and value) (§§ 14, 16, 18, 26), the body and its parts affected by pleasure and pain (§§ 11, 17, 18), thoughts and memories of thoughts, happiness (and unhappiness) (§§ 17, 18, 25, 26), salvation and punishment (§ 18). It may equally be supposed that God concerns himself with our happiness or our sorrow (§ 13). It is essential to the Lockean doctrine of the self and its appropriation to determine the place of concern (*souci*) in the system of representations connected to the person and to establish its 'necessary' relation to consciousness.

Let me note first that concern is in a sense the *internal* counterpart of *external* imputation or attribution in relation to actions: Locke says that when we impute actions to ourselves or 'own' (i.e. confess) them to be ours, they become objects of concern for us; and inversely (as may be seen in the example of the 'little finger' in § 18), to 'localize' concern, or assign it to a 'part' of oneself is at the same time to localize responsibility. This is because concern is always already a concern to be happy (§ 26), and in consequence a concern with the happy or unhappy (*malheureuses*) consequences, including punishment and retribution, that may result from an action. In this way, an indissociably affective and temporal dimension of thought is introduced.

In effect, concern necessarily intervenes in the relation between consciousness and its own thoughts or 'actions', in particular its *past* 'actions', and therefore in the relation between consciousness and memory: in a certain sense, it is concern that 'binds' them by *means of imagining the future* (which is itself always the expression of an interest in or anticipation of happiness, combined with a feeling of its fragility). Accordingly, there can be no definition of the continuity of consciousness through which it would function as 'self-identical' or 'the same', without a force or power at work in the very tension of the moments of time, the 'fluxion' of their flow, as Newton would have said. This force is concern.

On the basis of these formulations drawn from the treatise (§§ 11, 17, 25 and 26 in particular), it should be possible to articulate the two great Lockean concepts of consciousness and uneasiness around the single problem of the *power of the mind*. But we are here at the limits of Lockean phenomenology, which remains split into two blocks, each nearly external to the other, out of a fear, no doubt, of reintroducing substantialist speculation. Significantly, this problem – which virtually occupies the empty place left by the critique of the idea of the soul – is not even formulated as such,[7] since the two corresponding 'treatises' contained in the *Essay* (II.xxi, 'Of Power', and II.xxvii, 'Of Identity and Diversity') were as if in isolation from each other, that is, without explicit communication (each carefully avoiding precisely the use of the other's central concept, or leaving its place empty).

DIVERSE, DIVERSITY: §§ 1, 2, 9, 23, 25, 28

In my French volume I had already translated the *title* of Locke's treatise ('Of Identity and Diversity') as *Identité et différence* ('Identity and Difference') as a way of inscribing it in a lineage that runs from Plato's *Sophist* to Heidegger's opuscule (*Identität und Differenz*) and to Deleuze's book *Difference and Repetition*, to highlight the important place it occupies there, namely that of having identified identity with the active recognition of a 'self' by itself, operating in the element of consciousness. Without Locke's contribution, neither Kant, nor Fichte, nor Hegel, nor even Husserl would have been possible, even as they took Locke as an 'empiricist', if not a naturalist, philosopher and turned away from him in favour of a more or less mythical Cartesianism. It remains to show that this modification of Locke's own title does not do violence to the text, and, conversely, what supplementary intelligibility it brings to it.

Concerning the first, I might invoke the consistency between the uses of the noun *diversity* and the adjective *diverse*: the latter in such expressions as *the same, or divers Substances* (§ 9), *the distinction of any thing into the same, and divers* (§ 28) is rendered much more naturally in contemporary French as '*différent*'.[8] It is otherwise with the adjective *different*, which Locke, in the vast

---

7   Unlike, for example, what happens in Spinoza concerning the relation between *conscientia* and *cupiditas* (*Ethics* III, proposition 9, Scholium and Définition 1 of the affects). See Balibar, 'A Note on *Consciousness/Conscience* in the *Ethics*', and the Postscript to this book.

8   The same would hold in English, I submit. In his recent volume *Locke on Personal identity: Consciousness and Concernment* (Princeton, NJ: Princeton University Press, 2011) – undoubtedly to count as a major contribution to Locke scholarship in the coming years – Galen Strawson has also provided a translation of Locke's treatise (i.e. chap. II.xxvii of the *Essay*) into . . . English. Strawson attempts to transform Locke's idiom into a more 'modern' one (but for how long? Since languages ceaselessly evolve), while at the same time correcting what he considers to be imprecisions or ambiguities obscuring the 'logic' of Locke's argument, or expanding what he sees as the author's 'shortcuts'. For what concerns the understanding of Locke's thought (if this is the goal, different from conventionally *calling by the name* 'Locke' a formal argument which would be worth discussing anyway), this has some inconveniencies, particularly its erasure of Locke's *writing*, for example his subtle play on syntactic and semantic properties of 'self', 'same', 'own', and his uses of possessives and referential words in the first or third person, on which I argue that much of Locke's philosophical inventions relied. But it also has (as a translation always does, if it is a genuine confrontation with the original text) some advantages: in this case, it draws attention to the range of meanings involved in the idea of 'diversity' and offers them up for analytical discussion. Thus, in Locke's § 9, Strawson translates 'the same, or diverse substances' as 'one or many substances'

majority of cases, employs to complete the antitheses that punctuate his argument: *the same or different* . . ., *at different times can be the same* . . ., *the same in different places* . . ., *a different beginning* . . ., *different names for different ideas* . . ., *the same life communicated to different particles* . . ., *different substances by the same consciousness* . . ., *remaining the same it can be different persons* . . ., *a man born of different women* . . ., etc. In the terminology of the treatise, *diversity* is the noun used to signify difference, and *diverse* is one of the adjectives opposed to the idea of '(being) identical', generally expressed by *same* and *the same*, while *identical* appears only once. (I will later return to *sameness*).

This is all confirmed by a key passage:

> *First*, as to the sort of Agreement or Disagreement, *viz, Identity*, or *Diversity*. 'Tis the first Act of the Mind, when it has any Sentiments or *Ideas* at all, to perceive its *Ideas*, and so far as it perceives them, to know each what it is, and thereby also to perceive their difference, and that one is not another. This is so absolutely necessary, that without it there could be no Knowledge, no Reasoning, No Imagination, no distinct Thoughts at all. By this the mind clearly and infallibly perceives each *Idea* to agree with it self, and to be what it is; and all distinct *Ideas* to disagree, *i.e.*, the one not to be the other: And this it does without any pains, labour or deduction; but at first view by its natural power of Perception and Distinction. (IV.i.4)

This explanation demonstrates that the positing of differences refers to a fundamental operation of the mind: *distinction*, that is, differentiation or the ability to differentiate, coextensive with all the activities of the mind and presupposed by all its other operations.[9] This, in turn, leads naturally to the second point.

Difference is undoubtedly opposed to identity, just as identity is to difference. They are thus 'defined' by each other or are, the one just as much as the other, indefinable. Each of the two 'relations', however, is the object of an explanatory path that concerns the knowledge of the whole they form, and therefore deserves on our part a careful description of each. I will show below the problem of interpretation that the term *identity* poses, that of choosing between an *analogical* interpretation and an interpretation based on the notion of equivocity of identity itself. For its antonym *diversity*, the question of analogy can have little meaning; as far as the question of equivocity is concerned, it is subordinate

---

(184-5). But in Locke's § 28, while keeping 'different substances and different modes' unchanged, he translates/transforms 'the distinction of anything into the same, and divers' into 'distinguish what is the same as what, and what is different' (228-9). In my opinion, however – precisely because Locke's treatise is, among other things, a work of reflection on the meanings and uses of the notion of difference - it is not possible to a priori distribute these meanings into ready-made semantic categories.

9   The entirety of II.xi is devoted to *distinction* (or the ability to differentiate). On the possibility of linking all of this to a 'philosophy of ultimate resemblances', see Geneviève Brykman, 'Philosophie des ressemblances contre philosophie des universaux chez Locke', 439-54.

to the problem posed by the two possible modalities of the negation of the 'same': either an *external negation* encompassing every situation in which the 'same' is opposed to what from the outside limits it or is opposed to it (a difference that Locke calls 'numerical' and which we may call 'multiplicity'), or an internal negation encompassing every situation in which 'the same' is called into question by the intrinsic differentiation of its 'parts' (we might say an 'alteration', in particular a change over time of its shape, composition, qualities, etc.).

In the case of external difference, it cannot be denied that Locke's argumentation runs the risk of a regression to infinity: for in the absence of a 'principle of indiscernibles' having an *absolute* value, the difference of 'time and place' to which existences refer (§§ 1–3) itself lacks criteria: What is 'another place'? What is a 'different moment'? More simply, what do the questions of 'where' and 'when' mean? The clarification we might look for in the chapters Locke devotes to the ideas of space and time (II.xiii–xv) leads instead to *circles* that, however, do not function in exactly the same way.

The circle inherent in the idea of space arises from the fact that different places are identified through different bodies (in the last analysis, particles of matter), even though the criterion of the difference between bodies is the impossibility of superimposing them in the same place. At the very least, this shows the extent to which the difference between the ideas of space and of matter is essential to Locke's system: without it, the very structures of perception (of external sense) would collapse.[10]

At the same time, the circle inherent in the idea of time is connected to the fact that its origin is entirely *subjective*: it is the succession and distinction (or discreteness) of ideas in our mind that alone furnish its model (II.xiv.3, 6, 12–13). The different, 'regular' physical movements functioning like standards in chronometry intervene only retroactively to *determine* this fundamental idea. The difference *between times* thus refers to the difference *between thoughts* that can only be perceived by reflection or the 'internal sense' of a mind characterized by its consciousness and memory, which perceives itself as *unity passing through difference*. This in turn raises the questions of the identity of consciousness and of the phenomenological circles it contains. It is far from certain in any case that these circles are *defects* in the Lockean system: it may be that they quite simply constitute its *object*. In fact, we see there one of the most obvious indications that, ultimately, the question of the external differences inevitably leads to the consideration of *internal* differences (or the problem of the multiplicity of existences [*étants*] leads to the alteration of and distinction between parts).

---

10   As the critical remarks on Malebranche's 'vision in God' confirm, for Locke there is no 'modification', therefore no determination (figure) of space that would be truly distinct if there were no bodies occupying the space. Cf. Locke, 'Examination of P. Malebranche's opinion', § 48.

This can be seen clearly in the remarkable *elenchus* in II.xiv.13, showing that the mind *cannot not change ideas* and that it is therefore in itself 'in motion':

> If it be so, that the *Ideas* of our Minds, whilst we have any there, do constantly change, and shift in a continual Succession, it would be impossible, may anyone say, for a Man to think long of any one thing: By which if it be meant that a Man may *have one self-same single* Idea *a long time alone in his mind without any variation at all*, I think, in matter of Fact it is *not possible*, for which ... I can give no other Reason but Experience: and I would have anyone try, whether he can keep one unvaried single *Idea* in his Mind, without any other, for any considerable time together.

How, then, to explain internal difference? As I have indicated, the problem is knowing how one part can be said to be different or differentiated from another in the 'same' unity, or in what sense there may be a question of the identity of this 'same' unity whose parts or moments change or differentiate themselves (including when this unity is not fixed, but that of a flow or a unitary experience, as in the case of life or consciousness). Formally, the question could be resolved if we discovered the possibility of describing the play of the *same* and the *other* in such a way that differentiation is precisely that of a recognizable unity, and unity that of a determinate multiplicity. This is, to put it another way, the analogical aspect. But it is secondary in Locke, who ultimately privileges a 'material' point of view based on equivocity: accordingly there is no single concept of the unity of a multiplicity of parts or aspects. In consequence, *there can be no single univocal* concept *of 'internal* difference', but there are at least three, just as there are three meanings of 'self-identity' (*identité à soi*). The fact that one of them – namely, that which attaches the identity of consciousness to the internal perception of the difference between ideas in *the train of thought* and therefore to their numerical multiplicity for the subject and thus to the idea of time and the mind's perception of its own 'history', etc. – is privileged (anthropologically, psychologically), can never abolish this *difference of difference*. It is this fact that prevents any consideration of Locke's 'subjectivist' system as an absolute idealism. The *esse* and the *percipi* never meet.

See also IDENTITY, MEMORY, TIME AND SPACE

I, I AM, THE *I*, THE WORD *I*: §§ 16, 20

Coste translates the word I (*Je*) as 'moi' or 'le moi'. We may see by bringing together the two relevant paragraphs (§ 16 and § 20):

1. That English too offers the possibility of nominalising the pronoun (and

Locke undoubtedly follows the 'French' model of Descartes and Pascal here), but does not necessarily privilege the reflexive.[11]

2. That for Locke the reference of the 'I' and the 'I am' remains equivocal in that it may designate both individuality or personality, terms he seeks to hold in opposition. Although the distinction between the two terms is not always rigorous in his work, it is worth remarking that he calls the 'I' a word and not a name.[12] Words are the sounds of language insofar as they are means of communication which are expected to allow us to be understood by others. Names are these same words *referred to ideas*: III.i.ix. It might thus be argued that the 'I' is essentially the way *the 'self' (soi) designates itself for others*, which involves the risk that the use of such a term is empty and does not represent any 'self'.

Locke develops his own theory by putting into play quite different possibilities (always already reflexive) of the word *self* as adjective, adverb, noun and quasi-pronoun. This is not to say that he blurs the difference between the first and third person: on the contrary, one might say that he incorporates this difference in the very concept of personal identity, which thus becomes not a pure redundancy of the 'I' but a reciprocity of the 'I' and the 'he', and even of the 'that' (*çela*).

Implicitly, it is this reciprocity that is lacking in the ironic story (or tale) of the speaking parrot, called a 'rational animal' in § 8, which is striking in its multiplication of statements in the first person. Locke goes far in playing with the ambiguity of the 'I', given that he, without any attempt at refutation, cites the passage in the narrative in which the 'loquacious' animal (*zôon logon ekhôn*, in other terms) attributes to itself the responsibility of guarding the hen house.[13]

There is an anti-Cartesian moment in the narrative by William Temple included by Locke. In a letter to the Marquis of Newcastle on 23 November 1646, Descartes wrote: 'There is nothing in our external actions that can assure those who examine them . . . that there is also in it [our body] a soul that has

---

11   English thus finds itself in the same situation concerning this point as the German with *das Ich*. However, this possibility will not be exploited by contemporary psychology and psychoanalysis – which will have recourse to the Latin *the ego* (before establishing the antithesis of the ego and the self) – undoubtedly because in English the syntactical function referring to the speaker as 'I' is perceived much better here than any designation of an instance of the 'psychical apparatus' or even a substance. But these differences in connotation, rather than constraining history, are its result.

12   While person is the 'name' of the *idea* that is the 'self' ('soi') (§ 26).

13   Dr Michela De Giorgio pointed out to me that the fad for owning parrots and the corresponding trade in England date back to the end of the seventeenth and beginning of the eighteenth centuries. The portrait of Maurice of Nassau in Brazil with his parrot may be found in the Louvre. In the seventeenth century, Maurice de Nassau was one of the most well-known sceptics (allegedly one of the models imitated by Molière for the phrases attributed to his *Dom Juan*). Descartes enrolled temporarily in his army and quotes him cryptically in the First Meditation when it comes to subjecting to doubt even the elementary mathematical truths. See Mariafranca Spallanzani, 'Bis bina quatuor', *Rivista di filosofia* LXXXIII: 2, August 1991.

thoughts, except for words, or other signs made for a purpose [*à propos*] . . . I say that these signs have a purpose in order to exclude the speech of parrots, without excluding that of the insane.'[14]

But neither is it impossible that in dissociating the idea of the recognition of the self from the self-referential 'I am', Locke sought to distance himself from the blasphemous element contained in the Cartesian *Ego sum, ego existo*, in that this utterance is the 'name of God' par excellence.[15]

See also SELF.

IDENTITY: §§ 1, 2, 3, 4, 5, 6, 7, 9, 10, 11, 12, 14, 18, 19, 21, 23, 25

The theorization of identity in Locke raises a double problem: 1) Is this simultaneously logical and ontological notion univocal or, on the contrary, must the diversity of its uses or applications be considered irreducible? 2) Did Locke himself recognize this problem and if so how did he confront it?

It is interesting to note that while two recent readers (perhaps the most significant) of Locke's treatise, Michael Ayers and Paul Ricoeur, defend opposing positions on these issues, both ultimately accuse the philosopher of inconsistency. According to Ayers, the notion of identity must be regarded as fundamentally univocal. It must thus be capable of being defined in an abstract or formal way, and extended *by analogy* to different 'cases' or 'situations in which it is meaningful to speak of identity (which also means that the notion of identity makes it possible to conceive of an analogy between all these situations). Ayers thinks that while this is effectively Locke's point of view, Locke did not succeed in remaining faithful to it, particularly in what concerns the identity of bodies and more generally of substances.[16] At the same time, Ayers praises Locke for having, at least up to a certain point, developed the analogy between *life and consciousness*, which he sees as the theoretical centre of the treatise:

> The analogy between life and consciousness supplied the main framework for Locke's argument that the identity of the moral agent is conceptually independent of any particular theory about the nature, number and continuity of whatever, at the substantial level, underlies that phenomenal identity . . . just as life is an organizing principle which unites a variety of 'fleeting' or ever-changing parts into one

14 Descartes, *Œuvres philosophiques*, tome III, 694.

15 Cf. Hobbes: 'For there is but one Name to signifie our Conception of His Nature, and that is: I AM' (*Leviathan*, chap. 31) and Balibar, '*Ego sum, ego existo*. Descartes au point d'hérésie.' For Descartes, the 'I' autoreferentially denotes what or who *is neither God nor (animal) body*, but who at every moment has this 'other' in him, or around him in a proximity that causes his power of distinction to waiver. Locke, in *The Reasonableness of Christianity* (*The Works* Vol. VII, 89–90), affirms that in the Gospel according to John and elsewhere, the utterance *egô eimi* signifies nothing other than, in a cryptic fashion, 'I am the Messiah' (he who has been announced).

16 Ayers, *Locke*, II, 210 ff.

continuing animal, so consciousness is a principle which unites what is at least possibly a variety of fleeting parts into one person . . . Locke was in effect following [Hobbes] in claiming that life, although a mechanical process, is not a mere accident of matter but a principle of substantial unity and continuity. Yet Locke differed from Hobbes in finding another such principle in consciousness.[17]

However, as Ayers will later claim, we must recognize that Locke could not maintain his initial point of view: above all because of the necessity that arises from taking into account the 'intentionality' of consciousness at work in recollection, for which there is no equivalent in life. Locke would then turn to another, much more dubious, analogy: that of the identity and property in oneself.[18]

For his part, Ricoeur thinks that identity is fundamentally equivocal and he undertakes to separate the two opposing notions that it includes, even if he will then show why their interference is not arbitrary: that of the *idem* or the 'sameness' (that applies to things) and that of the *ipse* and the 'ipseity' (that applies to persons):

Locke introduces a concept of identity which seems to escape the alternatives of sameness (*mêmeté*) and selfhood (*ipséité*); after having said that identity results from a comparison, Locke introduces the singular idea of the identity of a thing with itself (literally: of 'sameness with itself'). It is in effect by comparing a thing with itself in different times that we form ideas of identity and diversity . . . This definition seems to join together the characteristics of sameness by virtue of the operation of comparison, and those of selfhood by virtue of what was the instantaneous coincidence of a thing with itself maintained over time.

But what follows in the analysis decomposes the two valences of identity. In the first series of examples . . . it is sameness that prevails; the element common to all these examples is the permanence of organization – which nevertheless involves no substantialism, according to Locke. But as soon as Locke comes to the personal identity that he does not confuse with that of a man, it is instantaneous *reflection* that assigns the 'sameness with itself' adduced by the general definition. It remains only to extend the privilege of the instant to duration; it suffices to regard memory as the retrospective expansion of reflection . . . Thus Locke believed he could introduce a caesura in the course of his analysis without having to abandon the general concept of 'the sameness [of a thing] with itself'. And yet the turn to reflection and memory in fact marked a conceptual reversal in which selfhood (*ipséité*) was silently substituted for sameness.[19]

---

17   Ayers *Locke*, II, 261–2.
18   Ibid., 265–8. See 'Appropriate' and 'Own' in the Glossary.
19   Paul Ricoeur, *Oneself as Another*, trans. Kathleen Blamey, Chicago: University of Chicago Press, 1992, 126–7 [translation modified].

In contrast, I will not ask if identity in itself is an analogical or equivocal concept – perhaps this question is undecidable or circular, analogy or equivocity being always already among the connotations of 'identity'. But I will seek to specify the way Locke uses the notion of identity. It seems to me that if we cease to pose the problem in terms of *definition* (comparing Locke's statements with given 'definitions') and instead regard the 1694 treatise as an 'inquiry into the question of identity', directing our attention to the dialectical *movement* that characterizes its unfolding, the following interpretation may be proposed:

1. Locke, *in order to begin his inquiry*, refers to a formal characteristic of identity, stated in § 1, which has a quasi-tautological character: no comparison and therefore no assigning of differences in existence would be possible if the existences themselves (or existing 'things') were not considered identical to themselves; but, reciprocally, a thing identical to itself is nothing other than a thing that does not differ from itself or presents no differentiation from the point of view of existence. Identity and difference thus form a circle and in any case to assign or specify identity would be also 'identically' a way of assigning and specifying relevant differences.

At the same time that he postulates this formal characteristic, Locke has *already* introduced a specification by judging that existences are distinguished in relation to a *moment* in time and to a *place* occupied in space. But this clarification, which signifies that the notions of identity and difference are not absolute but relative (to the 'conditions of experience', as Kant would later say), entails in its turn a hierarchization of two aspects: the principle aspect is the *temporal*, for the identity and difference of places appears to present no difficulty. Two things, whatever they may be, never occupy the same place if they are 'of the same kind', and if they occupy different places they are necessarily distinct. Identity and difference in time, in contrast, present the particular difficulties to which the inquiry will be devoted.

2. After § 2, Locke begins to change the way the problem was posed by introducing a point of view that is no longer 'formal' but 'material', grounded in a successive examination of the different kinds (*genres*) of being. In § 3, he shows that the same criterion of identity cannot be applied to the conservation in time of a substance whose model is the material body, or to that of a living individual or an organized body: 'The reason whereof is, that in these two cases of a Mass of Matter, and a living Body, Identity is not applied to the same thing.' In § 7, he begins to show that the notion of 'man' covers two types of identity in an equivocal fashion and that it is consequently necessary to introduce a third notion alongside the other two: 'It being one thing to be the same Substance, another the same Man, and a third the same Person, if Person, Man, and Substance, are three Names standing for three different Ideas.' After the crucial experience (real or imagined) of the 'storyteller parrot', (§ 8) which challenges the Aristotelian definition of the rational animal as *Zôon logon ekhôn*, the

distinction between *the individual* and *the person*, whose criterion is precisely consciousness, is definitively confirmed. Thus begins the examination of the problems posed by personal identity, by far the most difficult. (§ 9) It will lead to a redefinition of 'person' as 'the name for the self'. (§ 26)

From this moment on, the examination is conducted not only as a function of the difference between individual identity and personal identity, but also as a function of the difference between the latter and the identity of substance which closes the circle of possible analogies. The result of this analysis is that none of the three ideas of identities, related to the three kinds of being (or three points of view concerning existence), can be reduced to any of the others. *Envisioned materially, identity is thus fundamentally an equivocal notion*: such is Locke's essential thesis. It leads to the 'decomposition' of the pseudo-unity indicated by the current conception of *man*. (§ 21) Of course, this equivocity extends to all notions that one way or another play a role in the recognition of identity or are its correlatives: sameness and diversity, unity and multiplicity or the relation between a whole and its parts (belonging, participation, etc.: the concept of the parts of a body differs from the concept of the parts of an organism, which themselves differ from the concept of the parts or moments of a consciousness).

Let us thus return to the theses defended by the commentators whose testimony I have taken. In what concerns Ayers, it is surprising that he considers the notion of a 'material assemblage' of the same corpuscles, which Locke regarded as the criterion of the identity of physical bodies, as contradictory. For this amounts to attributing to Locke a physics or natural phenomenology different from what is in fact his. Ayers's discussion has the merit of highlighting the provocative nature of the theses articulated by Locke regarding the identity of substance: the elimination of the model of divine identity, the a priori reduction of the case of spiritual substances ('finite minds') to that of material bodies.[20] In contrast, his discussion becomes misleading when he seeks to demonstrate that Locke, despite his efforts, did not succeed in maintaining *the analogy* between life and consciousness (or between organic life and the life of consciousness). Such an analogy is undoubtedly a great philosopheme that traverses the entire history of modern philosophies. But it is precisely what Locke refuses, fundamentally because organization and consciousness present different relations to *temporality*: in the first case, an invariance that subtracts the unity of the organism as a whole from the change in which its parts are caught, which Locke calls the flow of continuous substitution; in the second, on the contrary a continuity

---

20   This reduction does not resolve the indecisiveness that hangs over the the entire second part of the treatise concerning the independence of substantial and individual identities, of the soul and consciousness insofar as the substances in question here are immaterial. What 'saves' Locke in a certain sense is that he is in dialogue with a (Christian) religious metaphysics in which minds (*esprits*) themselves are supposed to *occupy a place* in the world and in history.

or a tension that makes each part, whether representation or mental operation, a *moment* of internal temporal succession. This radical disjunction is at the heart of the reformulation of the anthropological problem.

For this reason, it may be assumed that Ricoeur more closely corresponds to Locke's position because he begins by posing the equivocity of identity. However, this is not the case, because Ricoeur immediately reduces this equivocity to the opposition of two terms: sameness and ipseity. Which is to say that he reconstitutes a dualism analogous to that of matter and mind, of the *in itself* and the *for itself*, of the *what* and the *who*, etc., even if it appears on a phenomenological, rather than metaphysical, plane.[21] Thus, in opposition to Ayers, the question of the relation between consciousness and life as referents of identity is completely eliminated.[22] It occupies a central place in Locke, however, not only in the negative sense, as we have just seen, but by opening the possibility of another way of posing the anthropological problem in which the unity of man, living individual and conscious person would not be constructed as a 'composition' or 'union', but through the detour of his practical activity (cf. 'Appropriate').

3. Ricoeur's discussion and the accent he places on the question of the 'self' (or of identity as ipseity) has the advantage of allowing us to identify one last characteristic of the Lockean position: the privilege that it finally confers on personal identity, insofar as 'identity to oneself' ('*identité à soi*') is constituted in the element of consciousness. This privilege can be expressed in different ways:

– either by supposing that in the last instance *every concept of identity* or of being 'the same as oneself' ('*le même que soi*') rests, from the point of view of its formal intelligibility, on an idea of reflexivity whose model remains the relation of consciousness to itself (cf. SAMENESS);

– or by recalling that consciousness is itself the 'site' of the definition of temporality in relation to which all the 'material' questions of identity and difference are posed (cf. MEMORY).

The difficulty then does not derive from Locke's allowing a 'naturalist' or 'objectivist' concept of identity to overwhelm and predetermine the examination of personal identity, ipseity or reflexive identity as containing within itself its own alterity. Rather, the difficulty derives from the opposite, from the fact that Locke tends to regard – without ever reducing them to the same ontological situation – the reflexive identity of consciousness, immanent in internal

---

21   It is true that Ricoeur's objective is not primarily to interpret Locke and that he is justified in developing his own point of view independently of the theses of Locke's *Essay*. Nevertheless, out of a concern for exactitude, he is led to attempt to define the Lockean conception of 'personal identity' at a certain moment in his study. (In a subsequent book – *La mémoire, l'histoire, l'oubli*, Paris: Éditions du Seuil, 2000, 123 ff.) Ricoeur referred to my argument in this book in a very positive manner. I was honoured and pleased, but I could not but notice that he in fact attributed to me his own position – the one that I had criticized here.

22   It will only be discussed at the end of Ricoeur's book, in the course of a brief discussion of Spinoza.

duration, as the epistemological or intellectual presupposition of all the others, and therefore of all thought of an identity between any existences whatsoever.[23] In this sense, there would be not only a psychologism but also, taking the term in a strictly etymological way, something like a Lockean 'personalism'.

INDIVIDUAL: §§ 4, 6, 10, 13, 21, 23, 25, 29

'Individual' as an adjective is applied to substances (in particular minds), actions, men. But the *concept of individuality* has a much more limited definition in Locke's text. Individuality, based on the invariance of the living organization, is one of three fundamental types of identity (the others being substance and person). His terminology is rigorous on this point. An examination of all its contexts allows us to set aside the thesis (maintained above all by Ayers) that the horizon of Lockean theory would be constituted by a *general concept of individuality*, applicable to all categories of beings.[24] *Individual* or *individuality* are not synonyms of *singular being* (to put it more precisely, all individuals are beings, but not all beings or existences are individuals). And individualization (not to be confused with a generic concept of individuation) (§ 3) is nothing other than the process of organization that assures a living being both of the permanence of its form and the possibility of perpetually occupying different places.

The critical thrust of this thesis obviously lies in its application to the 'particular case' of man. This case, however, leads us to distinguish two levels of argumentation and writing. The first concerns the animality of man. Locke's thesis here is so radical that it leaves no place for any dualism. Not only is the human species one among other species of animal (which has as its correlate the fact that species cannot be confused or mistaken for each other, even in the case of a man and a speaking parrot), but the problem (common from Plato's *Alcibiades* to Descartes' Sixth Meditation) of knowing if man's essence lies in the soul, the body or a composite of the two, is deprived of its object. For the answer is given in advance. But it is equally given that this identification of human individuality with the form of its corporeal organization is essentially linked to the constitution of another plane of identity, that of consciousness, and thus to the conceptual distinction of *humanity* from *personality*.

It would be wrong, however, to believe that Locke's treatment of the problem of human individuality in the treatise is limited to this generic thesis (which is fundamentally negative: the human individual is *nothing other than* a specific living

---

23   In the same order of ideas, see 'Locke's Treatise on Identity' above for a discussion of the relations between the 'principle of identity' and 'personal identity'.

24   Ayers, *Locke*, II, 208: 'Locke evidently felt the need to present his version of the mechanist treatment of individual substances within a more ambitious theory of the identity of individuals of any category whatsoever.' Based on this postulate, Ayers then feels able to reproach Locke for being inconsistent with his own premises.

thing). In fact, there is a second level of writing that is not thematized in concepts but whose narrative insistence cannot be disregarded: it concerns the use of *proper names* (Socrates, Plato, Pontius Pilate, Augustine, Caesar Borgia, Nestor, Thersites, the mayor of Quinborough, Melibeus, and even, where history and fable merge, the story of the prince and the cobbler, 'the Day-Man' and 'the Night-Man').

The identification of individuality with life here takes on a supplementary value: the category of individuality is applied to the continuity of the living body (through the typical moments of growth, health and illness, and ageing). But it is also to a given living individuality that *a proper name is attributed* (Socrates dying is still the same individual as Socrates the child).[25] Thus, it is possible (and, I would add, necessary) to read things in another way. The only answer to the question 'What is human individuality?' is that it is the sum or conjunction, not of a body and a soul, but of *a living body and a proper name.*[26]

This does not create a new reality, transcending the sphere of life, but shows that life is overdetermined by the actions and laws of civil society from which derives the attribution of names. We might well ask (and this question, it must be said, is far from absurd, even without taking into consideration the 'post card' found by Derrida) if *Socrates and Plato would not be the same person* if their 'consciousness' was common to them both.[27] But we can be certain that the *names* of Socrates and Plato, corresponding to living bodies that name themselves and are named by others differently (just as 'I' name myself differently than 'Nestor' or 'Thersites'), *refer to different men.* Humanity – a concept elsewhere regarded by Locke as enigmatic – is thus reduced to the articulation of what we would today call the biological and the symbolic. The question is whether this can take place in an *autonomous way*, without the 'mediation' of consciousness and personal identity.[28]

---

25 We may see here the critical point: using the same reasoning we may be sure that the infant Jesus and the crucified Messiah are one and the same individual, but the same guarantee cannot be extended to the resurrected Christ with whom, according to the Evangelical promise, we will be 're-united' beyond the grave.

26 Bringing together the suggestions concerning proper names associated with living individualities and the complex theory of proper names discussed in Book III of the *Essay* lies beyond the scope of this work.

27 Jacques Derrida, *The Post Card from Socrates to Freud and Beyond*, Chicago: University of Chicago Press, 1987.

28 The question is also posed, correlatively, of whether such an articulation can take place independently of *labour*. We have here the other side of the theory of appropriation that forms the basis, at least in a latent way, of the Lockean variant of 'individualism': legal property is obviously attached to the *name* of the proprietor (and to the symbolic order of the registration of property titles under names) but it concerns things with which the individual mixes his *body*, bringing about the specifically human mediating reality of labour, that is, appropriation as material transformation. We should note in this regard the inverted homology between the invariance of individuality living through the 'substitution' of parts in a natural flow and the process of the increase of property or the acquisition of things by a 'mixture' of the forces of the body and natural forces. These questions deserve a separate study.

We might assume the answer is no, for although Locke seeks essentially to *distinguish* these orders, he also furnishes suggestions concerning their articulation (especially the way in which language is based on mental life). But it must also be noted that the function of names is not so much to identify individuals but to *differentiate* them, avoiding the possibility that they be mistaken for one another. Fundamentally, we each perceive ourselves as a *person*, that is, as a 'self', and perceive others as *human beings* with a proper name before attributing a personality to them. What is emerging here is thus an anthropology of human relations, and not only of human nature.[29]

MEMORY: §§ 20, 23, 25, 27

We might begin the discussion of the problem of the relations between memory, consciousness and identity in Locke (and in consequence, the problem of the Lockean conception of the relations between temporality and interiority) by recalling that it is precisely on this point that, immediately following the publication of the *Essay*, his critics thought they had discovered a *logical circle* and attacked the validity of Locke's 'criterion' of personal identity. As early as 1736, Joseph Butler, in an appendix to his *Analogy of Religion,* observed that the continuity of consciousness cannot be made the criterion of personal identity without presupposing precisely what is in question, namely whether it is indeed the same 'self' that consciousness maintains.[30] But this critique assumes the adoption of precisely the substantialist perspective that Locke seeks to eliminate. In contrast, for Hume (*Treatise of Human Nature*, I, 4, sect. VI: *Of personal identity*), who regards the 'self' not as a substance but as a fiction constructed by habit, the argument based on circularity is reduced to the essential: memory can only provide consciousness with the means of recognizing identity to the extent that it first contributes to its constitution. Memory only postulates its own ability to actualize past perceptions or to integrate them into an existing 'belief'.[31]

I propose here to explore the following thesis: without any doubt this critique touches on an essential point, but fails to grasp its meaning because it does not see that the 'circle' of consciousness and memory, or their relation of

---

29   It is also important to specify the differences between Hobbes and Locke: in many ways the combination of living individuality and naming is precisely what Hobbes himself called identity and which he made the basis of the mechanisms of 'representation' (authorship and acting as a representative of the author). The necessary mediations are not furnished by consciousness, but by the passions, imagination, rational calculation and law (see 'Person' in the Glossary).

30   Joseph Butler, 'Of Personal Identity', in J. Perry, ed., *Personal Identity*, Berkeley: University of California Press, 1975, 99–105.

31   David Hume, *A Treatise of Human Nature* (1739), Analytical Index by L.A. Selby-Bigge, Second Edition with text revised and notes by P. H. Nidditch, Oxford: Oxford University Press, 1978, 251–63.

reciprocal presupposition and the presence of each term at the heart of the other, far from being an unnoticed weakness in Locke's reasoning, constitutes the *very object* of his discovery and his analysis. This is not to say that his analysis contains no other philosophical difficulty, but it inaugurated a problematic of temporality whose terms would remain under discussion at least through the work of William James, Husserl and their interpreters today.

Let us begin by laying out some terminological points.[32] A comparison with II.x, 'Of Retention', shows an evolution in Locke's formulations. In this chapter, he still reserves the term 'memory' for the 'passive' faculty by which we *keep* the traces or imprints of our past perceptions and ideas, making them available for their eventual revival (called here *recollection* or designated by the verb *to retrieve*). It is this that, identified with *secondary perception* (II.x.7) constitutes the active faculty. Having thus completed the cycle, Locke takes another step, showing that (§ 8) the play of memory and recollection is indispensable *to the use of any of our intellectual faculties* precisely because they all involve the concatenation of perceptions or operations on already existing perceptions and therefore the selective 'retention' and reactivation of 'dormant' thoughts.

It is necessary to keep this argument in mind in order to appreciate the construction of II.xxvii: on the occasion of the discussion of identity, Locke postulates a much more intimate relation between consciousness and memory that will finally lead him to employ the doublet 'operations of thinking and memory' (§ 27) as another name for consciousness, thus conferring a quasi-transcendental function on memory.[33] This derives from the fact that every consciousness in reality contains an internal temporality, a movement that passes from virtuality to actuality and the reverse. To reach this point, however, it will be necessary to make two points of clarification:

1. The first concerns the status of 'forgetfulness': the discussion in § 23 shows that what is important is not to think the continuity of consciousness as the availability of an infallible memory of its acts or past thoughts, but to show that the availability of memory precisely 'limits' or 'measures' the possibilities of the recognition of personal identity.[34] The line of demarcation thus passes between those subjects whose recollections, more or less abundant and easy to recall, are inserted into a single continuum and those whose memory is 'split', such that their memories are systematically distributed among several 'lives'

---

32   I have benefitted from Marc Parmentier's comments on an earlier version of this argument.

33   Or in any case a function that pertains to a 'transcendental psychology' rather than an 'empirical psychology'.

34   In II.x.9, Locke reports (not without some irony, perhaps) the memory attributed to the child prodigy Pascal, adding that the brilliant mathematician nevertheless shared with the great mass of people the limitation (or finitude) of having to recall his memories in *succession*.

isolated from each other (which leads to the theory of multiple personalities). It thus appears that it is, properly speaking, memory that scans or divides life and thus also constitutes it as a unity. But it can only do so to the extent that it is capable of actualizing the past, which leads us to the second question, that of *representation* or *presence*.

2. The difficulty here derives from the fact that it is difficult to determine the modality according to which Locke thinks 'recollection' as the reactivation of the past, which is marked by the ambiguous expression employed in § 25: *memory or consciousness of past actions*. It seems to me that in reality Locke developed a first analysis, but suggested another, different analysis through the examples and fictions that he multiplies. In any case, 'to recover past actions' of course means to recover their representation or idea, that is, the way they are or were perceived by the one who performed them in the framework of the mind or 'internal sense' (§ 13). But whereas the most explicit thesis suggests that it is a question of a repetition by which a 'consciousness' or conscious self-representation that has already occurred once is reproduced nearly identically and thus put once again at the disposal of the subject, the series of examples and fictions (all of which, of course, have something of the fantastic about them) suggest instead that recollection is the consciousness of an action *insofar as it is* past, that is, the consciousness – necessarily fragile or 'uneasy' – of a survival or memory trace that binds the present to the past and to which identity remains attached.

The argumentation in § 13 is encumbered by this difficulty, since it evokes without resolving (but by referring it to an unknown relation between soul and consciousness) the dilemma of a 'representation' that may be transferred from one substance to another independently of the action that it represents, and a 'representation' that would remain forever dependent on the 'reflex action of perception' of the specific action from which it arises:

> But it being but a present representation of a past Action . . . how far the conscious-ness of past Actions is annexed to any individual Agent, so that another cannot possibly have it, it will be hard for us to determine, till we know what kind of Action it is, that cannot be done without a reflex Act of Perception accompanying it . . . But that which we call the *same consciousness* [is] not . . . the same individual Act. (II. xxviii.13)

While it is clear that these two modalities are not equivalent, it is probable that Locke needed them both: the first gave him the guarantee that consciousness is capable of 'joining' (§ 24) representations, *irrespective of the objective distance that separates them,* and thus of having them present to the mind simultane-ously to recover them, while the second allowed him the possibility of attribut-ing a 'historicity' to consciousness, that is, a *representation of the temporal distance* that 'accompan[ies] our representations'.[35] The double orientation of Locke's descriptions affects both the way he understands the connection between consciousness and temporality and the articulation of this link to the idea of the 'self'.

The idea of a *repetition of the past* in the operations of consciousness (assuming that something like a repetition of the identical is possible) tends to inscribe time, as we have already seen, in the succession of the mind's operations. It is not a matter of lived time (*un temps vécu*), but of a virtual time, prior to any consciousness, which could even perhaps be understood as unconscious.[36] Against the specific modality of a consciousness of 'lived time' and its flow, the distances it introduces in the midst of 'self', the incertitudes, interruptions and lacunae from which it fashions the 'material' of our internal history, are at the heart of the idea of a consciousness of the past.

If Locke did not feel the need to clarify this difference, it was not simply because of the difficulties it posed for his thought. It was perhaps also because this difference served to resolve the problem of the concept of *duration* itself insofar as it is a 'subjective' concept. For such a notion assumes that consciousness, prior to any external experience, either by 'neutralizing' the exteriority of the objects of its thought or by locating itself on the sole basis of the succession of its own thoughts, has both an idea of the flow of time or a 'continuous movement' occurring within itself, and of a marking of the temporal distance between differentiated moments:

> 'Tis evident to any one who will but observe what passes in his own Mind, that there is a train of *Ideas* which constantly succeed one another in his Understanding, as long as he is awake. *Reflection* on these appearances of several *Ideas* one after

---

35   We find a striking illustration of this phenomenological ambiguity, which is in fact the essence of psychologism, in IV.i.9, where Locke discusses the memory of theorems which is at the same time a revival (or reactivation) of their truth indispensable to mathematical certitude: 'He remembers, i.e. he knows (for remembrance is but the reviving of some past knowledge) that he was once certain of the truth of this Proposition, that the three Angles of a Triangle are equal to two right ones. The immutability of the same relations between immutable things, is now the *Idea* that shows him, that if the three Angles of a Triangle were once equal to two right ones, they will always be equal to two right ones. And hence he comes to be certain, that what was once true in the case is always true; what *ideas* that once agreed will always agree; and consequently what he once knew to be true he will always know to be true, as long as he can remember that he once knew it.'

36   It appears that this is Leibniz's assumption, both in the *New Essays* (II.xxvii.9) where he describes the 'immediate [temporal] transition' (*passage prochain*) from one idea or mental state to another and (II.xx.6) where he understands *uneasiness* as 'imperceptible little urges' (*petites sollicitations imperceptibles*)' or as 'tiny aides, imperceptible escapes and releases of a thwarted endeavour' (*petites aides ou petites délivrances et dégagements imperceptibles de la tendance arrêtée*). But what is possible for Leibniz is not possible for Locke insofar as he is committed to a strict phenomenological description of what is immediately accessible for consciousness. It is what Leibniz calls in opposition '*the appearance of self*'.

another in our Minds, is that which furnishes us with the *Idea* of Succession: And the distance between any parts of that Succession, or between the appearance of any two *Ideas* in our Minds, is that we call *Duration*. For whilst we are thinking, or whilst we receive successively several *Ideas* in our Minds, we know that we do exist; and so we call the Existence or the Continuation of the Existence of our selves, or any thing else, Commensurate to the succession of any *Ideas* in our Minds, the *Duration* of our selves, or of any such other thing co-existing with our Thinking. (II.xiv.3)[37]

But in addition – and the two problems are closely linked – it was also because the notion of an equivalence between consciousness of duration and the recognition of the self contains a tension within itself between the idea of a 'self' that would be in a certain sense the invariant or *fixed point* of all its transformations and transitions, and that of a 'self' which would be nothing but *fluxion* itself, the inheritance each thought bequeaths to its successor (to use Leibniz's expression) or each thought's 'recommendation' to that which follows it (to cite the Stoics' metaphor) and the retrospective appropriation of the earlier by the later.

The problem is present more than ever in Locke's twentieth-century heirs. Thus Françoise Dastur summarizes the form this problem takes in Husserl:

Each phase not only has before it, but also in it, all the preceding retentions of which it is itself the retention: it is the latest moment in the moving of the initial point away from itself. There is thus a living solidarity between the different phases in relation to each other because they are all, as retentional phases, shadows cast by the incessant renewal of the same initial point, the differentials of a temporal identity, that of an extended *now* that comprehends *in itself* its own movement away *from itself*. It is this which explains Husserl's use on two occasions of the image of the comet to represent continuity in separation (*éloignement*).[38]

There is also William James, whose formulations David Lapoujade examines in the following manner:

Each conscious thought is essentially like a bamboo stem connecting past and future in the same continuous present – what James calls the 'specious present'; but this also means that there exists a point of the pure present whose thought does not

37   Of course, Locke admits that in the last analysis, the ideas in question here originate in external sensation. But it is clear that this origin is completely neutralized, the only thing intervening in the production of the idea of duration being their internal differentiation. It is precisely what Kant will attack in his 'Refutation of Idealism' in the *Critique of Pure Reason* (B 274–9), arguing that I can perceive the 'internal' temporality (*Zeitbestimmung*) of my thought (*Denken*) only inasmuch as it is simultaneously affected by 'external' perceptions and by their objects.

38   F. Dastur, *Husserl des mathématiques à l'histoire*, Paris: PUF, 1995, 65.

or at least does not yet belong to consciousness; it is separated from consciousness by the flow of temporal continuity . . . In the interval, a process of appropriation is completed: the thought that follows appropriates or inherits the preceding thought; it is the act of the retrospective appropriation of thought, even if this act is equally aimed at the future. 'Each pulsation of consciousness . . . each thought is born possessing and dies "possessed", transmitting all it was able to realize to the next owner'. It is in this way that the thought-event becomes *my* thought, the thought of my consciousness by an immediate retrospective labour of interpretation that integrates or appropriates the preceding thoughts.[39]

But for Locke (in opposition to Husserl), just as there is really an 'originary impression' from which retention would proceed as modification-conservation, so (unlike James) there is no 'pure present' heterogeneous to consciousness or preceding its movement of appropriation. There is only the '*train of* Ideas' with which Locke sought to engender the duality of the measuring and the measured or the virtual and the actual.

MIND: §§ 1, 8, 10, 13, 14, 15, 23, 25

The translation – and in consequence the knowledge – of the term *mind*, the key concept in Locke's *Essay,* presents us with one of the great 'untranslatables' of philosophy, given the absence of a term in the French language that corresponds exactly with the Latin *mens* (as is the case with *mind*, both etymologically and semantically). This lacuna has not ceased to produce confusing effects, leading to its translation, depending upon the context, as '*âme*' or '*esprit*' (*psuchè* vs *pneuma*; *anima* vs *spiritus*; *soul* vs *spirit*).[40] It is all the more surprising given that the adjective *mental* and its derivatives have existed in French for a long time. It is unfortunately too late to hope to be able to introduce a neologism, even in the form of a noun ('*le mental*' exists, but its uses are limited to the contexts of sports or parapsychology) that moreover cannot agree with all the English expressions.[41] We may at least attempt to take

39   D. Lapoujade, *William James. Empirisme et pragmatisme*, Paris: PUF, 1997, 32–3. The cited passage is taken from 'The Place of Affectional Facts in a World of Pure Experience', in *Essays in Radical Empiricism*, rééd. Cambridge, MA: Harvard University Press, 1976.

40   This confusion could have devastating consequences when Philosophy of Mind is becoming an established discipline, and for the discussions to which it leads. The case of German was similar given the fact that the word *Gemüt*, which Kant used in opposition to both *Seele* and *Geist*, fell into disuse (see my article 'Âme/Esprit' in Cassin, ed., *Vocabulaire*.

41   In the classical age, the same problem was posed by the use of *mens* by Descartes and especially Spinoza, who represented, in opposition to Locke, the other great attempt to 'desubstantialize' the faculty of thought through the 'parallelism of the attributes'. In his recent commentary on the *Ethics*, Pierre Macherey proposes 'la réalité mentale' (mental reality), and brings together expressions like 'le mental' (the mental), 'le psychisme' (psychism), 'la réalité psychique' (psychic reality), even 'l'appareil psychique' (psychical apparatus), to avoid the term *esprit* 'because of its

advantage of this difficulty to explain the stakes and consequences of this discrepancy.

Let me recall the essential meanings of the word *mind* in English according to the Oxford English Dictionary, a word whose predominance may clearly be seen in Locke's surprisingly frequent use of the term. The Indo-European etymology is the same as that of the Greek *ménos* (the soul, the principle of life and will) and the Latin *mens* and *memini* (to have in mind, to recollect, to mention).[42] Its first meaning is the state or faculty of recollection, which later became that of commemoration. The second is the action or object of thought, judgment and opinion. The third, a later usage than the others, is the seat of consciousness or intellectual capacity. In Locke's *Essay*, there is, in this respect, an oscillation between the uses of *mind* and *understanding*: in the strict sense, the understanding is simply one of the two faculties or operations characteristic of the *mind*, the other being the will or volition.[43] But the understanding also signifies the *mind* in its totality, which corresponds to Locke's 'cognitivist' orientation, that is, to the primacy of perception over all the other activities of the mind, in practice identified with thought in general, of which the mind is the source.[44] What is obviously most striking here is the way in which Locke's theorization of consciousness allows him to unify thought and memory as correlative aspects of the mind, instituting a temporal dynamic that sets aside the metaphysical problems associated with the notion of 'substrate'.

---

spiritualist connotations' (see the *Introduction à l'Ethique de Spinoza. La seconde partie: La réalité mentale*, Paris: PUF, 1997, 10–13). We cannot adopt such a solution here because the Lockean mind is not a 'mode' of thought or even less an idea or complex of ideas, but a 'power' that knows itself through the consciousness of its operations. See also Emilia Giancotti, 'Sul concetto spinoziano di *mens*', in *Ricerche lessicali su opere di Descartes e Spinoza*, Lessico Intellettuale Europeo, III, Roma: Edizioni dell'Ateneo, 1969. Both the Italians and the Spanish forged the term *la mente* without any problem. The deficiency in the French language is undoubtedly the rebound effect of the imperialism of the word 'esprit' and the numerous associations of ideas it has authorized.

On the fundamental importance of the distinction between *mind* and *spirit* after Locke (in particular in Berkeley), see. G. Brykman, *Berkeley et le voile des mots*, Paris: Vrin, 1993, 93 ff.

42   In the theological tradition, *mens* functioned as the equivalent of the Greek *noûs*; it was either considered the 'superior' part of the *anima* (*psuchè*), or tendentially autonomized as the image of God in man (as in Augustine's *De Trinitate* where the Human 'trinity' of Memory, Intelligence, and Will as different instances or hypostases of the Soul is said to reproduce the divine essence).

43   Locke, *Essay*, II.xxi.5 and 6, where he calls them 'powers of the Mind'.

44   The extensively revised chapter 'Of Power' (II.xxi) constitutes a 'Treatise on the Passions' in an abridged form. At its centre is the theory of 'uneasiness', which suggests that the primacy of mind can be overturned, or that Locke's most profound thought lay in the idea of the mutual envelopment of perception by uneasiness and uneasiness by perception, or, better still, in their respective *movements* or *flows*. But, as I have indicated a number of times, this point is the limit of the Lockean critique of the idea of the soul, the point at which he would need to produce a non-substantialist theory of power, which remains largely virtual.

Coste's extreme difficulty here should be noted, a consequence both of the deficiency of French in relation to English and of the predominance of the idea of the soul (*âme*) for which Descartes, when writing in Latin, had used the word *mens*. It is true that in his case it was a question of emphasizing less its immateriality or transcendent destiny than its essential attribute as a 'thing that thinks'. In fact, Locke persistently uses the Cartesian expression *thinking thing* (II.xvii.9, 10, 12, 17, 23, 27), and does so precisely in order to be able to pass from the substantialist point of view to that of the mind and its operations:

> I am apt enough to think I have in treating of this Subject made some Suppositions that will look strange to some Readers, and possibly they are so in themselves. But yet I think, they are such, as are pardonable in this ignorance we are in of the Nature of that thinking thing, that is in us, and which we look on as our 'selves'. (II.xxvii.27)

It is understandable that Coste, despite his lucidity, might have been troubled by the presence of a new idea and by the confusion caused by his native language. Thus, his lapse into 'âme' to translate not only 'soul' but even *mind*, and his hesitation to render both *mind* and *spirit* as '*esprit*'.[45]

The use of a specific term allowed Locke to express with ease the idea of an instance that was neither soul nor body (or an instance that did not need to be determined as one or the other), but that had to be thought as a set of independent operations linked to each other in internal time. The notion of operation here is fundamental: it excludes any consideration of 'parts' (ideas that exist in the memory like parts of a whole and can thus be the object of an 'appropriation').[46] It is also tendentially separated from the old notion of 'faculty', although Locke on occasion employs the pair *faculty* or *operation* (II. xi.14), which finally leads to the substitution for a classification of faculties of an analysis of the *power of operation*, or a reflexive analysis of the powers from which proceed these actions of the mind which are these operations (perceptions being in fact the first level and origin of all these operations). But this analysis is co-extensive with consciousness, given that, as we have seen, it

---

45   There can be no doubt that Locke, through his use of 'thinking thing' as a means of transition between the point of view of substance and that of mental operations, was, well before the Kant of the 'Paralogisms', responsible for the reproach directed against Descartes, rightly or wrongly, by modern philosophy for having substantialized thought.

46   On this question, it is certain that Descartes' insistence on the idea that 'the soul has no parts' (against the Platonic and Aristotelian traditions taken up by theology) opened the way to the Lockean point of view. But it is equally clear that his position encouraged modern philosophers and historians to project retrospectively the Lockean conception of 'consciousness' on Descartes, even to the point of lamenting that he had burdened this conception with 'substantialist' survivals or prejudices. It is all the more amusing to note that his 'disciples' (e.g. La Forge) who were the first systematically to use the term *conscience* as consciousness were also tempted (under the influence of Augustinian theologemes) to reintroduce the idea of inferior or superior 'parts of the soul'.

extends throughout the space between sensation or primary perception and reflection and abstraction. The point of view of consciousness is thus what allows Locke to think mental reality, in its intelligible structure, as distinct from the structures of living organization (the mental is opposed to the vital) as from those of language (the mental is opposed to the verbal); to think it as an *action without substance* (at least without a *determinate* substance, whether material or spiritual, etc.). But not, obviously, as an *action without a subject*. We might even say that here the revocation of substance liberates the point of view of the subject (even if the term *subject* does not appear in this sense before Kant).

ORGANIZATION, ORGANIZED: §§ 4, 5, 6, 8, 27

The term *organization* has been in use since the end of the fifteenth century (in English since 1450, according to the *Oxford English Dictionary*, and in French since 1488, according to the *Trésor de la langue française*) in the sense of 'the state (or action or condition) of an organized body', an idea itself of Aristotelian origin (the totality of the *organa* or instruments of the body). In any case, it was not until the second half of the seventeenth century that life began to be conceptualized as a fact of organization, first at the level of the anatomical disposition of the organs, and later at that of their functionality.[47] And only after the middle of the eighteenth century was the idea of this functionality extended from metabolism to growth and reproduction:

> Until the seventeenth century, the exemplary organized body was the animal body . . . The microscopic examination of plant specimen preparations permitted the generalization of the concept of organization, even inspiring fantastic analogies between plant and animal, regarding their structures and vital functions . . .
>
> The Greek *organon* designated both the musician's instrument and the artisan's tool. The assimilation of the organic human body to an organ was more than a metaphor in the seventeenth century . . . For Descartes, the organic organ functions without an organist. But for Leibniz, the structural and functional unity assumes an organist. Without an organizer, that is, without a soul, there can be nothing organized or organic . . .

---

47   The *Encyclopédie* of Diderot and d'Alembert still gives only a short and imprecise definition, without any epistemological development: '*Organization*, s.f.: the arrangement of the parts that constitute living bodies. The first principle of organization is found in seeds. The organization of a body once established is the origin of all other bodies. The organization of solid parts takes place through mechanical movements. *Organize*, v. act.: an organist's term, meaning to unite a small organ with a harpsichord or other similar instrument'. Between 1664 and 1706, the *Oxford English Dictionary* lists three references for *organization*, one of which is to Locke's treatise (II. xxvii.17).

The history of the concept of organism in the eighteenth century, through the research of naturalists, physicians, and philosophers, had recourse to semantic substitutes for or equivalents of the soul to account for the increasingly established fact of the functional unity of a system of integrated parts. In such a system, the parts maintain among themselves relations of direct or mediated reciprocity . . . such that the term 'part', strictly speaking, no longer serves to designate the organs of which the organism may be said to be the totality but not the addition.[48]

Locke – who, it should be recalled, had a medical education initiated in England and completed in France – was situated mid-way in this evolution. In § 5 of his treatise, he makes organization the equivalent of a 'Construction of Parts, to a certain end'. *Construction* here means anatomical *structure* (a meaning in currency from the time of Vesalius's *humani corporis fabrica*); *end* refers to an internal finality in the sense of functionality, the ensemble of physiological functions carried out by an organism. The difficulty of grasping his position arises from two points: first, the difference between an organization and a material structure (a living 'body' and a physical 'body' [*un 'corps' physique*]); and secondly, the exact relation between the reference to organization and the reference to life (not in the sense of a soul).

Concerning the first point, a reading of the treatise leaves no doubt: the principle of the totalization or arrangement of the parts of a solid body that makes its 'cohesion' and that of a living organism are rigorously opposed. The unity of the cohesion of solid bodies, which allows them to remain identical to themselves as long as they are not destroyed, is made analytically on the basis of *elements* or *parts* (which are in the last analysis particles of matter) and resides in a composition. It is thus essential that the parts *remain the same*, even if the whole itself shows no change. In contrast, the unity of the organization of living bodies, in particular animals – the foundation of what Locke calls 'individual identity' or 'the identity of life' – is made synthetically, on the basis of the form that subsumes *parts or organs*. This form is the link between the individual and the species (§ 4), but resides in the individual itself.[49] It is its permanence in time (its 'continued organization') which has primacy over the material identity of its constituent parts and allows movement in and out, and growth and diminution (even amputation, provided that the general form is saved). It is also

---

48   Georges Canguilhem, 'Vie', *Encyclopaedia Universalis*, 1ère édition, Vol. 16 (1973), 768. Canguilhem then shows how Leibniz's ideas made possible the definition of the organism proposed in 1769 by Charles Bonnet: 'this profusion of varied relations that so closely link all the organic parts and by virtue of which they all conspire to achieve the same general end: I mean to form that *unity* that is called an animal, that organized whole that lives, grows, feels, moves, preserves and reproduces itself'.

49   Locke will later insist again on this point in his debate with Stillingfleet: 'Mr. Locke's Second Reply to the Bishop of Worcester', *Works* IV, 316 ff. (concerning the resurrection of the body).

what permits us to understand the living individual as *imposing the law of its organization* on its environment (§ 6: 'constantly fleeting Particles of Matter, in succession vitally united in the same organized Body').

On the second point, it might seem that the expressions employed by Locke sometimes seem to support the thesis that organization is *the means employed by life* to distribute itself among the parts, inspire their solidarity and insure the continuity of form ('which is fit to convey that common Life to all the Parts so united'), and at other times seem to support the thesis that *life is precisely nothing other than the permanence of organization* (or it capacity to perservere) ('such an Organization of those parts, as is fit to receive, and distribute nourishment, so as to continue, and frame . . . in which consists the vegetable life') (§ 4). But what is essential is perhaps not there: it is rather in the way Locke subsumes the *continuity of the organs' adaptation to a series of functions* under the concept of an arrangement of parts having in itself the principle of its movement. It is equally important that growth (if not reproduction) is counted among these functions, understood as the addition of matter within the permanence of form.[50]

We are now in a position to understand how Locke was able to make life/organization a *specific mode of identity* reducible neither to the identity of substance (in particular material substance), nor to personal identity (which does not consist of a synthesis or subsumption of parts according to the law of a synthetic form invariant in time, but, on the contrary, of the mobile continuity of experiences or ideas linked into the present and recalled by memory). Life, thus represented as the *invariance of the form* common to parts 'in motion' in relation to each other, is in fact *identity* in the strong sense and in the original meaning of the term, but it is neither the analogue of cohesion nor of consciousness (even a 'drowsy' or 'obscure' consciousness as in Cudworth). It is not surprising that Leibniz rejected this representation:

> PHILALETHE. This shows of what the identity of the same man consists, namely in that alone which enjoys the same life, continued through particles of matter in a perpetual flow, but who in this succession are *vitally* united in the same organized body.

---

50   Dr Françoise Nicolas-Barboux, author of a thesis completed at the Université de Paris X on Locke's medical thought, has pointed out to me various indications in the text of the *Essay* suggesting that Locke adhered to the preformationist theses promoted by Leeuwenhoek (with whom he associated during his sojourn in Holland) rather than the epigenetic position of Harvey: above all, his insistence on the continuity between the plant and animal kingdoms and on the analogous nature of their mechanisms in the unique domain of living beings. But, as Nicolas-Barboux herself remarks, these indications are weak and it is very likely that Locke, on this point as on so many others, observed an agnostic neutrality – in any case, as concerns the processes of embryonic development, whose knowledge appeared to him to be of little practical import. Cf. K. Dewhurst, *John Locke (1632–1704), Physician and Philosopher: A Medical Biography*, London: Wellcome Historical Medical Library, 1963.

THEOPHILE. This can be understood according to my way of thinking. In effect, the organized body is not the same beyond the moment: it is only equivalent. And outside of the relation to the soul, there can be no single life nor any *vital* union. In this way, there would only be the appearance of identity. (Leibniz, *New Essay*, II.xxvii.6)

The alternative proposed by Leibniz (*equivalence* instead of *identity*) would be more interesting if it did not render the specificity adduced by Locke nothing more than *appearance*, behind which it would be necessary once again to seek a soul or substance, expressed to various degrees in all the forms of identity. It confirms, if only *a contrario*, the importance of the conceptualization of life in the Lockean construction: personal identity, for Locke based on the continuity of consciousness, does not refer to an ontological or ethical dualism. It is opposed as much to a (material or immaterial) substantial identity as to an organic individual identity. Consciousness is therefore neither a 'thing' nor a 'life of the mind'.

The correlate of this double demarcation is the dissociation of the different aspects confusedly gathered into the image of *man*, and the restriction of the use of this term to designate the *individuality* that he has in common with all animals (see INDIVIDUAL).

Locke is clear in his use of the word 'life', which does not introduce any confusion into the three accepted uses of it that he employs: life as a property of individual organisms (§ 12: 'Identity of life'), life as the flow of human experiences (in particular, 'past life', § 15, 20), and finally 'this life' and 'another life' (§ 26: that in which a person places his hope of happiness, about which he will continue to be concerned). In contrast, the adjective *vital* that, together with *material, immaterial, personal, mental, verbal*, etc. forms a system, is always employed in the sense of a 'living' animal and human, particularly in the expression 'vitally united' (forming a living unity or a unity of life).[51]

OWN, TO OWN: §§ 8, 14, 15, 17, 18, 24, 26

As in the case of SELF (the two problems being in truth closely linked) Locke put into play the totality of the semantic and syntactical resources that the English word *own* offered him, by binding together – not only at the level of

---

51 Ayers (*Locke*, 256–7) indicates that the expression 'vitally and personally united' emerged from the discussions on the unity of the persons of the Trinity which took place in the years 1680–1690, marked by a confrontation between Anglican theologians, the Cambridge Platonists and 'Socinian' heretics. From this Ayers derives an argument that Locke favoured an analogy between life and consciousness. From the same historical premises, I arrive at the opposite conclusion: such an analogy or conjunction is impossible in Locke's treatise on identity, which systematically *dissociates* 'living unity' and 'personal unity' (see 'Identity' in the Glossary.)

theory, but also at the level of the expression and the utterance itself – the different aspects of a theory of *identity* as *appropriation*. The uses of *own* and *to own* are thus situated at the centre of a constellation that also includes the terms *belonging, imputation, concern, recognition* and *recollection*, and little by little the totality of the treatise's characteristic notions.

This play (wordplay, in the strong sense of the term), when confronted by a commentator familiar with the analysis of 'ordinary language', has often been regarded as abusive. Accordingly, Ayers maintains that Locke could not have connected his definition of *consciousness* (a cognitive term) to the moral and juridical doctrine of conscience without playing on the double meaning – 'recognition' and 'property' – of the word *own*, as well as on the two ways the idea of *appropriation* may be interpreted: property in oneself or property in goods (that cannot be confused without abolishing the distinction between person and thing).[52] But it is perhaps necessary to take up the question again by examining much more closely the way Locke worked with language.

In English, *own* is both an adjective and a verb. As adjective (the equivalent of *proprium*, but also simply of *suum*) it is generally used with possessive adjectives such as *my, his* and so on as an intensifier: *my own house* (my house, the house I own, that is mine), *I am my own master* (I am master of myself, I am mine and no one else's). This can perhaps be absolutized: *my own*, 'my own self', is practically synonymous with *my self*. And to conclude, it allows the subject to designate himself reflexively to the exclusion of all others: *I am on my own*. As a verb, *to own* has an entire spectrum of meanings, from 'to possess' to 'to confess', and including such synonyms as 'to recognize', 'to declare' and 'to claim': it is thus in general the fact of making or saying something to be 'one's' ('*sien*'), accompanying a 'care of the self', being concerned with oneself ('*souci de soi*').[53] In a different language (French, for instance) it is not always easy to choose one nuance over another, since any nuance will be projected onto a context where it is not actually required (which is why we sometimes need a gloss when Locke makes use of repetition, as at the end of

---

52   Ayers, *Locke*, 265 ff.

53   Concerning the use of *to own* as a signifier of confession (*aveu*), today unfamiliar to the French (and even perhaps the English) reader, a sampling of passages from Locke himself may be useful: 'And had I told you in plain words, that I was the Messiah, and given you a direct commission to preach to others, that I professedly owned myself to be the Messiah; you and they would have been ready to have made a commotion, to have set me upon the throne of my father David, and to fight for me.' (*The Reasonableness of Christianity as Delivered in the Scriptures*, in The Works of J.L., 1923, Vol. VII, 95): this is the *prosopopeia* of Jesus, in fact paraphrasing John, XVI, 17–18); 'I must own, that I think certainly grounded on ideas.' (*A Letter to the Right Reverend Edward Lord Bishop of Worcester*, IV, 57); 'My Lord, I do not remember that ever I declared . . . that I did not own all the doctrines of the Christian faith', (*Mr. Locke's Reply to the Bishop of Worcester's Answer*, 119); 'The owning of this to your Lordship in my former letter, I find, displeased your Lordship'. (Ibid., 180).

§ 17: 'owns all the Actions of that thing, as its own', which literally exhibits the wordplay).

Locke makes use of all these significations and corresponding constructions, both separately and in combination (as in the passage just cited). The result of these absolutely idiomatic turns of phrase, whose frequency cannot be a matter of chance, is a remarkable fusion (and not confusion) of the paradigms of *being* and *having*.[54] Fundamentally, 'me' is (=I am) 'mine' and what is 'most properly mine' is myself (*moi-même*) (just as what is most properly 'yours' or 'his' is 'yourself', 'himself', etc.). But is this not exactly what Locke wanted to explain?[55]

From this, three consequences follow:

1. The relation to the self is thought as a relation of appropriation that might be called *recurrent* or *retrospective* (from a term that, as we have seen, Lapoujade applies to William James: only here what is in question is consciousness and not belief, and that the recurrent appropriation exists in embryonic form from the first 'storing' operation, that is, perception). Appropriation is fundamentally the appropriation of *my thoughts* and thus of *myself insofar as I think*. We know its mechanism: it resides in the reciprocity of memory and

---

54 After adapting into French my essay quoted above ('My Self, My Own: One and the Same?') I received a commentary from Jean-Jacques Lecercle (the linguist and emeritus professor of English Literature at Université de Paris-Nanterre), from which I draw the following passage, which I reproduce 'for those who read French' (as Coste would say): 'Le rapprochement entre "self" et "own", malgré la distance syntaxique qui sépare les deux termes, me semble s'imposer. Ce que je ne parviens pas à déterminer, c'est si ce rapprochement a été inspiré à Locke par le mouvement de la langue même, ou s'il en a été l'initiateur, ou un des initiateurs (par le passage de "self" de morphème grammatical à nom, la chose est claire). D'où ces quelques réflexions de linguisitique spéculative. Sémantiquement les deux termes s'opposent. Dans le langage de Culioli, l'un, "self", est du côté de "be", marqueur d'identification, et l'autre, "own", du côté de "have" marqueur de différenciation/localisation. Sauf que la langue est sans cesse en mouvement, d'où le rapprochement, que je propose de formuler ainsi : avec "self", un se divise en deux . . . tandis qu'avec "own", deux se fondent en un. "Self", qui est le pronom réfléchi, a syntaxiquement besoin d'un antécédent dans la même proposition, dont il donne l'image en miroir (ce dédoublement est encore plus clair dans l'usage emphatique, dérivé du réfléchi, "although I say it myself"). Le "self", c'est donc l'ego en miroir. "Own", au contraire, est issu d'un participe passé (de "owe") transformé en verbe à deux arguments (d'où la différenciation/localisation): ce que je possède est localisé par rapport à moi (I own a car) et l'ego en tant que "own" résulte de la fusion de ces deux éléments séparés, fusion telle que "own" en est venu à désigner la solitude (he is on his own). Je crois que ce rapprochement a dû se produire au XVIIe siècle. Mon dictionnaire étymologique me susurre que le sens du verbe "own", "reconnaître comme sien", donc "accepter comme vrai", est lui aussi apparu au XVIIe siècle' (*Citoyen Sujet et autres essais d'anthropologie philosophique*, Presses Universitaires de France, Paris, 2011, 153–4).

55 This fusion comes from afar: from Greek discourses on the *oikeios* and the *idios*, describing the particularity of the 'self'. (On the Greek 'self' see J.P. Vernant, *L'individu, la mort, l'amour. Soi-même et l'autre en Grèce ancienne*, Paris: Gallimard, 1989, 211 ff.). It has continued into our own time, confirmed even in Heidegger's liminary thesis in *Sein und Zeit* (§ 9), which identified the existential particularity of human *Dasein* with *Jemeinigkeit* (literally, 'being each time mine') ('*être à chaque fois [le] mien*') (later developed as the play of the self's belonging and loss, and of the 'proper' and the 'improper').

consciousness, and of virtual and actual operations. It is therefore legitimate to describe my thoughts as 'being a part of me' or 'belonging to me' without these diverse formulations introducing any gap or distance, but only on the condition that it is understood that the very course of consciousness constitutes a totalization of parts according to a specific, purely transitive mode. But we must go farther and postulate that, through the intermediary of ideas from reflection (what Locke calls in § 13 'a reflex Act of Perception'), *my actions are appropriated by me or become part of me.* Locke makes use here of an idea that Descartes incorporated into his definition of the *cogitatio* (*Principles of Philosophy*, I, § 9): all the modalities of thought, including those that express the internal perception I have of my actions (or the perception I have of my actions 'from the inside', precisely what distinguishes them from the actions of *another*) are, according to the same principle, *cogitationes* which are thus related to the *ego* as its own 'acts of thought'. Accordingly, 'I walk' or 'I dream' or 'I write', etc. But this leads in Locke to an indirect or modal incorporation – which Descartes did not carry out – of every action into the unity of the 'self', thereby rendering it a totality rather than a singularity.

2. The appropriation of my actions, past and present, insofar as they are also my thoughts (or may become so again), also has as its consequence a radical solution to the question of *my relation to 'my' body* that from the outset short circuits every problematic of the 'union of the soul and the body'. Here Locke turns against Descartes. Of course, the latter in the Sixth Meditation offered a remarkable phrase:

> *Non etiam sine ratione corpus illud, quod speciali quodam jure meum appellabam, magis ad me pertinere quam alia ulla arbitrabar.* (It was also not without some reason that I believed that this body [which by a certain particular right I called mine] belonged to me more properly and more closely than any other.) (*Ce n'était pas aussi sans quelque raison que je croyais que ce corps [lequel par un certain droit particulier j'appelais mien] m'appartenait plus proprement et plus étroitement que pas un autre* [trans. Luynes].)

But the entire movement of Descartes' meditation on the 'one's own body' (*le 'corps propre'*) aims to transfer the question from the register of having to that of being, which leads to a particularly contorted form of the dilemma of identity and alterity (put into practice in the study of the passions), given that at the same time *I am my body* (and even, I am *not other than* my body) and *I can always think (myself) without my body.*[56] There is nothing like this in Locke, where the relation to the body appears as the site par excellence of the reconciliation between being and having, since *my body is nothing other than that which*

---

56   See D. Kambouchner, *L'homme des passions.*

my consciousness presents to me as myself, bringing it about that all *its* actions of thought belong to *me*.[57]

3. Finally, the thematic of 'own', 'owning' and 'ownership' entails (as we have already seen in the case of the terms *appropriate, impute,* etc.) a parallelism of responsibility and property, of self-consciousness and 'property in oneself'. Such a parallelism can be seen as paradoxical or even intolerable. Thus Paul Ricoeur (criticizing Peter Strawson):

> Is the possession implied by the adjective 'mine' of the same nature as the posses-sion of a predicate by a logical subject? There is, to be sure, a semantic continuity between *own, owner,* and *ownership* (possession), but it is relevant only if we confine it to the neutrality of *one's own.* And even under this condition of the neutralization of the self, the possession of the body by someone or by each one poses the enigma of an untransferable property, which contradicts the usual notion of property. This is a strange attribution indeed, that of a body that can neither be made nor taken away.[58]

Inspired by Locke, one might respond with the following argument: on the one hand, the possession of the body does not correspond to a 'neutralization of the self', but on the contrary represents an experience of it or one of the modes of its constitution. Locke does not say that the conscious experience I have of the actions of the body as 'my actions' is more important than my experience, for example, of the operations of my thought. But having arrived at this stage in his reflection, Locke nevertheless accords it a fundamental importance. This is why the experience of my body's actions belongs at once or indistinctly to the sphere of responsibility and to that of property. Further, it is limited or bound in the same manner (just as I am not responsible for the constitution of my organism, but for what it does or what I do 'through it', so I am essentially 'the proprietor of myself' insofar as I am the proprietor of my actions and their effects). From this point of view, the existence of an untransferable (or inalienable) property which represents an incompressible minimum constructed around 'the body proper' (*le corps propre*) in the sphere of action (as well as around the idea of the 'self' in the sphere of thought, memory and opinion)[59] thus constitutes not an enigma or

---

57   It would be very revealing to compare in detail how the development of the theme of ampu-tation varies in Descartes and Locke: Descartes is preoccupied with the hallucinatory illusion that it can entail (I keep feeling sensations in a missing arm: see *Metaphysical Meditations,* Sixth Meditation), while Locke imagines that consciousness might have its seat in one or the other of the separated parts (either the whole body or the little finger: a striking illustration of the radical difference between 'indi-viduality' and 'personality' which also shows Locke's mastery of 'counterfactuals').

58   Ricoeur, *Oneself as Other,* 37.

59   The Lockean doctrine of *tolerance* as an institution necessary to civil society is constructed around the preservation of a 'proper realm' of private thoughts which are inalienable: or the self as (my) own, or (my) property, which ought never to be invaded or alienated.

paradox, but, (for Locke at least) the *condition of possibility* of any external property or property 'in things'. It was another name for liberty. The real 'danger' of alienation for the personality does not come from external possessions or their return against the self, but from its internal divisions, such as amnesia and 'multiple personalities' (see PERSONALITY).[60]

PERSON, PERSONAL: §§ 7, 9, 10, 11, 12, 13, 14, 15, 16, 17, 18, 19, 20, 21, 22, 23, 25, 26

Locke says that the word 'person' is a 'forensic term' which Coste translates as '*un terme de Barreau*' (the bar) and which I translated as '*un terme (du langage) judiciaire*' (a term taken from judicial language). But he specified: 'as I use it', to mark that this is, for him, a position whose philosophical, as well as religious and political, stakes are fundamental. It would be useful to follow its trace through the very writing of the treatise. I propose the thesis that there is a double demarcation there: the first on the theological front, the second on the political front.

The theological demarcation set Locke against almost the totality of the orthodox tradition in which the term referred to the doctrine of the Trinity, or more precisely to the latter as the operator par excellence of speculation on the analogy between divine nature and human nature since Augustine (the image and resemblance of the creature in relation to the creator). This in turn entailed the possibility of representing the entire economy of salvation – from original sin, the incarnation and passion of Christ, to the judgment and resurrection – as the road that leads to a reunification of the two natures, at once similar and unequal and therefore separated throughout the history of the world.

The sign of this background appears in Locke's treatise through the formula offered in § 9, the first (provisional) 'definition' of the *person* whose identity will be sought: 'we must consider what *Person* stands for; which, I think, is a thinking intelligent Being, that has reason and reflection, and can consider it self as it self'. What is the provenance of this definition? Leaping over intermediary references (More, Cudworth, Stillingfleet,[61] etc.), we may proceed directly to

---

60   See my essay 'Possessive Individualism Reversed: From Locke to Derrida' (*Constellations* 9: 3, 2002), in which I argue that 'property in one's person' (or self-ownership) is not a particular application of a formal concept of 'property' which, among other 'things', could apply to 'oneself', but the transcendental condition of possibility of every appropriation through labour. It is on this that later critiques (or 'reversals') of possessive individualism (Rousseau, Marx, Derrida) are based.

61   Locke found the 'definition' of the person (inspired by the Thomist tradition) that Stillingfleet opposed to his own utterly insufficient: 'a complete intelligent substance with a peculiar manner of subsistence'. (Cf. *Mr Locke's Reply to the Bishop of Worcester's Answer*, 172 ff.; *Mr. Locke's Second Reply*, ibid., 303 ff. See as well [335] the reference to a possible contradiction between Locke's definition and the dogma of incarnation.)

Boethius's famous formula: *rationalis naturae individua substantia*, 'the individual substance of a rational nature', reproduced by Thomas Aquinas as the heading of his exposition on 'Divine Persons' (*Summa Theologica, Part I, Question 29*). After having justified the fact that the term could not be found in the Scriptures themselves, Aquinas assigned its origins to the Greek *hupostasis* employed by the Church Fathers and present in the discussion of the relations between 'essence', 'substance' and 'person' that allow the mystery of the One God who is Three to be thought.[62] We should note that the term *hupostasis* was also translated more literally by the theologians as *suppositum*, and therefore as 'support' or 'subject', which inscribes the entire discussion at the heart of the genesis of the conception of the individual as a subjectivity forever implicated in a (religious) symbolic order.

We may now regard the entire development of Locke's treatise from § 9 to § 26 as a *transition* from the initial (anthropo-theological) definition to the new 'judicial' definition, or rather as a *transformation* of the initial definition. It is a matter of incorporating a new anthropology whose theoretical core is constituted by the relations between 'consciousness' and 'responsibility', such that each one can find them in himself and can 'own' (*avouer*) them. Such an anthropology is not based on the hierarchical relation between the human image and the divine model, or between time and eternity, but on the very movement of experience: it may be represented as an always new acquisition of property and knowledge which, however, presupposes (and develops or effectuates) an orginary *self-appropriation*[63] present in the very constitution of the mind (see APPROPRIATE).

In relation to this fundamental objective, the subtlety of the reasoning that demonstrates the *independence* of the point of view of substance from that of the person throughout the treatise (even if it is 'reasonable' and 'plausible' to assume a hidden relation between them) and thus undermines in a more or less direct way the metaphysical foundations of Trinitarian doctrine (in particular the identity of human and divine essence in Christ beyond the Crucifixion and the Resurrection), may appear to us a secondary element. This, however, is not the case for at least two reasons. One, which I will discuss below, is the relation of these arguments to the problem of 'multiple personalities' (see PERSONALITY); the other is the way they ultimately lead to a revision of the representation of the Last Judgment, which adds an indispensable *moral*

---

62 Thomas Aquinas, *Summa Theologica*, I. The difficulty arises from the fact that, etymologically, *persona* does not correspond to *hupostasis* but to *prosôpon*, designating at first, as in Latin, a theatrical mask or character. See E. Hendricks, *Introduction au De Trinitate de Saint Augustin*, Bibliothèque Augustinienne, Œuvres de Saint Augustin, Vol. 15, *La Trinité (Livres I–VII)*, Desclée de Brouwer, 1955, 32 ff.

63 It is, of course, in no way incompatible with the fact that Locke elsewhere insists on the created nature of the human person and on the divine *workmanship* whose product it is (see Tully, *A Discourse on Property*).

complement to the idea of juridical responsibility, making consciousness the very element in which the subject is related to the 'ultimate ends' of his condition (see RESURRECTION).

Of course, the relation of the notion of the person (the Latin *persona*) to a juridical and moral context is not new. Such a notion is in fact the oldest: anterior to its theological uses, but benefitting retroactively from their terminology and distinctions. The association of the notions of personality, responsibility and civil obligation (according to the status of the person) is systematized in the *Corpus Juris Civilis.*[64] It was closely tied to an ontology of Stoic inspiration which distinguished *persons, things,* and incorporeal *actions.* It is certain that, in reformulating this ontology through a postulation of a concept of consciousness that allowed the interiorization of actions by a 'self' and making them the moments of its self-recognition, Locke's treatise on identity (and the *Essay* more generally) forms an essential moment in the invention of the modern subject, a moment from which the theorizations of the subject and the moral person, such as those of Kant and Hegel, are directly derived.

At the same time, there emerges a second line of demarcation or second front which sets in opposition the point of view of *the person as the (proper) name of the 'self'* and that of the *person as fiction.* Concretely, this takes the form of an opposition between Locke's use of the concept of the person and that of Hobbes some decades earlier.[65] Locke's treatise must also be read as a response to Hobbes carried out at the level of philosophy, but with political and social consequences. Here, we discover a point of heresy at the heart of what has been called the paradigm of possessive individualism (Macpherson). For Hobbes: 'A person is he whose words or actions are considered, either as his own, or as representing the words or actions of an other man, or of any other thing to whom they are attributed, whether truly or by fiction.' In effect, the definition offered by Hobbes is fundamentally an *exterior* one that does not proceed from

---

64   A vast compilation of codes, glosses and manuals compiled in the sixth century in Constantinople on the basis of classical Roman law, on the order of the Emperor Justinian. On this see Michel Villey, *Le droit et les droits de l'homme*, Paris: PUF, 1983, and 'Esquisse historique sur le mot responsable', in *Archives de philosophie du droit* 22, 1977 (*La responsabilité*); Jean-Marc Trigeaud, 'La Personne', in *Archives de Philosophie du Droit* 34, 1989 (*Le sujet de droit*). Finally, Jean-Pierre Baud (*L'affaire de la main volée. Une histoire juridique du corps*, Paris: Éditions du Seuil, 1993, 59 ff.) shows how, throughout the history of law, the relations between individuality and personality have varied ('the person may die after or before the body', which led the jurists of the time to elaborate in a completely secular manner the category of *resurrection* in order to organize the regime of physical separation and its legal consequences).

65   Above all in chapter XVI of *Leviathan*, 'Of Persons, Authors, and Things Personated' (Thomas Hobbes, *Leviathan*, Edited with an Introduction by C.B. Macpherson, London: Penguin Books 1968, 217 ff.). See Yves-Charles Zarka, 'Identité et ipséité chez Hobbes et Locke', *Philosophie* 37, Hiver 1993, and Frank Lessay, 'Le vocabulaire de la personne', in Yves-Charles Zarka, ed., *Hobbes et son vocabulaire*, Paris: Librairie Vrin, 1992, where the Hobbesian conception of the person as distinction between 'actor' and 'author' in the process of the representation that constitutes it is discussed in detail.

the subject himself, or a fortiori from his consciousness, but from the way he is described by a juridical system lying outside of him.[66] Hobbes' objective is to ground the relation (as necessary in the private as in the public domain) of the *representation* (associating an author and an actor) or *delegation of power* (trust) that occurs through the codified exchange of words and not through the experience of a consciousness. Hobbes can thus generalize the medieval notion of the *persona ficta*, or moral person, and apply it in turn to the human individual itself understood in its social role or function.[67]

We should not be fooled by Locke's reference to judicial language: it is not a matter of an undifferentiated legal category. Locke grants predominance to a sphere of judgment in which, in the last analysis, decisions are legitimate only with reference to the identity and interiority (the confession or owning [*aveu*]) of the subject over that of representation and convention in which written laws and offices are determinant. In so doing he traces a decisive line of demarcation in philosophy and politics.[68] On the one side (Hobbes) we have a doctrine of *moral personality* (and, at the limit, for Hobbes even 'physical persons' are 'moral persons' or *personae fictae* to the extent that they enter into relations of representation and make use of the corresponding legal fictions); and, on the other (Locke), a doctrine of the *morality of persons* (based on their capacity to preserve a natural or authentic identity through self-consciousness, within every 'role', in the *intermediary space between things and words*). Two divergent conceptions of society and of the state follow from this, even if they might both be considered, in a formal sense, 'individualist'. We would have to wait until Kant to see a reciprocity of legal and moral definitions of the 'person' substituting this antithesis.

PERSONALITY: §§ 22, 26

The term *personality* (*personalitas*) – an abstraction formed on the basis of *persona*, itself liable to hypostatization – is not of recent origin, but is highly

---

66   This is perfectly congruent with Hobbes' reduction of 'conscience' to opinion, characterized in a highly pejorative way as a 'rhetorical term', in chapter VII of *Leviathan*.

67   The 'moral person' was an invention of thirteenth-century jurists which allowed them to attribute legal capacity to corporations and states, but it was anticipated by the doctrine of 'the person of the Church' (or Church as person), itself derived from Trinitarian theology. On this see in particular J. P. Canning, 'Law, Sovereignty, and Corporation Theory, 1300–1450', in J. H. Burns, ed., *The Cambridge History of Medieval Political Thought*, Cambridge: Cambridge University Press, 1988, 454–76; and Ernst H. Kantorowicz, *The King's Two Bodies: A Study in Medieval Political Theology*, Princeton, NJ: Princeton University Press, 1957 (chapters VI and VII).

68   But the position he occupies is anything but simple to uphold. His disciples would experience this, caught between two extremes: a return to substantialism (as in Leibniz, for whom Lockean identity was nothing more than the appearance of the person) and a movement toward fiction, that is, towards the idea of the person as habit or social convention (as in Hume). See R. C. Tennant, 'The Anglican Response to Locke's Theory of Personal Identity', *Journal of the History of Ideas* 43, 1982, 73–90.

charged with references to controversies over the meaning of the individual and its unity or multiplicity. It is this which makes its appearance at two strategic moments in the treatise particularly interesting. It acquires a supplementary signification for the contemporary reader who has inherited the long history of the problem of 'multiple personalities'. Locke's text appears to us to be situated at the exact point of a reversal through which, leaving a 'theological age' and entering a 'psychological (or anthropological) age' – while preserving a significant number of the intellectual instruments forged by the first for the use of the second – the 'modern' question of multiple personalities has been substituted for the ancient question of the persons of the Trinity in the elaboration of the notion of the subject (see PERSON).[69]

The transition between the two is assured by the question of the 'transmigration of souls' which Locke's treatise repeatedly subjects to an examination in order to submit it to the rational criterion of personal identity. It is well known that this question occupied the Cambridge Platonists as well as Leibniz (who alluded to it in II.xxvii.14 of the *New Essays*, citing the opinions of Van Helmont).[70] From a contemporary point of view, it is tempting to say that the many questions between which the Lockean treatise moves are not situated on the same plane: the Trinity is a *symbolic* (religious) structure, transmigration is a myth or *imaginary* representation to which one may refer to prove the meaning of certain 'suppositions', while multiple personalities are a *real* problem, or an enigma drawn from experience, to be resolved.[71]

---

69   It is by no means certain that the 'psychological' and 'theological' contexts are not intermingled from the outset, as Augustine's reflections in the *Confessions* suggest. The question is whether on both sides of the 'conversion' we are dealing with the 'same' man, for the certitude of the difference remains troubled by the experience of nocturnal hallucinations arriving from the past and the involuntary pleasures – discharges of seminal liquid – to which they give rise. 'My Lord God, am I not now what I was before? And how can it be that there is so great a difference between me myself and me myself (*tantum interest inter me ipsum et me ipsum*), as there is between that moment when I am asleep and that in which I am awake?' X, 30, 41). It is to God alone to ultimately assign the division between Night-Man, who rebels against him, and Day-Man, who is his servant.

70   Henry More, in his *The Immortality of the Soul* (1659), moved from one extreme to the other, opposing to this 'transmigration' theory the idea of a transitory participation of individuals in the soul of the world. (See his association of 'Personality, Memory, and Conscience', 284). On the Cambridge Platonists' interest in spiritualism, see also A. Rupert-Hall, *Henry More*.

71   See Mikkel Borch-Jacobsen, 'Who's Who? Introducing Multiple Personality', in Joan Copjec, ed., *Supposing the Subject*, London and New York: Verso, 1994. On the history of the problem see also, Henri F. Ellenberger, *Histoire de la découverte de l'inconscient*, Paris: Fayard, 1994, 156 ff. In the tradition of French psychiatry the question of multiple personalities confers a particular interest on the work of Pierre Janet (*L'automatisme psychologique*, 1889), and in the Anglophone tradition on William James (*Principles of Psychology*, 1890; *Exceptional Mental States*, Lowell Lectures, 1896). (To these we might now also add Ian Hacking, *Rewriting the Soul: Multiple Personality and the Sciences of Memory*, Princeton, NJ: Princeton University Press, 1995, which I had not read at the time of this essay). James annotated Locke's chapter on identity, which he refers to as a model of a pragmatist reformulation of metaphysical problems through the elimination of the idea of 'substance' and through a reference to 'experience' (*Pragmatism* and *The Meaning of Truth*, Cambridge, MA: Harvard University Press, 1975, 47–8).

The question of multiple personalities is not confused with that of *amnesia* or *simulation* (or 'bad faith'), both of which are discussed by Locke and have not ceased to occupy an important place in judicial casuistry. But it constitutes in a certain sense the antithesis of the argument for the lived continuity of life (or experience) that permitted Locke to resolve the old aporia of 'the identity of man through the ages': it must in effect be acknowledged that this continuity can be broken by a division that does not abolish the mechanisms of memory and self-recognition, but distributes them among distinct 'selves', each one of which is the pole of identification for a consciousness. In § 23 Locke writes:

> Could we suppose two distinct incommunicable consciousnesses acting the same Body, the one constantly by Day, the other by Night; and on the other side the same consciousnesses acting by Intervals two distinct Bodies: I ask in the first case, Whether the Day and Night-man would not be two or distinct Persons, as *Socrates* and *Plato*?

It is impossible to read this argument today without effecting a certain rapprochement, not only with Augustine's anxious questions (in the *Confessions*, Book X) concerning his 'other self' who is sexually excited during his nocturnal fantasies, but with Robert Louis Stevenson's celebrated novel *The Strange Case of Dr. Jekyll and Mr. Hyde* (1886), that is itself inscribed in a tradition at once literary and psychiatric (two domains that cannot with certainty be distinguished).

This convergence shows that Locke carefully avoided marking the difference between the phenomena of consciousness considered 'normal' and those that might be regarded as 'pathological' (amnesia, paramnesia, misidentification syndromes, split personality). The role of this neutrality in the argument is to allow the isolation of the question of the relation between consciousness and responsibility in a 'pure' state. It leads to a series of consequences.

We see first that Locke's theory of identity is also indissociably a theory of the *alterity* or *alteration* of consciousness. It would be interesting to compare it in detail with the utterly different way Descartes encountered this problem in the course of his analysis of self-certitude, in the form of the double problem of 'substantial' union and distinction: a first problem concerning the union and distinction between my finite thought and infinite divine thought, the idea of which I find within myself, and a second concerning the union and distinction between thought as 'sensation' and the corporeal movement of which I have a sensation. As we know, Descartes makes a very strange use of the category 'substance', which essentially serves to allow him to understand differences (between the finite and the infinite being, or the intellectual and the extended beings): the combined differences, however, form a 'union', which is his enigmatic solution to the problem of the specific human individuality. In Locke, the reference to substance has not simply disappeared but, at the end of the 'reduction' of which it was the object, and by means –which prove to be essential – of a fiction, it appears instead to be much more a *concern for consciousness itself* (which finds it 'reasonable' and normal to be permanently bound to substance, but without being able 'to be certain of it', reduced on this point to 'assumptions') than a problem for philosophy. This is a kind of existential or imaginary 'paralogism' that Locke attempts to critically resolve.

At the same time, however, the fiction that Locke pushes so far reveals a weakness or at least a difficulty in the argument which assumes the radical dissociation of the points of view of substance, the individual and consciousness. In order entirely to enclose the latter in interiority, and in concert with his theory of language as a secondary institution, Locke attaches the *proper name* to the *individual* (to the 'man') and not to consciousness, which in this sense has no other name than the generic name that it gives itself internally: 'My Self'. Locke is no less obliged to mark the difference between consciousnesses by the difference of a name, even if it is a matter of convention and chance (The Night-Man, The Day-Man). And it is not certain that this verbal trace can be eliminated from consciousness or from the way it recognizes itself as 'itself' (*se reconnaît comme 'soi-même'*), imputes and appropriates actions to itself, projects itself into the past of its actions and in its concern for its happiness, etc.[72] With some mischeviousness, we may wonder whether he would not have had to identify himself *for himself* through a name, e.g. as 'the author of the *Essay on Human Understanding'*, in the form of a 'mental utterance': 'I, John Locke, imagined and wrote this book.' But we also know, with certainty, that in his correspondence he would make use of the *anonymous* publication of other texts (notably the *Two Treatises of Government*) to treat his own authorship as an *alias*, at the same time distancing himself from the book and commending its content to readers . . .

RESURRECTION: §§ 15, 20

The closely linked questions of the Last Judgment and the Resurrection occupy a remarkable place in Locke's treatise. There are good reasons to think that it was the acuity of the controversy in the years 1690–1693 centred on theological problems in which his positions were cited or alluded to that determined Locke (after the personal intervention of his friend William Molyneux) to write Chapter XXVII of Book II for the second edition of the *Essay*. In the course of these debates, the accusation of 'Socianianism' was regularly made against Locke, who was forced to defend himself against it. The term was used very

---

72   As Borch-Jacobsen has correctly noted ('Who's Who?', 60–1), but referring to Descartes and Husserl, rather than Locke, in whose work the problem is much more apparent.

loosely at the time, amalgamating every denial of the doctrine of Christ's divinity, or of the resurrection of the body, and every attempt to propose a 'reasonable' interpretation of fundamental Christian dogmas; it designated a spectre that covered everything from libertinism to natural religion. The idea of a 'reasonable' religion is in effect fundamental in Locke (and suggested the title of his 1695 work *The Reasonableness of Christianity*, translated into French by Coste in 1715), and although Locke never explicitly took up unitarian arguments (against the Trinity), the fundamental article of faith for his denomination tended in this direction, given that it was centred on the messianicity of Jesus, 'son of God' (and eventually also on the idea of Christ as the person whose existence pre-exists all humanity), but not on his divinity in the strict sense.[73] The detour through the question of the dogma of the Trinity, whose refutation was at the heart of the radical thought of Socinus, allows us to see an essential link with the ideas expressed in Locke's treatise on identity concerning the Resurrection and the Last Judgment (that have the character, Locke tells us, of a 'reasonable' supposition: something that 'it may be reasonable to think' [§ 22]).

It is crucial to understand that Locke's theses on the Judgment and the Resurrection (explicitly present in §§ 15, 20, 22 and 26, and underlying every discussion about the character, whether necessary or not, of the personality's attachment to a 'substance', either corporeal and therefore mortal or spiritual and immortal) do not constitute, from a *theoretical* point of view, a foreign element within the treatise's problematic. The most powerful argument for such a position may be found in § 22: confronted with the objection that, if the criterion of identity (and therefore of the imputability of and responsibility for its acts) was simply consciousness, there would be no reason to condemn a drunken man for crimes committed while he was under the influence of drink and of which he claims to have no memory, Locke responds that this objection is without merit. For while the human court applies a rule of prudence in not accepting the word of an individual who has every interest in concealing his misconduct, in God's tribunal, judgment applies to hearts whose secrets are laid bare. This argument proves that for Locke the truth of consciousness (or self-consciousness) and that of absolute judgment, freed from the veils that communication and language impose, constitute one and the same problem: that of the *last instance of judgment*. It is possible to take this as a kind of myth, but it would be more accurate to see in it an *ideality*: precisely the ideality that Locke, through the concatenation of the terms

---

73 On this question see Osier, *Traité de Morale*; J. Lagrée, *La religion naturelle*, Paris: PUF, 1991 (who devotes a discussion to Locke, 52–5); and Marshall, *John Locke*. The most important discussions of Resurrection are found in *The Reasonableness of Christianity*, 9 ff., 91 ff., 126 ff (no one can be punished for his 'unbelief', but only for his '*misdeeds*'), 203 ff. and 340 ff.

consciousness, memory, identity, 'self', responsibility and judgment, seeks to place at the limit of his theory of mind.

Given these conditions, it appears possible to specify the theses outlined by Locke (or which he has given to us to puzzle over), without attributing to him a strategy of dissimulation or double language. On this point, most commentators, having adopted a narrowly *contextual* and fundamentally *defensive* view, have assumed that Locke sought either to propose new arguments – paradoxically founded on a bracketing of the question of substance – in favour of the immortality of the soul (an immortality, in some sense, without substance), itself required by the idea of the Last Judgment (Ayers); or to propose arguments in favour of the idea (known as 'mortalist' in the history of religious ideas) that the Resurrection will not necessarily be that of the body, by suggesting that the 'same consciousness' might be associated with a new body (Marshall).[74] I want to argue that Locke's most profound and riskiest idea in reality concerned the eschatology of the Last Judgment and the Resurrection itself.[75]

It is sufficient to extend the arguments of §§ 21 to 24 – concerning the impossibility of uniting within the same 'person' consciousnesses-memories that do not have a common content – to see the collapse of the notion of the *reunion of human persons in the person of Christ* beyond death and the end of time. The death of the individual does not exclude a resurrection or the transtemporal continuity of consciousness, but it does exclude any possibility that I can recover or recollect the internal trace of the life of Christ, of his thoughts and actions, in 'my consciousness', any more than I can recover those of Socrates, Nestor or Caesar Borgia. And if for his part Christ was well and truly a person endowed with a consciousness and his own 'self', there can be no possibility of his ever finding in his own consciousness the trace of my thoughts (in order, if necessary, to pay for them though his own death). The first consequence of Locke's theorems thus profoundly subverts any theological conception of an *economy of sin* in which the crime requires redemption, leading to a mystical union in the spiritual body of Christ.

Locke, however, adds a second, even more significant consequence. He tells us that only the continuity of consciousness, or the internal unity of consciousness and memory that constitutes the 'self' and appropriates to a man his actions, also allows him to impute merit or fault to them or to render him responsible for them. But he also says that on 'Judgment Day' 'The Sentence shall be justified by the consciousness all Persons shall have, that they *themselves* in what Bodies

74   Locke spent many pages arguing over this point in his dispute with Stillingfleet: cf. *Mr. Locke's Second Reply*, 303 ff.

75   John Yolton outlines a similar interpretation in *Locke: An Introduction*, Oxford: Blackwell, 1985, 31, and now more extensively in his *The Two Intellectual Worlds of John Locke: Man, Person, and Spirits in the 'Essay'*, Ithaca: Cornell University Press, 2004.

soever they appear, or what Substances soever that consciousness adheres to, are the *same*, that committed those Actions, and deserve that Punishment for them.' (§ 26) Thus Locke is not content merely to inscribe the Judgment to come in the continuity of consciousness, but demonstrates that this Judgment is the result of the *very consciousness that subjects have of having done good or evil.* In any case, the Judge's justifications will remain indiscernible from the subject's consciousness. It is not so much, then, that – as Plato maintained – 'no one is intentionally bad', as that consciousness is the witness and the medium of the judgment that each 'self' passes on 'itself'. In a profound sense, the idea of immortality thus becomes pointless, while that of a Mediator of the Divine Law, directed according to the Gospel to recognize sin and goodness, no longer has any but an external and allegorical function. It is in the intimacy of consciousness, in the testimony that it gives, or the truth that it manifests to itself, that the essence of Judgment resides and from which rewards and punishments follow as logical consequences. At the very least, it may be postulated that the representation of God's judgment conveyed by theology only has meaning to the extent that it passes through the interiority of each consciousness.

It would be instructive to confront this interpretation with two others that it excludes in a symmetrical manner: on the one hand, that of the Stoic tradition, taken up notably by Spinoza, for whom 'virtue is its own reward' (and crime its own punishment) without judgment (see *Ethics,* Part V, prop. 42) and, on the other, that of Pauline and Augustinian orthodoxy. In *The Search After Truth,* Malebranche devoted a section at the end of Elucidation Eleven to the same texts by Paul on which Locke comments:

> Saint Paul says that his conscience gives him no reproach, but he does not claim that because of this he is justified. He claims, on the contrary, that this does not justify him and that he dares not judge himself because it is the Lord who justifies him. But given that we have a clear idea of order, if we also had a clear idea of the soul through our inner sensation (*sentiment intérieur*) of ourselves, we would know clearly whether the soul conformed to order; we would know whether we are righteous or not. We would even be able to know with precision all its inner dispositions to good and evil when having a sensation of them. But if we could know ourselves as we are, we would not be so liable to presumption.

We see not only that Malebranche maintains the necessity of a transcendent instance for Judgment (even and especially if it must be sought 'in the innermost part of ourselves' and our conformity to order), but that he adds to the representation of the eschatological event that of an overturning of the alienation that produces the obscurity of the human soul to itself.

In contrast, for Locke – because, in practice, it is consciousness that judges itself – there is no structural reason for the Great Day to be situated at an 'end of time': it is much more 'reasonable' to suppose that the judgement of consciousness can take place *at any moment in time*. For what counts is the time of consciousness, not cosmological time. Again, the eschatological theme of the 'end of time' designates allegorically nothing else than the moment of truth, whatever it may be, where consciousness totalizes its own experiences in the modality of a judgment. But it is precisely consciousness that intrinsically *is* that resurrection or that operation of totalization which, as memory, recalls in the transparency of the present the 'self's' entire past. It is true, though, that we might also attribute to consciousness and to its own concern an inverse movement of 'protension': it perpetually defers the resurrection, or indefinitely projects the moment towards a ' beyond'.

SAMENESS: § 9

While the adjective 'same' appears constantly in the treatise on identity, the abstract noun 'sameness' only occurs once and is employed only one other time in the entire *Essay*.[76] These two occurrences are finally reduced to one, given that the passage in I.iv.4 is a prefiguration of the treatise on identity:

> If *Identity* . . . be a native Impression; and consequently so clear and obvious to us, that we must needs know it even from our Cradles; I would gladly be resolved, by one of Seven or Seventy Years old, Whether a Man being a Creature, consisting of Soul and Body, be the same Man when his Body is changed? . . . it will appear, that our *Idea of sameness*, is *not* so settled and clear, as to deserve to be thought *innate* in us . . . For, I suppose, every one's *Idea of Identity*, will not be the same, that *Pythagoras* and Thousands others of his Followers have; And which then shall be the true?

At the moment Locke was writing the *Essay*, the term 'sameness' was not a neologism, since the OED lists an occurrence in 1581 ('the sameness of time'), before jumping to Cudworth in 1678 (in the sense of 'the quality of being the same', the signification 'absence of variety' noted as occurring in 1743). This is obviously a term that is still problematic (although Locke contributed to its currency, as shown by the fact that Hume in the *Treatise of Human Nature* would employ *identity or sameness* as a doublet). To render it in French, Coste made use of periphrasis ('*Ce qui fait qu'un être* . . . *est toujours le même*' [what makes it that a being . . . is always the same]). Paul Ricoeur (*Oneself as Another*) proposes '*mêmeté*' – modelled on '*altérité*' (alterity) – and uses it systematically to mark the difference between *la mêmeté and l'ipséité* (*idem* and *ipse*), or the

---

76   Dr Paulette Taieb has kindly verified this intuition for me by performing a word search on the English text of the *Essay* available on the internet.

same and the *self*, which he claims Locke tended to confuse despite his contribution to 'personal identity'.

Why did Locke have recourse to this rare and 'technical' term? Two reasons might be cited: the first is stylistic, while the second takes us to the heart of the problem. Locke was compelled to ask if *identity is identically conceived* by everyone or, to put it another way, if there is a *sameness of the (idea of) identity*, and he used two roots (Germanic and Latin) to mark the change of discursive level. This is the first reason.

But it leads to a second question: *sameness* connotes the *relational* character of identity, and designates in fact (as Ricoeur understood very well) the relative or relational essence of identity. It thus refers to the diverse constructions of *same* and *the same*: either oppositives (same and distinct, same and divers, same or different, etc.), comparatives (the same with, the same which), or intensives (the same identical). Sameness allows a 'deduction' of what makes identity a relation and specifies it in the face of its contrary (in other terms, the difference between identity and difference which no 'thing' or 'being' escapes, § 26). But, even as it marks this universality, it is also required in order to classify the different modalities of the 'being the same (as)' that lead to the equivocity of identity itself.[77]

It seems to me that in this regard, Locke's text is traversed by a constant tension that might connect, in modern terms, to two quite different modalities of the passage from the *general* expression in the form **x R y** to the particular, reflexive expression **x R x**, depending on whether the latter is considered to be a 'particular case' – that is, an application of the former – or instead a 'limit case' and a reversal.

Inscribing identity explicitly among the 'relations', Locke was compelled to respect the concept thereof that he had developed (in II.xii.7 and II.xxv.5: 'The *nature* therefore *of Relation*, consists in the referring, or comparing two things, one to another; from which comparison, one or both comes to be denominated'). In a number of respects this concept appeared as a primitive, undefinable notion, but one whose consequences ought to be explained. To begin with, relations as Locke conceived them were, according to Russell's terminology, exclusively 'external', that is, they proceeded from 'comparisons' between terms or, as Locke said, they were 'superinduced' over the terms themselves (II.xxv.8),

---

77   In the important sections IV.i.3–4 that I cited earlier (see DIVERSE, DIVERSITY), Locke juxtaposed the ideas of *Identity, or Diversity* and *Relation*, going so far as to inscribe the latter as secondary in relation to the two others. There is therefore, if not a circle, at least some hesitation regarding the logical hierarchy of these quasi-primitive ideas. We have seen a primary aspect of the difficulty in our discussion of the passage from the general operation of distinction, inherent in all ideas, to the specific idea of difference. We now have its reverse side: the difficulty of separating the idea of identity, in one of its meanings, from the general notion of the reflexivity of relations.

expressing therefore neither their 'nature' nor the 'intrinsic properties' of the terms that would contain in advance, as it were, the idea of the whole that they together form (as Leibniz, in contrast, would maintain).[78] The question will thus be to know what 'to compare a thing with itself' means. Further, the idea of comparison in this sense apparently refers to the even more primitive idea of *difference*, and in this sense, if identity is a relation, this means that it *presupposes difference*, or that it is – paradoxically perhaps – a certain way of resolving difference and discussing it: by 'reducing it to zero'.

We should note at this point that this illuminates a fundamental characteristic of Locke's treatise on identity that is far from being simply a stylistic or rhetorical trait: the fact that there is a persistent question of describing differences, including the differences between (the kinds of) differences – in short, that it is in practice a *treatise on diversity* and the 'fixed points' that organize it. In this respect, the impossibility of thinking identity as anything other than 'what differs from the different' is thus not a discovery of the Hegelian dialectic!

There are, however, two possible ways to develop this cancellation of difference which engenders identity on the basis of an operation of comparison, and it seems that both are present in the text. The first consists in *applying the relation x R y to the 'particular case' in which x and y are 'the same'*. In order for such an operation not to be meaningless, we must first determine the type of identity that we are looking for, or specify the circumstances in which it has significance (that is, finally, to distinguish an object language from a metalanguage). It seems to me that this is what Locke does when he characterizes identity as the fact of something 'being the same as itself over time', that is, when he identifies identity as what *neutralizes the course of time*. It is thus possible to say: two apparently distinct existences are in reality only one, or everything that conserves itself in time, under one heading or another, is 'identical' or 'the same as itself'. But we might well ask whether this reasoning is not finally circular, since it can only restore a 'deferred' ('*différée*') identity, once it has demonstrated the possibility of an abstraction from the time that itself constitutes 'pure' difference. This in turn leads to the second line of thought Locke develops in the text. Instead of thinking **x R x** as an 'application' to a particular case, it will be thought as a limit-case. And this limit is, in fact, a reversal: every 'comparison' destined to exhibit a relation (for example, that of father and son, big and small, etc.) presupposes a difference, a possibility of 'discerning', *but it can be the case that difference is annulled, and becomes ungraspable ('insaisissable')*: the operation of discrimination (*discernement*) leads instead to a fusion of terms. The interest of the limit-situation in which difference is transformed into identity is to bring

---

78   J. Vuillemin, *La philosophie de l'algèbre*, Tome Premier, Paris: PUF, 1962, Note III, 547, 'Le principe des relations internes'. Against Russell's interpretation, see Hidé Ishiguro, *Leibniz's Philosophy of Logic and Language*, 2nd edition, Cambridge: Cambridge University Press, 101ff.

necessity onto the scene: what is 'identical to itself' is not so arbitrarily, by virtue of convention or from a particular point of view, but is so *in itself* (which does not mean outside of the world of experience or the sensible world).

There is no doubt in my eyes that in his inquiry into the criteria of identity, Locke sought, in a number of different situations (or on the basis of concepts describing several kinds of being, including the being of thought or mental activity), to grasp, on each occasion, the point at which a reversal of this type (from difference to its contrary) occurs. But in the case of *personal identity* or the identity of (and through) consciousness, it is possible to argue that he takes one more step. There is something like a dialectical overcoming in relation to the two explanations of sameness we have just presented. In this case, the being identical to itself is precisely the 'self'. It is therefore nothing other than the concept of identity present *in differences* ('*dans les différences*') and reproduced *by these differences* themselves. This may also be specified in relation to time: it is nothing other than the continuity of the 'same time' which has the structure of a consciousness, linking together its successive moments. In this sense, the reflexivity of the 'self of consciousness' (*soi de la conscience)* or *self-consciousness* appears to be the model of all reflexivity or the originary reference that allowed Locke to gain access to the nucleus of signification presupposed by all predication that takes the form 'x R x', 'something is identical', or '*the same with itself*'. Such an idea of the self (or of the folding back of the self upon itself) does not pose difference and identity next to and apart from each other, but the two together, each being the condition of the other.[79]

It might be said, yet again, that this is subjectivism or psychologism. But it might also be asked if the means employed by others to avoid this position, and therefore to 'objectify' or 'formalize' identity, can do anything other than indefinitely defer its explanation to a metalanguage that would be 'final'. The choice would seem to be between the solution to which Locke was inclined – namely, to clarify the meaning of 'sameness' and 'identity' through the experience of 'being oneself', as the donor of the originary reflexivity that is at work in every 'identification' – and, in opposition, a general axiomatic of the relations in which identity would implicitly either be defined by a postulate, or given as a pure *indefinable.*

See also DIVERSITY, IDENTITY

SELF, THE SELF: §§ 9, 10, 11, 14, 16, 17, 18, 20, 21, 23, 25, 26, 28

In *An Essay Concerning Human Understanding*, and more particularly in the treatise on identity included in it, Locke invented two of the great concepts of

---

79 Of course, it would triumph in the transcendental formalizations in the manner of Kant and Fichte, in which A=A must immediately be interpreted as 'I am I' (*Ich bin Ich, Ich gleich Ich*).

modern philosophy: *consciousness* and *the self*. The invention of the latter more than the former (although the two are inseparable) would not have been possible without utilizing the resources proper to the English language to transform, from within, the philosophemes at his disposal in other languages (Greek, Latin, French). This process, to whose consequences we are still subject, does not refute Locke's epistemological theses because it is situated at another level: it contains, however, an ironic aspect, when we recall the way Locke sought to devalue the verbal element and radically isolate the mental or purely cognitive element of knowledge. For it took considerable labour on words and syntax to make possible the anti-linguistic 'turn' I discussed in the introduction.

The conceptualization of the *self* in Locke has its origin in the complete set of nouns, adjectives and possessive and reflexive personal pronouns in Greek and in the Latin or Germanic languages denoting the subject and allowing its qualification. But its immediate background is constituted by the invention of the expression 'le moi' in French philosophy in the face of the complexity of the uses of *self* in English.

It was in fact Pascal, as Coste noted, who introduced the neologism 'le moi' into French philosophical and literary language: 'I feel that I might not have been, for the self consists in my thought'. [*Je sens que je puis n'avoir point été, car le moi consiste dans ma pensée*] (B.469/L.135); 'The self is hateful . . . I will always hate it'. [*Le moi est haïssable . . . je le haïrai toujours*'] (B.455/L.597); 'What is the self? . . . Where then is this self, if it is neither in the body nor the soul? How is it possible to love the body or the soul, if not for these qualities which are not what make the self, since they are perishable. [*Qu'est-ce que le moi? . . . Où est donc ce moi, s'il n'est ni dans le corps ni dans l'âme? et comment aimer le corps ou l'âme, sinon pour ces qualités, qui ne sont point ce qui fait le moi, puisqu'elles sont périssables?*]' (B.323/L.688).

Descartes, however, in the *Discourse on Method* (Part IV) already wrote: 'this self, that is, the soul, through which I am what I am' (*Ce moi, c'est-à-dire mon âme, par laquelle je suis ce que je suis*). And this striking formula was interpolated later by the translator (the Duc de Luynes) in the course of the Sixth Meditation.[80] Descartes in no way identified subjectivity with consciousness, and the nominalization of the statement 'I think' to make it a transcendental principle proceeds entirely from later developments. It is clear, however, that the nominalization of self-reference (this [my] self, *ce moi, Ego ille*) is at the heart of the Cartesian interrogation of identity and alterity. It imposes a very powerful grammatical constraint on philosophy in the French language: undoubtedly '*le soi*' (the self) was also introduced (by Coste, Locke's translator,

---

80   When de Luynes (revised by Descartes) interpolated the formula from the *Discourse*, he changed 'l'âme' for 'mon âme' (my soul). I thank Prof. Vincent Carraud for drawing my attention to this important nuance.

and taken up many times subsequently, either on the basis of English, or the German *das Selbst*), but it is not universally useable. Thus the tension between '*moi*' and 'myself' or 'my self' remains very powerful, for in French one cannot very easily write '*mon soi*', nor a fortiori use this pronoun as a noun in the plural ('our selves').[81] What must particularly interest us here is Locke's negotiation between the French model of reflexive expression, strictly attached to the first person, and the tendency in English to reintroduce the marks of possession and internal distantiation into all self-reference.

Classical English in effect did not develop any expression analogous to *das Ich* (in fact, English later had to create the esoteric expression *the ego*) or *le moi* (which, as grammarians explain, marks an intensification of the subject by means of the 'oblique case': *me, moi*). In opposition it offers an astonishing variety of uses for the word *self* and its compounds, which allow for the conceptualization of the subject according to a plurality of instances.

The etymology of *self*, in the last analysis, is obscure, according to the OED. The term included both a pronominal use (corresponding to the Latin *ipse*), and its use as an adjective (corresponding sometimes to the Latin *ipse* and sometimes to the Latin *idem*: thus, 'myself' and 'itself' or 'the same', 'the same thing'; a movement of reference and a movement of comparison). But very early there existed uses of *self* as a noun in the position of a subject or a complement, with or without an article (*self, the self*).[82]

Further, there exist combinations of *self* with other words which develop in two major directions:

– Combinations with pronouns and possessives, on some occasions written as one word (*itself, himself, myself, oneself*), and on others, as two (*it self, him self, my self, one self*), which tend to be substituted for the pronoun *itself*, in a movement of persistence or intensification (which may in its turn be duplicated: *I myself*). The written double (*myself* vs *my self*) authorizes its understanding either as a pronominal function or as an adjective (or a noun).[83] And the latter contains a virtual subject-object duplication or distantiation that may be noted

---

81   Let us recall that the uses of the English *self* and those of the French *soi* by which Coste proposed to translate it (the reflexive pronoun *se, soi*, having a function analogous to *me, moi*, or *te, toi*) in no way coincide (as the juxtaposition of *one-self* and *soi-même* shows fairly clearly). This is why, in my attempt at a new French translation, I gave in to the temptation to paraphrase, having failed to find a precise equivalent: in return I hoped to reveal the influence of linguistic constraints on conceptual elaboration.

82   The noun without an article is found in Hume: 'after what manner, therefore, do they [= the perceptions] belong to self; and how are they connected with it?' (*Treatise of Human Nature*, 252).

83   To which is added the passage from the singular to the plural: *our selves*, meaning (an insistent) 'we', but also, if the term is nominalized: 'the self that is ours [our own]'. Inversely, the word *self* remains neutral from the point of view of gender, and it is not easy to see how it would be possible to differentiate it, as the poet Paul Valéry did for the 'moi' in French, using the feminine form of the adjective: 'Harmonieuse moi . . . Mystérieuse moi' (*La Jeune Parque*).

or not according to emphasis. It is particularly the case if it coincides with a context in which the noun is linked to moral and metaphysical predicates (as is also the case in French with *le moi* [the self]): 'the self is hateful', the self is conscious', the self is autonomous'.[84]

– Combinations with nouns or adjectives to form notions marking reflection, the application of action to the subject itself, as in the Greek terms formed with *auto-* and with *heauto-*: thus, *self-conscious* and *self-consciousness* (where the Latin languages employ a genitive construction: *causa sui, compos sui, 'cause de soi', 'maîtrise de soi', 'conscience de soi'*).[85]

The final important characteristic: the nearly total equivalence between the expressions *my self* and *my own* when the subject of the utterance addresses himself or designates himself by what is most proper to him.[86] It is thus possible to say that *self* 'travels' between *same* and *own*, and overdetermines their meanings (while in French, in the absence of such a term, we are condemned to dissociate them).

Let us see how these virtualities are employed in the three passages in the treatise in which the doctrine of the 'self' is constructed by a progressive enrichment.

The first decisive moment is constituted by sections §9–11, whose crucial formulation I will again reproduce:

a *Person* . . . is a thinking intelligent Being, that . . . can consider it self as it self, the same thinking thing in different times and places . . . And by this every one is to himself, that which he calls *self:* It not being considered in this case, whether the same *self* be continued in the same, or divers Substances . . . it is the same *self* now it was then; and 'tis by the same *self* with this present one that now reflects on it, that that Action was done . . . we have the whole train of our past Actions before our Eyes in one view . . . our consciousness being interrupted, and we losing the sight of our past *selves* . . . For it being the same consciousness that makes a Man be himself to himself . . . as far as any intelligent Being can repeat the *Idea* of any past Action with the same consciousness it has of its present thoughts and actions, that it is *self* to it *self* now, and so will be the same *self* as far as the same consciousness

---

84   Thus, the suggestion that the subject is haunted by a double: 'Is it not like the King? As thou art to thy selfe' (*Hamlet*, I, I, 59).

85   Interestingly, in contemporary Italian, the combination of idiomatic possibilities and the internationalization of philosophical discussions (i.e. translations) has led to a shift: from the more 'natural' *coscienza di se* to the more 'technical' *autocoscienza*. And now even in French translators of Kant and Hegel try 'auto-conscience', which nevertheless sounds extremely artificial: 'Frenchified German' as it were . . .

86   I have taken up this question in order to correct a mistake that I initially made in my essay 'My Self and My Own: One and the Same?', as well as in the letter from Jean-Jacques Lecercle on uses of 'self' and 'own' from a professional linguist's standpoint in É. Balibar, *Citoyen Sujet et autres essais d'anthropologie philosophique*, Paris: Presses Universitaires de France, 2011, 153–4.

can extend to Actions past or to come . . . are a part of our *selves: i.e.* of our thinking conscious *self* . . . Thus the Limbs of his Body is to every one a part of *himself* . . . it is then no longer a part of that which is *himself* . . . we see the Substance, whereof *personal self* consisted at one time, may be varied at another, without the change of personal *Identity*.

In this passage, the idea of identity as simple *sameness* (§ 9) evolves into that of a *reflexive identity*, which is precisely what the word *self* designates: it thus becomes a noun (which Locke begins to italicize). This occurs by means of a slippage (*glissement*) from comparative expressions, such as 'the same with itself' and 'consider it self as it self', to the reflexive expression 'that is self to it self'. From this point on, it becomes possible to qualify or quantify the self, which also results in the transformation of personal pronouns into possessives (note the parallelism of 'our past actions' and 'our past selves', and the passage from 'our selves' to 'a part of our selves'). In § 14, there is another consequence marked in writing: 'he is no more one self with either of them' (hence he is not the same as them, but also: with neither of them does he form a single self). It is thus possible to exchange the expressions 'to be one (identical) Person', and 'to be one self'.

The second moment corresponds to §16–17, in which *self* plays a role in relation to the first person as either its substitute or an other or double, with which it carries on a dialogue (as already in §15: 'having resolved with ourselves what we mean'):

Had I the same consciousness . . . I could no more doubt that I, that write this now . . . was the same *self*, place that *self* in what Substance you please, than that I that write this am the same *my self* now whilst I write . . . that I was Yesterday. For as to this point of being the same *self*, it matters not whether this present *self* be made up of the same or other Substances, I being as much concern'd . . . appropriated to me now by this self-consciousness, as I am, for what I did the last moment . . . *Self* is that conscious thinking thing . . . concern'd for it *self* . . . the little Finger is as much a part of it *self* . . . and constitutes this inseparable *self* . . . That with which the *consciousness* of this present thinking thing can join it self, makes the same Person, and is one *self* with it, and with nothing else; and so attributes to it *self*, and owns all the Actions of that thing.

This passage brings about a slippage (*glissement*) of *self* as a common noun to *self* as a quasi-proper noun (without the article), while it preserves the possibility of its functioning as a possessive. But even more, through the equivalence of expressions such as 'I am my self', 'I am the same self', 'I am the same my self', Locke makes the *self* the representation (if not the concept) of the 'self' for 'the self', or, to put it another way, the term to which (or to whom) I attribute what I attribute to myself, what I am concerned with when I am concerned with myself ('*Self* . . . is concerned for it *self*'). Locke attempts here to square the circle, by forging *a generic expression for self-reference in the first person* which the self may make use of in order to think itself (or objectify itself) without leaving itself. It is aided in this by the fact the *self* can be placed in apposition with the subject in a phrase written in the first person. But we may also say the inverse: this quadrature is the very movement by which, paradoxically, I 'attribute to myself' some thing, some thought, etc. and 'confess' ('own') or 'perceive' it as mine. It is a matter of escaping the quasi-tautology 'I think, I am', (or 'I write, I am') – or, to put it another way, to fold it back upon itself.

Finally, the third moment corresponds to § 24–6 in which Locke universally calls 'person' the *self* that he himself had used to clarify the singularity of 'personal identity':

> that consciousness whereby I am my *self* to my *self* . . . join with that present consciousness, whereby I am now my *self*, it is in that part of its Existence no more my *self*, than any other immaterial Being . . . by this consciousness, he finds himself to be the *same self* which did such or such an Action . . . In all which account of *self*, the same numerical Substance is not considered, as making the same *self* . . . Thus any part of our Bodies . . . makes a part of our *selves* . . . that, which a moment since was part of our *selves*, is now no more so, than a part of another man's *self* is a part of me . . . *Person*, as I take it, is the name for this *self*. Where ever a Man finds, what he calls *himself*, there I think another may say is the same Person . . . This personality extends it *self* beyond present Existence . . . whereby it becomes concerned and accountable, owns and imputes to it *self* past Actions.

Here, Locke appropriates Descartes' expression (or the expression derived from Descartes by his translator: *ce moi, c'est-à-dire mon âme, par laquelle je suis ce que je suis*) for his own use, that is, he 'translates' it into the language of the *self*. But he also takes advantage of this expression to substitute 'consciousness' for 'my soul' in order to identify 'that by which I am what I am', which allows him to turn once again to the possessive: 'whereby I am now my self', and 'whereby I am my self to my self', that is, 'for my [own] self', or again, if we want to employ the denomination that Locke presents as its conceptual equivalent: 'for my [own] person'.

The idea of being oneself for one's person, or being 'a self' for oneself by perceiving oneself as an identical person, obviously contains an element of duplication or internal distantiation. It therefore introduces an uncertainty into the question of whether the identical, identity, *is really myself* or *is represented in me* as an image or a verbal simulacrum – albeit one which would precisely never give rise to a reification or splitting. For, in Locke, the self cannot be anything other than an identical 'appearing to oneself' or 'perceiving oneself': it would not be able to *really* duplicate itself either into subject and object, or into real self and apparent self.[87] This is why I propose to call this distantiation a *vanishing distantiation,* proper to the expression of the subject in its own proper sphere, in its own proper language. It is the developed form of the 'tautology' of the subject and corresponds closely to the idea that the theorization of consciousness attempts to establish, marked as we saw by the tension between the idea of a fixed point to which the entire appropriative succession of the ideas would be attached, and that of a flow of representation whose very continuity would lead to identity.

Must we, in the face of such conditions, assume that Locke bent language to his concept? Or that it is the work of language (in part realized as translation) that clears a path for the concept? Perhaps such a question is undecidable. And, perhaps, beside the point.

SUBSTANCE: §§ 2, 3, 7, 9, 10, 11, 12, 13, 14, 16, 17, 18, 19, 21, 23, 24, 25, 26, 27, 28

While, as we know, for Locke the idea of substance is confused, this does not mean we can simply disregard it: instead, its use must be critical, restricted or hypothetical.[88] I cannot here enter into a detailed examination of Locke's swinging between arguments that tended to represent the soul as a material substance which was the source of the power of thinking and feeling, on the one hand, and arguments that tended to see it as an immaterial substance capable of surviving the decomposition of the body, on the other. Still, I will offer three remarks on the argumentation found in the treatise:

1. The definition of substance to which Locke always refers is Scholastic rather than Cartesian. It thus concerns the inherence of properties (or accidents and modifications) in a subject and not the relation of opposition between several incompatible substances (as the opposition between thinking substance and extended substance or, on another plane, the opposition between infinite and finite substance were for Descartes). Locke rejected the Cartesian idea of a 'principal attribute' of substances (thought for the soul, extension for the body: *Principes de la philosophie,* § 53 ff.), of which we would have, according to Descartes, an immediately clear idea. He also rejected the *problems* formulated on the basis of this notion, above all that of the 'union of the body and the soul' as the necessary substantial liaison that paradoxically remained all the more obscure as the terms that it joined were absolutely clear. In fact, the union (like the presence of the divine infinite or of

---

87 In other terms, no dialectic in the form of 'I = I and non-I', which issued from the formula elaborated by German Romanticism (Fichte, Jean-Paul: *Ich bin [ein] Ich*), has yet emerged.

88 See in particular Chapters II.xiii, II.xxiii and xxiv, II.xxxi, III.xi, IV.iii, IV.vi of the *Essay,* as well as the debate with Stillingfleet (*Mr. Locke's Letter to the Bishop of Worcester*, Vol. IV, 25 ff.), to which Coste dedicated a long presentation and commentary in a note to his translation (440–7).

the 'incomprehensible' in the soul's clear idea of itself) was the paradigm of the Cartesian theorization of the *alterity* that intrinsically characterized the very identity of the subject.[89] Does this mean that Locke, for his part, ignored questions of alterity in this sense? Clearly not, but whereas Descartes posed them in the form of a dramatic tension, it seems that the literary way in which Locke envisioned them was essentially *narrative* (*de façon essentiellement* romanesque):[90] it is the play of 'multiple personalities' and 'the fusion of personalities' that forms the essential basis of the argumentation concerning the difference between substantial and personal identity in the treatise (§ 14–25). In the end, this imaginary confers an authentically surrealist meaning on the very idea of the person. And substance becomes no more than a spectre (see PERSONALITY).

2. At a number of different moments in the treatise (as in the rest of the *Essay*) Locke took up the expression, of Cartesian origin, of 'a thinking thing' (§ 9, 10, 12, 17, 23, 27). It is fairly difficult to determine if he does so in an ironic fashion or if the question that is contained in it is taken up by him for his own purposes. Taken literally, the text renders it either another designation of the 'self' (a way for consciousness to represent to itself the unity of its own operations), or an expression of the question that consciousness cannot fail to pose to itself regarding the mysterious origin of the *power* whose effects it observes within itself. In this sense, Locke's formulations constitute an indispensable link between Descartes' *affirmation* – 'I am a thing that thinks, that is, *that* . . . ' – and Kant's *problem* of the (practical, regulative) use to which we must put the idea of the 'being that thinks in us' (*das Wesen, welches in uns denkt*), an object of thought, certainly, but not an object of knowledge (think of the paralogisms of pure reason). In Descartes, the expression 'thinking thing' designates that which is absolutely clear in the 'thought of thought', while in Kant, in contrast, it is that which remains mysterious. Locke alternates between the two.

3. In § 2 of the treatise, Locke examines three kinds of substance ('we have the *Ideas* but of three sorts of Substances'): God, finite (or created) intelligences and bodies. We might expect that the three cases will be compared to each other. We might even expect, given that 'God is without beginning, unalterable and everywhere' and that 'concerning his Identity there can be no doubt', that the light of divine identity, and the idea that corresponds to it, might constitute a paradigm for all subsequent discussion.[91] But nothing of the kind appears:

---

89   This is what Kambouchner, in *L'homme des passions*, calls the 'developed cogito'.

90   Of course, we might extend the range of the comparison: in Pascal this mode is the tragic, in Malebranche, the pathetic, etc.

91   We might compare these formulations with those of the General Scholium of Newton's *Principia*, which contains a very strong statement about divine identity ('God is the same God, always and everywhere') that authorized the passage from the soteriological concept of God as 'omnipotent Judge' to a cosmotheological concept of God (whose *sensorium* is identified with material space). On this moment in Newtonian philosophy, see F. Regnault, 'De deux dieux', in *Dieu est inconscient. Etudes lacaniennes autour de saint Thomas d'Aquin*, Paris: Navarin Éditeur, 1985,

that there is no doubt on the subject of 'divine identity' seems practically to mean that it holds no interest for us and teaches us nothing. In a certain way, this 'identity' is tautological and the philosophical problem of identity begins to be posed only after it is set aside. Let us go even farther: the *problem of identity is the problem of all that is not God*, a problem that is posed 'in the absence of God'. Even further: the retreat of divine identity – absolutely non-problematic or tautological – beyond the limits of the question of identity, which in reality concerns the objects of the world and the relation of consciousness to itself, also determines the disqualification of the ideas of univocity and analogy: the entrance of equivocity onto the scene, as I have already noted.

Michael Ayers expresses a similar idea: identity as Locke thinks it 'supplies what is missing', all identities are *identities by default*, even quasi-identities, continuations of identity manifested in time, given the lack of intemporal permanence.[92] This insistence on the fact that Locke's problem concerns existence and not essence seems correct. But Locke's theorization must be completely *detached* from the relation to essence. In reality, temporal identity 'lacks' nothing, but is instituted in the domain of corporeal substances, living individualities, or conscious personalities, for these existences concern only themselves (in the enigma of their two opposing sides: multiplicity and unity, difference and identity). Finally, I prefer the suggestions of Remo Bodei: Lockean identities are the correlatives of a 'fragility of being' in the element of time; better, they are un-easy (*malaisées*) in both senses of the term.[93]

31–47.
  92 Ayers, *Locke*, Vol. II, 209.
  93 Remo Bodei, 'Migrazioni di identità. Trasformazioni della coscienza nella filosofia contemporanea', *Iride* 8: 16, December 1995, 628–71.

CHAPTER THREE

Postscript: A Note on 'Consciousness/ Conscience' in Spinoza's *Ethics*

In the course of the foregoing book, which arises from a critical edition, translation and commentary on Locke's treatise on personal identity (Book II, Chapter XXVII of An Essay Concerning Human Understanding*), I had several occasions to refer to Spinoza's conceptions of 'conscience' and 'consciousness'. I presented them allusively as forming an alternative to the Lockean 'invention of consciousness', albeit based in good part on similar premises and references (notably the Cartesian idea of a criterion of certainty immanent to the intellectual procedures of thinking, best exemplified by mathematical reasoning, and the methodology of the 'analysis' and 'composition' of ideas also exposed by the* Logique de Port-Royal, *which partly derived from Descartes and may have been one of Spinoza's indirect sources of inspiration). They clearly belong to the same classical* episteme *(to borrow the well-known Foucauldian category), but they go in opposite directions. I was not only pushed towards that comparison by the customary taste of historians of ideas (and some philosophers) for symmetries and antitheses, or by the fact that I had devoted quite a bit of time in my career to working on and 'with' Spinoza.*[1] *Rather, I had two intrinsic reasons, which at some point should inevitably overlap, but remained autonomous. One of them belongs to the history of contemporary disputes over the function and understanding of the idea of the 'subject' in philosophy (from metaphysics to ethics to epistemology), as a founding or constituent, if not a transcendental, subject, in which a whole generation (albeit with notable exceptions) defended the idea that 'subjectivist philosophies' can be traced back to the influence of the Cartesian* cogito, *whereas 'structuralist philosophies' owe more than a symbolic debt to the author of the* Ethics, *whose central axiom asserts that 'the order and connection of ideas is identical with the order and connection of things' (or causes) (Ethics, II, Prop. 7). However, as I was increasingly led to question a traditional image of Descartes as the father of the idea of subjectivity qua 'consciousness' (as explained at length in the preceding essay), and to fully picture Locke as a theorist of 'self-consciousness', whose ideas and problems irrigate every philosophy of the 'inner sense' and the 'reflective self' from Kant to modern phenomenology, it was inevitable that I should begin wondering about*

---

1 Cf. Pierre Macherey, *Avec Spinoza. Études sur la doctrine et l'histoire du spinozisme*, Paris: Presses Universitaires de France, 1992. I refer throughout this Postscript to the following edition: Spinoza, *Éthique, Texte original et traduction nouvelle par Bernard Pautrat*, Paris: Éditions du Seuil, 1988.

the precise terms in which a comparison of Locke's and Spinoza's theories of 'mind' or mens should be undertaken. This met with my second reason, because it seemed to cross the fact that Locke's and Spinoza's conceptions of 'mental operations' or a 'spiritual machine' (automaton spirituale), embodying different ways of endowing a mechanism of the association of ideas with a dynamism that makes it possible for the intellect to develop (or 'grow') out of its intrinsic 'power', could be considered without arbitrary projection of another terminology, a seminal dilemma from which a modern 'philosophy of mind' keeps drawing its inspiration.[2]

It is this overdetermined 'point of heresy', traversing philosophies and sciences from the seventeenth century to our own time, which I would like to help clarify in this Postscript, taking advantage of Stella Sandford's suggestion to complete our book (with its two successive parts: the introduction to Locke's treatise on identity, and the 'philological-philosophical Glossary') with an additional piece or postscript. Instead of 'replying' to her generous introduction, at the risk of making more obscure what she seems to me to have greatly clarified, I decided (with her agreement) to bring in my little essay on Spinoza (published somewhat earlier, but prepared and written essentially in the same conjuncture as the Locke commentary).[3] *I give it in its original version (keeping some inevitable repetitions with the previous texts), only correcting some stylistic mistakes and adding a final section to highlight the points of comparison which, in my current view, deserve special attention.*

1. No doubt, much has been written about Spinoza's theory of *consciousness* (as a psychic agency or a faculty, be it identified or not with the mind itself) and *awareness* (a disposition of the mind regarding some objects, some states of affairs, some 'internal' or 'external' processes). At the same time, one of the main reasons why certain currents in modern philosophy, in spite of their divergences (logicists, structuralists, vitalists . . .), are so specifically interested in Spinoza is precisely that they view him as an adversary of 'subjectivity', a critic of that 'primacy of consciousness' which, so it is believed, would run from Socrates to Husserl, through Descartes and Kant, among others. One could even suggest that this has been the main focus of the debate on Spinoza in the second half of the twentieth century, where Spinoza's *objectivism* was discussed from Cavaillès and Koyré to Canguilhem and Althusser, much as his *naturalism* had been in the eighteenth, or his *pantheism* in the nineteenth.

---

2   The possibility for contemporary philosophy (and physiology) of mind to fruitfully 'return' to Spinoza has been popularized among non-philosophers by Antonio Damasio's book *Looking for Spinoza: Joy, Sorrow, and the Feeling Brain*, New York: Vintage, 2003. (Damasio is also the author of *Descartes' Error: Emotion, Reason, and the Human Brain*, New York: Harper Perennial, 1995). But there are more interesting suggestions: see Pascale Gillot, *L'esprit: Figures classiques et contemporaines*, Paris: CNRS Éditions, 2007.

3   It was published in *Studia Spinozana*, Vol. 8: *Spinoza's Psychology and Social Psychology*, Würzburg: Königshausen und Neumann, 1992, 37–53.

There comes a day, however, where one acknowledges with some surprise that most commentaries discuss a theory (or a critique) of consciousness in Spinoza by referring to *loci* in the *Ethics* where he speaks neither of *conscientia* nor of *conscius esse* (nor uses any classical synonym of these terms), and cease to mention it where, on the contrary, these terms are present in the text. Whether these commentators agree or not with Spinoza's conception of the mind, the nature of ideas and affects, the various kinds of knowledge, etc. whether they simply agree or not that these conceptions are meaningful (which is not always the case . . .), one cannot but suspect that there could exist some basic misunderstanding here.

If this is the case, a more literal reading of Spinoza's arguments with regard to *conscientia* could be of primary interest. It could provide us with a significant test of the original link between 'epistemology', 'psychology' and 'ethics' in Spinoza's philosophy. But it could also help us to do away with the metaphysical illusion that every philosophy confronts the same eternal questions (albeit answering them differently), or – which is not so different indeed – the positivistic illusion that modern 'scientific' problems (the 'problem of consciousness' or 'self-awareness', the 'mind-body problem', etc.) provide a standard framework for discussing any philosophical theory.

The situation is all the more interesting because of the historical conjuncture in which Spinoza was writing. It is the very conjuncture in which the crucial terms mentioned above were created or underwent a profound transformation in their use and meaning. Nearly all the significant tendencies of classical philosophy were involved in this highly conflictual process. Although Spinoza does not seem to have taken part in any direct controversy, he certainly provides us with an important counterexample. He might also have had an indirect influence on such authors as Locke, Leibniz and the later Empiricists and Materialists. Let us recall briefly some linguistic facts here.

The classical Latin term *conscientia* had an exclusively 'moral' meaning, both in theological and philosophical contexts. It was widely used in the scholastic and the (neo-) stoic traditions (sometimes referred to the Greek *synderesis*), expressing a faculty or state of mind for which, in modern English, the word *conscience* has been kept. To be sure, the correlative expression *conscius esse*, or more precisely *alicujus rei sibi conscius esse*, had psychological connotations (which derived from the idea of a 'private' knowledge, or the personal experience arising from such a knowledge), but always with regard to moral matters and problems.

In Descartes, *conscientia* is very seldom used, especially not in such major texts as the *Meditations*. (It can be found in one passage, admittedly crucial, of the *Principles of Philosophy*: Part I, § 9.) Above all, the French transcription *conscience* was never used by Descartes or accepted by him in the translations of his works (with two marginal exceptions, one of which is rather dubious).[4] However, it was introduced after his death in a 'psychological' sense by 'minor Cartesians', discussing the autonomy of the soul with respect to the body (La Forge, *Traité de l'esprit de l'homme*, 1666), and more importantly by Malebranche, in his *Recherche de la Vérité* (1674 to 1678), where *conscience* is an equivalent for the *sentiment intérieur*, i.e. a confused perception of one's own ideas and feelings.

The English word *consciousness*, on the other hand, is a neologism from the late seventeenth century. Together with many other philosophical terms, it was invented by Ralph Cudworth in his *True Intellectual System of the Universe* (1678), a lengthy refutation of the atomistic/materialist tradition from Democritus to Hobbes, where it encompasses all the degrees between the confused perception of the environment proper, to any living individual and the reflexive activity of the superior intelligence. From there, albeit with a decisive shift in meaning, it passes to the empiricist/rationalist philosophy of John Locke. In *An Essay Concerning Human Understanding* (1690), the attribute of being *conscious* (and *self-conscious*) is cut off from any reference to *conscience*. It becomes a correlate of *consciousness*, for which Locke has provided a definition relying upon the clear distinction of the 'inner' and the 'outer' experience, later to be adopted or discussed by the whole metaphysical and psychological tradition ('Consciousness is the perception of what passes in a Man's own Mind', *Essay*, II.i.19). As is well-known, the main application of this new definition, which proved much more influential than Cudworth's original, is to provide a criterion for *personal identity*, which liberates it from any dependency on the scholastic notion of substance, while avoiding at the same time the perilous moral, religious and juridical consequences of accepting a 'multiple' self. *Consciousness* in Locke is a synthetic agency, which binds together the experiences of oneself. The consequences would be decisive, not only in the Insular tradition (say, from Berkeley, Hume and Reid to James and Ryle), but also in the Continental (from Condillac and Kant to Husserl).

Interestingly, it is through the translation of Locke's *Essay* – published in 1700 by a Protestant, Pierre Coste – that the word *conscience* (initially written *con-science*) was reintroduced as a French equivalent for *consciousness*. However, it took almost a century for this novelty to be fully accepted, mainly in the empiricist, but also in the spiritualist current. In the end, however, it would be projected back on Descartes, thus paving the way for a 'psychological' or 'transcendental' reading of his doctrine as a *philosophie de la conscience*. Notwithstanding, Leibniz on his side had rejected this novelty: after having

---

4   See Geneviève Rodis-Lewis, *L'oeuvre de Descartes*, Paris: Librairie philosophique J. Vrin, 1971; Glyn Davies, 'Conscience' as consciousness; and my 'L'invention de la conscience: Descartes, Locke, Coste et les autres', in Bloch, ed., *Traduire les philosophes*.

tried another neologism, *consciosité* or *conscienciosité*, in the *Nouveaux Essais* (his reply to Locke, written in French, as was much of his philosophical work), he would prefer a more specific term: *aperception*, which allowed him to stress the continuity with *perception* (both 'conscious' and 'unconscious') – whence *Apperzeption*, the Kantian equivalent for transcendental *Selbstbewusstsein*, evidently comes.

2. How does Spinoza fit into this conflictual pattern? We must be very careful not to project on his text any pre-established understanding of *conscientia*, *conscius esse, conscience* (French or English), and *consciousness*. Any philosophical work is indeed a confrontation with specific written words, loaded with history, but this is especially true when great philosophical alternatives are at stake. What is thus required first is a complete list of the occurrences of *conscius* and *conscientia* in Spinoza's works, and a precise description of the contexts. For reasons of room and consistency, I shall restrict myself to the *Ethics*.[5] This simple examination already shows that Spinoza's use of these terms is relatively scarce, but very systematic. In most places, a modern reader would translate *conscientia* as *consciousness* or *awareness* and *conscius* as *conscious* or *aware of*, but not always. Moreover, with the sole exception of IIP35S, which is a literal repetition of IApp, concerning the illusion of men (given as an example of *falsitas*) that their will is free of causal determinations, the Second Part of the *Ethics* (Of the Nature and Origin of the Mind: *De natura et origine mentis*) does not appear in this list.

This is a very remarkable fact. Negatively, it suggests that a theory of 'conscience/consciousness' in the *Ethics* has nothing to do with such problems as mind and body ('parallelism'), *idea ideae* (the 'idea of idea', often described as a general, or 'logical', concept of consciousness in Spinoza, by means of the notion of reflexivity), the kinds of knowledge (especially the third one), etc. Or better said, it would suggest that, according to the geometrical order, a reference to *conscientia* is not a prerequisite to discuss such problems.

Positively, it shows us that the terms *conscius* and *conscientia* are indeed crucial in the second half of the *Ethics*: more precisely, they strategically organize Part III, with precise consequences in the argumentation of Part IV and the

---

5 Here is the complete list, with the help of Emilia Giancotti-Boscherini (*Lexicon Spinozanum*, La Haye: Martinus Nijhoff, 1969): I App; IIP35S; IIIP2S; IIIP9, dem, S; IIIP18S2; IIIP30dem; IIIDA1; IIIDA17; IVPref; IVP8dem; IVP19dem; IVP47S; IVP64dem; IVApp32; VP31S; VP34S; VP39S; VP42S. I have deliberately ignored any distinction between 'moral' and 'psychological' uses (which indeed will prove irrelevant).

There are very few *loci* for *conscientia* and *conscius* outside the *Ethics*. The use of such terms as *Conscientie, bewust*, and *medegeweten* in the *Korte Verhandeling* is of unquestionable interest, but poses indeed different problems (see Mignini's commentaries in his critical edition: *Korte Verhandeling/Breve Trattato*, Introduzione, edizione, traduzione, commento di Filippo Mignini, L'Aquila: L.U. Japadre Editore, 1986, 621).

end of Part V. Seen from this angle, the only two uses of *conscius* before Part III (which indeed have exactly the same content), clearly appear as anticipations of the anthropological theory of (self-)awareness as a necessary (albeit inadequate, self-deceiving) expression of (human) desire.

I see no compulsory reason to interpret these facts in the light of a chronological hypothesis regarding the writing of various sections of the *Ethics*.[6] In a sense, it is enough and also more illuminating to interpret them in a purely systematic manner: provided we succeed in showing that they have a strong internal coherence. Which I think is the case.

Spinoza's first references are to *conscius esse* (IApp, IIP35S, IIP2S). They share exactly the same characteristics: it is here a question of showing (i) that men are conscious of their actions which aim at realizing their will, or desire, or the appetite of their utilities, (ii) that they ignore the causes or determinations of their wills/actions, (iii) that this ignorance itself becomes the cause of a specifically human illusion: the illusion of 'freewill', which would have human beings escaping the ordinary conditions of nature. Spinoza does not say that 'consciousness' and 'ignorance' are one and the same thing, neither does he explicitly say that the specific ignorance of the 'appetites', or causes of one's own actions, is the essential content of consciousness. But there is undoubtedly a strong suggestion here that these three notions are closely connected, since the antithesis *conscius* vs *ignarus* lies at the heart of the process which transforms a real action (*suum utile quaerere*: to look for one's own utility) into an imaginary one (to act out of free will, i.e. without determination).

This suggestion becomes ratified and explained when we reach Part III, with the introduction of the substantive *conscientia*. It should be noted right from the beginning that the main references – indeed the only three uses of *conscientia* as an autonomous concept, in IIIP9S, IIIP30dem, and IIIDA1 – aim at the very core of the anthropological doctrine. There is no formal definition of *conscientia*, but the term is used itself to indicate the difference between *appetitus* ('appetite') and *cupiditas* ('desire'), which in turn expresses the 'essence of man'. A number of characteristics are remarkable here, showing that Spinoza has very carefully combined the terminological, logical, and ontological aspects.

First, the 'subject' of this particular action called 'consciousness' is no longer directly the Human Being (*homo, homines*) in general, but the Mind (*mens*), which is said to be (i) 'conscious' of its own effort/endeavour (*conatus*); (ii) 'conscious' of itself (*sui sit conscia*) by means of the ideas of the affections of the Body; and finally (iii) 'conscious' of its own desire (*cupiditas*) – itself already

---

6   Although, if one adopted the idea that all these *loci* belong to a 'late' layer in the work of Spinoza, i.e. after the 'break' of 1670–1672, it could be interesting to imagine 'echoes' of the post-Cartesian discussion around *conscientia*, *conscience* and *consciousness* emerging during the same years in the French and English realm, which was certainly not ignored in Holland.

introduced as *appetitus cum conscientia* ('appetite with consciousness'). It is the complete series of these determinations which amounts to picturing the 'self-consciousness' of *Man*: to say that Humans are (self-) conscious means to say that (human) Minds are conscious of their own desire, i.e. their effort to preserve themselves, which means that they are conscious of themselves by means of the idea they have of the affections of the Body. Thus consciousness is undoubtedly an idea,[7] but it is unique as an idea inasmuch as it immediately identifies any affection in the Body with desire in the Mind. Moreover, there is no actual difference between being 'conscious' and being 'self-conscious': which is not only a particular application of the theory that any *idea* is also immediately *idea ideae*, but more precisely a consequence of the fact that to be 'conscious of one self' is never anything else than to be conscious of one or several affections of one's Body. Conversely, such an idea of the Body (through its affections, which always involve an effort to preserve itself, and even, as we will see later, a 'difference' in this effort, which is greater or lesser) is already enough to be 'self-conscious'.

The very same propositions involve another puzzle. In IIIP9S, it is *Appetitus* which is said to be 'nothing but the very essence of man' (*nihil aliud quam ipsa hominis essentia*), whereas in IIIDA1 Spinoza writes: 'Desire is man's very essence, insofar as it is conceived to be determined, from any given affection of it, to do something' (*Cupiditas est ipsa hominis essentia, quatenus ex data quacunque ejus affectione determinata, etc.*). In the following *explicatio*, he goes on to explain (in a remarkable move to avoid what he calls himself *tautologia*) that the concept of *appetitus* in general does not necessarily involve consciousness or self-consciousness (which could be rephrased: some appetites are voluntary, others not), whereas *appetitus* combined with an idea of the Body's affections is the same as *cupiditas*. Hence there is no difference between *cupiditas* ('desire') and specifically *human* 'appetite', and it can be said that 'desire' or 'human appetite' is the very essence of Man: not an abstract or formal essence, but an essence involving the idea of certain determined actions.Now it could seem that, in order to avoid a 'tautology', Spinoza has in fact entered a circle. I have quoted texts that explain that the human essence must involve consciousness, while admitting that consciousness is a specifically human kind of idea (or an idea of a specifically human Body, or of a specifically human mode for a Body to preserve itself). I shall without difficulty admit that there is this circle in Spinoza, because I see it not as a logical weakness, but as a philosophical strength. A nominal 'definition' of *conscientia*, which would make it a 'faculty'

---

7   Which is confirmed, if necessary, by the fact that IIIP30 and the corresponding demonstration substitutes *conscientia* for *idea*: 'he will be affected with joy accompanied by the idea of himself as a cause' (*is Laetitia, concomitante idea sui tanquam causa, afficietur*) then becomes: 'will be affected with joy, together with a consciousness of himself as the cause' (*Laetitia cum conscientia sui tanquam causa afficietur*).

in the metaphysical or psychological meaning of this term, is avoided. On the contrary, what we have is an *implicit definition* of 'consciousness', which (i) identifies consciousness with *the specific difference between appetite and desire;*[8] (ii) presupposes that *a specific quality (or 'complexity'?) of the Human Body is expressed* in (at least some) ideas of the affections of this Body in a Human Mind; and (iii) identifies an analysis of consciousness with *a theory of the determinations of the human essence inasmuch as they are expressed as ideas of the Body's affections.* This definition is implicit, but it has a very positive content, because it opens the door for a description and a causal explanation of conscious processes which actually coincide with the connexions, fluctuations and transformations of the human affects and their ideas: i.e. with the complete contents of Part III, a good deal of Parts IV and even some aspects of Part V.[9]

Bear in mind that we (twentieth-century readers) do not know what 'consciousness' is (or if you like, we have decided to forget what we have been 'taught' about it by philosophy, be it Lockean, Kantian, Husserlian or Jamesian, by psychology, physiology and cognitive science . . .) We want to learn something about it from Spinoza, better said from his use of the term *conscientia*, which proves to be both very systematic and very original. We are now led to several conclusions.

3. It is clear that Spinoza's implicit definition has a polemical aspect. IIIDA1, particularly, has a strong stylistic resemblance with Descartes' only systematic reference to *conscientia* (in the *Principles*, I, 9). Therefore it is all the more striking that the modes of 'thinking' or *cogitatio*, which had been listed by Descartes in order to show that they can be conceived by the sole power of thought, be substituted here by ideas of the affections of the Body, which express one and the same *conatus* of the human nature.

But the main conclusion is about the relationship between 'consciousness' and knowing, or knowledge. Initially, it seems to be purely negative. IIIP9dem refers to IIP23, where it is proved that the Mind has neither a direct nor an adequate knowledge of itself – a radically anti-Cartesian proposition ('The mind does not know itself, except insofar as it perceives the ideas of the affections of the body': *Mens se ipsam non cognoscit, nisi quatenus Corporis affectionum ideas percipit*). IIIP30dem again refers to the same proposition, and to

---

8   I think that we could clarify this in the following way: consciousness is the specific 'degree' or 'quality' which transforms appetite into desire. This formulation will become important as soon as we notice that the affects of Joy and Sadness are connected with Desire, not with mere Appetite, from IIIP11S onwards: therefore the 'dialectic' of ambivalence, which forms the structure of Part III as a whole, is undoubtedly a dialectic of Desire.

9   What I am proposing here is therefore exactly what Edwin Curley had suggested, but to declare it impossible: 'We might argue that part III of the *Ethics*, which discusses the origin and nature of the human emotions, is an attempt to work out the rudiments of this universal psychology'. Curley, *Spinoza's Metaphysics: An Essay in Interpretation*, Cambridge, MA: Harvard University Press, 1969, 120.

IIP19 ('The human mind does not know the human body itself, nor does it know that it exists, except through ideas of affections by which the body is affected': *Mens humana ipsum humanum Corpus non cognoscit, nec ipsum existere scit, nisi per ideas affectionum, quibus Corpus afficitur*). It should not be forgotten that this partial and inadequate 'perception' of the Body (through the affections, i.e. a mixture or combination of the Body's structure and its interaction with other things), identical with a partial and inadequate (self-) knowledge of the Mind, nevertheless expresses the actual *conatus* of the Mind's essence. We are back to the antithesis of 'consciousness' and 'ignorance', which had been emphasized in Parts I and II, but this time there is an explanation for their necessary combination, which indeed amounts to viewing them as one and the same expression of the Mind's power, inasmuch as (*quatenus*) it is limited or determined in a certain way. To be conscious goes along with being ignorant; nay, *it means to be ignorant*, provided we understand that both formulations refer to the same process of (inadequate) expression.

The same idea will acquire its full importance if we put it in the following way. What appeared as a 'negation' is indeed a determination. 'Consciousness' and 'ignorance' are names that refer to a positive power that is limited, or they refer to aspects of the (inadequate) idea which are like recto and verso. What is it, in fact, that our Mind is 'ignorant' of? Spinoza has only one answer, repeated again and again: we ignore *the causes* (the causes of the affections, and the affections as causes of the appetites, or determinations of the *conatus*: in short, we ignore the causal chain, *ordinem et connexionem causarum*). And what is it that we are conscious of? We are conscious *of the ends* (we have ideas of our actions inasmuch as they seek certain goals which we think are useful for us, or we have ideas of our actions as purposeful and intentional). To 'ignore' *is not a void, it means to 'know'*. More precisely, to ignore causes means to know ends and by means of ends, to have them in mind, or to have a Mind which is composed of ideas of ends, goals, and purposes connecting 'oneself' and a multiplicity of 'things'. Or if you like, it is to misunderstand everything inasmuch as it is causally determined, and to understand everything as finally determined (for, since 'man thinks', *homo cogitat*, there is no such thing as no understanding at all).

But this is exactly what a 'definition' of the 'human essence' is about: human beings perceive causes as ends (in an 'inverted' manner), or they 'know' of causes that they can imagine, picture, and think as ends, by referring to 'themselves' (or: to their Self). This is indeed a crucial conclusion, which we could also express by saying that, in Spinoza's doctrine, *conscientia* or consciousness and Human *voluntas* or will are practically equivalent concepts (with exactly the same range), as a new careful reading of IIIP9S will immediately show.

4. Now that we have identified not only the form of consciousness according to Spinoza, but also its content, we are ready to examine the two successive, and

quite distinct, *derivations* from this implicit definition (which could be called also *developments* of consciousness). The first and more developed is a rigorous equivalence (established in Parts III and IV) between what most of the philosophical tradition has considered distinct notions: *consciousness* and moral *conscience*, which in Spinoza's conception refer to exactly the same kind of ideas. The second, indicated more quickly, but no less decisive, is an aspect of the Third Kind of knowledge, presented in the second half of Part V, from which a new articulation of (self-) consciousness, knowledge, and ignorance will arise (where Spinoza will introduce the word *inscius*, as a counterpart of *sapiens*, or 'wise', but also 'learned'). I shall examine them briefly in the same order.

That Spinoza does not make a distinction between the two notions presented today as translations of the Latin *conscientia* should be no surprise to any reader who has kept in mind his denial that 'understanding' and 'will' are different realities. It is part of the same endeavour (expressed in the title *Ethics*) to go beyond the traditional distinction of 'theoretical' and 'practical' philosophy. But it now concerns a more specific point about human nature (or the 'model of the human nature', as the Preface of Part IV will say). Conversely, whoever has read IIIP18S2, IIIDA17 and IVP47S without prejudice should see no reason to understand this *conscientia* (in *conscientiae morsus*: remorse of conscience) in a different way from elsewhere. But of course this is only one particular use.

The 'moral' use of *conscientia* is indeed rooted in its being indiscernibly an idea and a 'mental' expression of the *conatus*, or more precisely, the 'differential' element of desire and appetite. IIIP30 adds an important piece of explanation: what are identical in fact are not isolated ideas and affections, but *connexions of* ideas and affections, best understood in this case as *polarities* in both realms: Joy and Sadness on the one hand, the affects which arise from an increasing or decreasing power to act; the representation of good and bad ends on the other hand, i.e. the ideas of Good and Evil (the idea of an end, or finalistic idea, can never be 'neutral': it is necessarily the imagination of something that should be sought *or* avoided, or, if transformed into an abstraction, the idea of the Desirable as such *or* the Avoidable as such). From there we can immediately deduce the definition of *conscientiae morsus* (a 'temporal' modality of this affect/idea).[10] But above all we can go to the extraordinary proposition IVP8 and its demonstration, one of the turning points in the *Ethics*, where the knowledge of Good and Evil (*cognitio boni et mali*) is expressly identified with the idea of a joyful *or* sad affection of the Body. But since there is no affection of the Body which is not *either* joyful *or* sad, this amounts to saying that the knowledge of Good and Evil is nothing else than the conscious affect in general ('nothing but an affect of joy or sadness, insofar as we are conscious of it': *nihil est aliud, quam ipse affectus, quatenus ejusdem sumus conscii*).

---

10   We can even suggest that a reference to *conscientia* is implicit in the definition of the passion opposed to *conscientiae morsus*, i.e. *Gaudium* ('gladness'), as in all affective polarities.

With this demonstration, all the elements are knit together. The knowledge of Good and Evil is the general concept of what the philosophical and theological tradition has called 'moral conscience' (usually conceived as an inner *voice*, because of its intrinsic connexion with the ideas of Law, Legislation, Legislator). From a Spinozistic standpoint, 'moral conscience' is, of course, a misunderstanding or misrecognition, following exactly the pattern of inversion noted above. But there is nothing more in this 'moral conscience' than what we found characteristic of 'consciousness' in general, i.e. the representation of ends with the affects they necessarily entail. And conversely, every 'consciousness', be it of the external world with its constituent objects, or of oneself – but in fact any consciousness is an idea of myself-in-the-world or an idea of the world as 'my world' – is always already a 'moral conscience', or if you like it is a 'moral worldview', a picture of the world permeated with 'values', where things are 'good' or 'bad', where there is 'order' and 'disorder'. This is indeed what the Appendix of Part I already explained, and the Preface of Part IV will again emphasize, by resuming the terms *conscii, ignari*.

As a consequence, an 'English' (or American) Spinoza would have no use of the distinction 'consciousness vs conscience' elaborated nearly at the same time by Cudworth and Locke. These two words for him refer exactly to the same phenomena. Just as Part III of the *Ethics* could be considered in its entirety an implicit 'definition' of consciousness, identified with the Essence of Man, or with the specifically human forms of an individual's idea of its own striving for preservation, Part IV (or a good deal of it) could be considered a phenomenology of moral conscience, or the analytic description of the 'moral view of the world' (including the 'self' as its imaginary centre or point of reference). But these are in fact one and the same problem. Accordingly, to analyse spontaneous morality, or to propose a phenomenology of consciousness-conscience, is tantamount to defining the Essence of Man.

5. Many commentators would stop here. But we still have some *loci* to give an account of: those in Part V. They cannot be read as a continuation of what has been just explained. Indeed, they are intended to show us that 'human nature', or 'human essence', has another aspect, contrasting if not contradicting the mainly passive life of the affections.[11]

---

11   See IVD8 : 'By virtue and power I understand the same thing, that is . . . virtue, insofar as it is related to man, is the very essence, or nature, of man, insofar as he has the power of bringing about certain things, which can be understood through the laws of his nature alone' (*Per virtutem, et potentiam idem intelligo, hoc est . . . virtus, quatenus ad hominem refertur, est ipsa hominis essentia, seu natura, quatenus potestatem habet, quaedam efficiendi, quae per solas ipsius naturae leges possunt intelligi*). From a logical point of view, a comparison of the various 'definitions' of the 'essence of Man' in Spinoza would be no less necessary than an explanation of what is 'implicit' in each of them (see a complete list, among others, in Gueroult Martial, *Spinoza: L'âme (Ethique, 2)*, Paris: Aubier Montaigne, 1974, Appendice n° 3). The next step would be a discussion of the *universal* and *singular* use of the expression *hominis essentia* itself (see Balibar, 'Spinoza: From Individuality to Transindividuality', in *Mededelingen vanwege het Spinozahuis*, 1993).

What is immediately striking is (i) that the uses of *conscius (esse)* are all located in the 'second part' of Part V, after Proposition 20, i.e. where Spinoza introduces again the 'Third Kind of Knowledge' and the 'eternity of the Mind', to deduce happiness and wisdom; (ii) that the final word of the *Ethics* (VP42S) is precisely an opposition which involves consciousness: ' The ignorant lives . . . as if he knew neither himself, nor God, nor things . . . On the other hand, the wise man . . . being, by a certain eternal necessity, conscious of himself, and of God, and of things, he never ceases to be . . .' (*Ignarus . . . vivit praeterea sui, et Dei, et rerum quasi inscius . . . Cum contra sapiens . . . sui, et Dei, et rerum aeterna quadam necessitate conscius, numquam esse desinit*).[12] The kind of consciousness we are dealing with here is thus clearly a form of knowledge, which in the latter case coincides with the 'Third Kind' or the 'intuitive science' (*scientia intuitive*). This use is totally opposed to the kind of consciousness which was defined above as a kind of ignorance, or necessarily involving ignorance. This would lead us either to admit that there are *two concepts* of 'conscience-consciousness' in the *Ethics*, or that *each kind* of knowledge can be accompanied by some sort or degree of consciousness – which would amount to understanding *conscientia* as an autonomous 'faculty' above the kinds of knowledge themselves. Neither is satisfactory. I think that a better solution can be indicated by taking into account the other *loci*.

Propositions VP31, VP34 and VP39, which lead to the use of *conscius* in their respective Scholia, are concerned with four 'objects' (the Mind, 'its' Body, God, the 'things' in general), and the way they are known *sub aeternitatis specie*, 'from the point of view of eternity'. Better said, they are concerned with the way *a relationship* can be built within knowledge between these different 'objects', which amounts to knowing them *sub aeternitatis specie*. This relationship is not mysterious: a knowledge or consciousness of 'itself' and of 'God' (which I think means to have the idea of a necessary connection *of itself with God*) for the Mind presupposes that it now conceive or be conscious *of its own Body* from the point of view of eternity; which in turn means that, for a given Mind, 'its' Body is conceived *as a Body*, with its singular essence and powers deriving causally from God (or Nature) as a proximate cause.

Again, we have a system of propositions involving a reciprocity of concepts. It should be clear, however, that what Spinoza wants to explain under the names of *scientia intuitiva*, or Third Kind of knowledge, or the point of view of eternity, is not a 'fixed' idea, or a single idea which could be expressed by several names to be mutually substituted *salva veritate*. Rather, it is a process (or, as he had said

---

12   If one has a reading of Part V which sees propositions 1 to 20, and 21 to 40, as two independent expositions of the 'same' doctrine in different languages, this location becomes even more important: VP42S will be understood as a real 'synthesis' of the two lines of argument (cf. Paolo Cristofolini, *La scienza intuitiva di Spinoza*, Napoli: Morano Editore, 1987).

in VP23S, an 'experience') equating all the terms in the chain by continuously passing from one into the others. As a consequence, the 'consciousness' or 'being conscious' which is pictured here is nothing else than the power of thinking (*potentia cogitandi*) which is expressed by this continuous process, or which immanently *circulates* among its terms. To keep using the words 'conscious' and 'consciousness' is justified, however, by the fact that one of these terms is 'my Body' (or if you like, for every singular Mind, 'its own Body'.) The Third Kind of Knowledge continuously transforms a perception of the ideas of the affections of my Body into an idea of the causes of these affections. *Thus, IIP23* (quoted above) *remains formally true*: 'The mind does not know itself, except insofar as it perceives the ideas of the affections of the body', provided we understand now: the Mind is able to explain what it is to perceive affections. It is not *a Body* (whichever Body) that is conceived from the point of view of eternity. It is 'my Body', or better said, *a Body inasmuch as it is 'its own Body' for some Mind* (which, conversely, is *this Body's idea*).[13]

A counter-proof is provided by VP34S, which I would translate: 'In their common opinion, Men already know of the eternity of their Mind, but they confuse it with duration, etc.' Apart from the implicit attack against the theological belief in the immortality of the soul hidden under the name of eternity, this proposition involves an extraordinary idea, namely that there can exist something like *an inadequate idea of eternity*, which is nothing else than *an inadequate idea of adequacy*, mixing it with something else. But, thinking more about it, this is perfectly normal: 'adequacy' or 'eternity', being ideas, are 'objects' for other ideas, which can be adequate or inadequate. The same suggestion was involved in VP23S, which juxtaposed two ways of *sentire* and *experiri*: one intellectual, by means of concepts and demonstrations, the other imaginative, by means of pictures in the memory.

6. Let us conclude that, in the process of consciousness (I should say: in consciousness as a process), two incompatible modes of thought are always counterpoised, in different proportions. Or, as Heraclitus and Mao Zedong would say: *One (Consciousness) is divided in Two.* But this quite simply expresses that the 'sage' is no superhuman figure. He is just a high degree in the development of humanity. The *sapiens* is not an instantiation of *sapientia*, an intellection or wisdom to which one has access by breaking with the determinations of human nature. He is a *homo sapiens*, i.e. a singular Man (or Woman) developing his (her) essence. We are back to the hypothesis stated above: to study the forms

---

13   As we see, Spinoza has lost nothing from Descartes' distinction, set up in the *Sixth Meditation*, between bodies in general and *body proper* or 'corps propre'. But, contrary to Descartes, he does not believe that the latter's idea must remain inadequate. This is because he does not see it as a 'mixture' of heterogeneous 'substances'.

of 'consciousness' is to define the human essence, or the specifically human power.

The same conclusion can be made in other words, which might help in clarifying the controversies I was alluding to at the beginning. One divides in Two: *conscientia* has two successive meanings, which do not result in inconsistency, but picture a process, or a polarity. *Conscientia*$_I$ belongs to the First Kind of Knowledge. It is an aspect of imagination, and it is practically identical with moral conscience, or a moral (more generally: value-loaded) view of the world, particularly inasmuch as it involves the illusion of 'free will'. *Conscientia*$_{II}$ belongs to the Third Kind of Knowledge, and it is an immanent consequence of 'intuitive science', which causally explains everyone's own Body (and its place within nature), or refers it to the idea of God, 'from the point of view of eternity'. Although these two forms are immediately juxtaposed in every human Mind, and although the Mind's *conatus* is nothing else than a transition from one form to the other, there is no continuity between them, but a gap or a break. In other words, to pass from *Conscientia*$_I$ to *Conscientia*$_{II}$ requires a detour, and a 'long' one, whichever unit you adopt to measure it: a detour through 'Reason', the Second Kind of Knowledge, or the science of causes founded upon common notions. I shall dare to say, in a more dialectical language: the proper process, or 'history', of *conscientia* passes *through non-consciousness* (i.e. scientific demonstrations, where consciousness in whichever sense does not apply, since in Spinoza's doctrine it is *never* associated with general terms or common notions).[14] This discontinuity in the history of modes of thought, which each for itself are 'continuous', we might name *a process of consciousness without a subject*. Such a formulation is intended to throw some light onto the embarrassments of past discussions about Spinoza's position with regard to the Philosophies of the Subject and the Primacy of Consciousness. It was widely believed that to exclude Spinoza from the range of Philosophies of the Subject would mean to deny that Consciousness was central in his doctrine. As a consequence, his anthropology became incoherent, since Consciousness to him is the primary feature of the Human Essence (more precisely: of every individual human's singular essence). But this implication is not necessary. Quite the

---

14   Consequently, there is nothing like a process of self-transformation *within* consciousness through reflexion. Not even a continuous process of *emendatio*. This is why commentators (like Robert Misrahi, *Le désir et la réflexion dans la philosophie de Spinoza*, Paris: Gordon and Breach, 1972), who may be right to read such a progress (starting with the definition of *idea ideae*) in the treatise on the 'emendation of the intellect' (*De Intellectus Emendatione*), are wrong when they project it on the *Ethics*. Moreover, it could help explaining why Spinoza abandoned the path he had tried in this early draft. In the *Ethics*, Spinoza has kept the notion of a *reflexivity* of the idea itself, but divorced it from the notion of consciousness; hence *certainty* (the reflexivity of the true idea) is also independent of *consciousness*, as IIP43 and Scholium clearly show. On this point I disagree with Gilles Deleuze (*Spinoza, philosophie pratique*, Paris: Les Éditions de Minuit, 1981) although his formulations on p. 82 come close to the idea of 'consciousness without a subject'.

contrary: it is Spinoza's doctrine of consciousness which makes it useless and, indeed, impossible to refer to a Subject. In the *Ethics*, we find something very odd in classical philosophy: an anthropology of consciousness without a subject.

EPILOGUE TO THE ENGLISH-LANGUAGE EDITION

I want now to return to my purpose of comparing Spinoza's theory of *conscientia* with Locke's 'invention of consciousness'. I can do it, of course, only in the form of hypotheses, submitted to further clarification and discussion. I will mention five of them, as concisely as possible.

1. Generally speaking, we can say that both discourses are formed historically on a 'threshold of modernity', or in a transition phase that begins when conceptions of the 'soul' and its hierarchical organization into inferior and superior parts, linked to different relationships with the vital functions and the spiritual aspirations of the mind (overdetermined by moral and theological concerns), begin to appear untenable or 'unthinkable'.[15] This transition made it possible to imagine a new kind of psychology, which would become 'psychology' in the *modern* sense, essentially aiming at the analysis of mental operations, schemes of the association of ideas, correlations between representations and affects, stages in the development of moral and cognitive faculties, 'normal' and 'pathological' modes of thinking, etc. As I argued here and in other places, Descartes' philosophy (in its entirety, ranging from the cogito as 'first metaphysical truth' to the theory of the 'substantial union' of body and soul which gives rise to the 'passions') was at the same time a necessary *condition* and an *obstacle* for the development of such a psychology, which therefore could only take the form of a critical reaction to Cartesian metaphysics (particularly through a 'de-substantialization' of the 'mind', however atypical – and in fact subversive – Descartes' use of the category *substance* had already been). But there is more: this new step could be taken in completely different ways, offering *radical alternatives*. For this reason, I have borrowed the Foucauldian notion of the 'point of heresy' – and also to indicate that the plane in which the alternatives unfold constitutes the reverse side of what Foucault called the 'classical episteme', which he defined as a domination of the scientific models of *mathesis* and *taxonomy* (or classification).[16] A complete comparison of the classical

---

15   I have used the expression 'threshold of modernity' (*seuil de la modernité*) in my articles 'Conscience' and 'Âme/Esprit' for the *Vocabulaire européen des philosophies*, already cited. I have no doubt that the 'unthinkable' character of Ancient and Medieval doctrines of the soul (particularly expressed by Descartes in his repeated assertion that 'the soul has no parts', but is neither *absolute* nor *irreversible* in all its aspects: just think of Freud's 'return' to a topography of 'instances' or 'regions' of the 'psychic apparatus') is linked to a complex 'crystallization' of heterogeneous causes: institutional, cultural, religious, scientific . . . But is not my aim to discuss them here.

16   See Michel Foucault, *The Order of Things*, London: Tavistock, 1970, Chapter 3: 'Representing'.

discourses on the 'soul', the 'spirit' and the 'mind' (of which I have sketched only some aspects here, taking Locke as a point of reference, and indicating as much as possible how he would reflect the oppositions, e.g. with Malebranche who in so many respects was his 'intimate adversary') should certainly include a great diversity of doctrines diverging or converging on specific problems. But it is particularly worthwhile to emphasize the differences between Locke and Spinoza, because they concern philosophers who, in some important respects (including political and religious matters), are *de facto* very close to one another. With their help, we can push the idea of a 'point of heresy' far enough to suggest that the 'common episteme' of the classical age is in fact not at all a stable, dominant paradigm, but an open-ended, essentially unstable space of controversy. The comparison also makes it easier to understand the radicalism of Locke's *own choices*, his astonishing capacity to open a 'modern' path that is in fact neither 'spiritualist' nor 'materialist' – even if it cannot exactly be called 'transcendental'.[17] On such issues as the articulation of 'consciousness' and 'knowledge', 'understanding' and 'affectivity', 'identity' and 'individuality', or *dominium sui* as 'self-ownership' or ethical 'liberation' of the mind's power, the two philosophies undoubtedly present us with the sharpest antitheses, albeit sometimes expressed in the same words, therefore in the greatest vicinity. *Eo ipso*, they offer an exceptional possibility to understand how philosophy operates within its own conflicts

2. A first antithesis is found in the relationship between 'consciousness' (as a reflective type of idea) and 'knowledge' (as a product of the *understand*ing and a result of its own development.)[18] For both Locke and Spinoza, this relationship is an intrinsic one, so it could be said that the idea of 'unconscious knowledge' is ruled out or is a contradiction in terms; and for both of them, *formally speaking*, this intrinsic unity of 'knowing' and 'being conscious' is linked with the fact that there is an essential *reflexivity* of the activity of knowing which must be made possible by the fact that the mind operates *in the second degree* on ideas or representations of objects (including 'internal' objects) of the *first degree*. However, in Locke, this unity is also an essential *continuity* in the 'natural history' of the mind, rooted in the fact that there is an *originary correlation* of 'perception' and 'reflection', from which all the subsequent acquisitions of

---

17 I leave aside, for the sake of this brief characterization, interesting hypotheses concerning the possibility of Spinozistic influences on Locke (which Wim Klever has pushed to the extreme, arguing that there is a 'disguised Spinozism' in Locke; see his essay 'Locke's Disguised Spinozism' at www.benedictusdespinoza.nl), because my object here is only the structural disposition of the arguments.

18 Understanding: it is important that, for both philosophers, this category is granted a central role. This explains in particular why both Locke and Spinoza in fact escape the simplistic distinctions between a 'rationalist' and an 'empiricist' point of view, which were projected retrospectively upon them by historians of ideas.

knowledge are derived (even if they have need of other means, particularly the 'social' means of language). This is indeed nothing other than consciousness itself as an 'operation'. Conversely, in Spinoza, this unity involves an essential *discontinuity* (or, as I have argued, it has to be recreated or rebuilt beyond an epistemological discontinuity), because the 'originary' form of consciousness is identified with a 'misrecognition' of the essence of objects (or, simply, their properties, which are understood in terms of an imagined 'value' for the subject). And more profoundly (as explained in the theory of the 'Kinds of knowledge'), knowledge has to exchange its primary understanding of 'things' as they are perceived through the affections of our bodies for an understanding of 'things' (including our body) as they are in themselves – in other terms, it must go through a reversal of the idea of causality, which is also a mental (and moral) revolution. In both of these doctrines, it is possible to picture knowledge in terms of a 'learning process' which originates in consciousness and ends with conscious ideas of reflection: but one of them has a *cumulative* figure, whereas the other has a *rectifying*, or a self-critical pattern. It would be just a matter of space to show that this also involves antithetic representations of the relationship between 'truth' and 'error'.

3. If we pass now to the correlative issue of the relationship between understanding and affectivity, we observe an almost inverted situation. It has to be said, foremost, that on the issue of the 'passions', and more generally the 'practical' side of his theory of the mind (as mainly exposed in the extraordinary Chapter XXI, 'Of Power', in Book II of the *Essay*), Locke has affinities with Spinoza which are hard to deny. One of them, of obvious moral and political importance, has to do with the refutation of a notion of a 'free will', or the idea that actions are born out of a radical spontaneity, and the absence of 'preexisting determinations', which is common to both. This also has consequences for the notion of 'responsibility', which in Locke will *not* become premised on an ideal capacity to choose between Good and Evil that ought to be protected from the influence of desires, but, in a much more pragmatic way, on a possibility for any person to 'identify' herself with the author of such and such actions, and therefore to 'acknowledge' the validity of any sanctions that they call for, be they external or internal (or even 'eschatological'). But it is even more interesting to study the affinities at the level of *desire* itself: a word which, in Spinoza, serves to identify the 'singular essence' of any man (or, even better, any man's *conatus in suo esse perseverari*, effort/endeavour to preserve himself or his own essence and existence), and in Locke is identified with 'a state of *uneasiness*' permanently disturbing one's rest, whether caused by the perception of the 'pain of the body' or by the 'disquiet of the mind' (*Essay*, II.xxi.31–2). Locke's coupling of desire and uneasiness, and Spinoza's coupling of desire and *conatus*, are remarkably close to one another, all the more because they serve to explain that there

is never a separation between a *train of affects* and a *train of ideas*: to be sure, one can always abstractly distinguish between a 'theoretical' representation and a 'practical' affect that is either a passion or an action, just as there are affective consequences of changes in ideas and intellectual consequences of affective processes, but essentially it is their mutual dependence that makes the 'life of the mind' (or gives a *dynamic* character to the analysis of the mental operations or processes). Notwithstanding, the analysis then goes into divergent directions, since for Spinoza the *conatus* underlying different forms of (unconscious) appetite or (conscious) desire is a constant as long as an individual's 'form' is maintained with respect to its environment. Therefore, it is also what makes it possible to recognize 'the same individual' at different stages of a life passing through diverse experiences and degrees of knowledge, because it is in fact what accounts for the individual's desire to 'increase its power to act and be affected'.[19] Whereas for Locke, *uneasiness* is in a dialectical relationship with consciousness, being originally rooted in the incapacity of the mind to 'think the same idea' for more than a single moment (which, as we have seen, is essentially a qualitative, phenomenological notion): it calls for a permanent exercise of memory to retain the mind's personal identity (or to subjectively reclaim the 'principle of identity' as its own condition of existence – with the possible limits of the 'pathological' cases, where identities are split and personalities dissociated or merged, studied by Locke in the 'thought experiments' which form an essential part of his treatise).

Epistemologically, there arises a great difference here, because for Locke memory has to be divided into two different levels (for which he uses the words *memory* and *recollection*): one purely empirical, where lapses and interruptions must be taken into account – as a kind of victory of uneasiness over consciousness – and another quasi-transcendental or 'virtual', which forms the condition of possibility for a 'normal' relationship between consciousness and its own uneasiness. It is the latter which determines *personal identity* (or the identity of the 'self'), inasmuch as it is grounded in 'interiority' or the 'train' of mental states. Quite differently, in Spinoza, memory names a persistence of *traces* from previous experiences in which the mind – essentially consisting of confused ideas of the body – has been affected by external objects which it has associated with ideas and signs: over time, either they reiterate and reinforce themselves,

---

19   This leads to considerable difficulties, but also to Spinoza's latent fascination with the problem of *childhood* and the kind of 'metamorphosis' involved in the transformation of a child into an adult, which had been profoundly discussed by François Zourabichvili (in his book *Le conservatisme paradoxal de Spinoza. Enfance et royauté*, Paris: PUF, 2002), who succeeded in showing that this is one of the keys to the understanding of Spinoza's conception of the relationship between power and individuality. Again, this is similar to Locke, starting with his 'strange' comprehension of the non-correspondence between memory and individuality mentioned above, which 'liberates' a place for the imagination of transgenerational identities (even if it is only a methodological fiction).

or they contradict and virtually destroy each other, thus producing the typical 'mental instability' (*fluctuatio animi*) which is the main object of Spinoza's psychology (*Ethics*, IIIP17S). In short, Locke's memory is synthetic and virtual, whereas Spinoza's memory is disjunctive and material. But above all, Locke's memory forms a circle with the postulate of 'mental isolation' or self-reference (albeit recognizing its possible limitations), whereas Spinoza's memory breaks the circle in the direction of *exteriority*, 'expropriating' the mind's states as much as 'appropriating' them (and therefore providing Spinozism with a kind of 'refutation of idealism' in the Kantian sense). But the ontological difference remains enigmatic, because in Spinoza the articulation of mental states (ideas and affects) with actions and affections of the body is explicitly problematized (even if through the notoriously difficult notion of a mind which is a collection of all the ideas of the body, whether adequate or inadequate), whereas in Locke it is suspended in a 'sceptical' manner, through a practical refusal to cross the 'border' of interiority and exteriority – which also separates causes of the affects from their effects, each being located on different sides of the divide. However, as we know, this blind spot in Locke (symptomatically illustrated in the writing of the *Essay* by the fact that *consciousness* and *uneasiness*, the two key notions, are materially absent from 'their' respective chapters) has a positive counterpart, which is the largely novel relationship that he establishes between the questions of 'identity' and 'property'.[20] This leads me to my third point of comparison.

4. If a correlation of the operations of the understanding and a 'difference' in the dynamic of the affects is a strong element of affinity between Locke and Spinoza, the articulation of identity and individuality, on the contrary, displays the strongest possible incompatibility. On one side (Spinoza), we have a complex but organic unity of the two notions, deriving from the idea that 'identity' with oneself is *a quality of the individual* (*qua* unity or superposition of a composed body and its own mental representations), which can be reached inasmuch as an individual (and here Spinoza usually writes *unusquisque*, 'anyone') acquires adequate ideas of himself as a 'cause' of his own actions, thus also producing the ethical affection of 'self-approval' (*acquiescentia in se ipso*).[21] It is important to note here that nothing in this definition implies that adequate ideas form a 'total' idea, involving the representation of the individual as an indivisible unity or a whole, whose actions would be the expression of a single cause, or to whom they would uniquely 'belong'. On the contrary, it is fully compatible with the

---

20 I say largely novel because in the background of Locke's newly established relationship is the Stoic theory of *oikeiosis* or *convenientia*. But the introduction of consciousness as a 'subjective' mediation in their articulation also completely recreates them.

21 Cf. *Ethics*, Part III, Definitions of affects, 25: '*Self-approval* is pleasure arising from a man's contemplation of himself and his own power of action.'

idea that different actions could be *unevenly* caused by ourselves, in combination with other causes (particularly the action of other individuals), or the idea that we can only *partially* reach an 'adequate' understanding of our power to cause our actions (a supposition fully consistent with the idea, at the end of the *Ethics* [VP39], that 'part of our mind' is 'eternal' inasmuch as the multiple capacities of our body generate a 'consciousness' of the mind itself and its relations to God and other things).²² Hence Spinoza's notion of identity (or perhaps we should rather say *identification*) is mainly a practical idea, mediated by 'common notions', meaning that we become aware of the extent to which, in the causal chain determining our actions, we are active and passive, or we influence the nexus of causes, progressing towards a greater autonomy (losing *dependency*, but not *interdependency* or reciprocity).

Locke's concept of identity is strikingly different, because it is based on a radical disjunction (methodological, if not ontological) of the *individual* (as a living organism) and the *self* (as a conscious person): as discussed at length earlier in this book, 'identity' for Locke is an *equivocal* notion, which allows for analogies between three types of 'identity-relations' (for substances, individuals and persons), but does not derive them from a single logical definition. Most important here, however, is the fact that personal identity becomes defined as a specific form of 'property' (namely the property or owning of our own thoughts and, more generally, our 'experiences', that is provided by consciousness, which *appropriates them to our selves*): this accounts for a 'pragmatic' relationship between individuality and (personal) identity (although not one that would be automatic and 'naturally' verified, as shown, once again, by the thought-experiments relating to 'pathological' disjunctions, whose possibility Locke does not exclude). This is the relationship provided by the (mental) fact that one individual's *actions* are also perceived or experienced by some consciousness as 'its own' actions – whence derives the fact that they are actions of 'its' body, and consequently (to that extent, indirectly), that *this is* 'its body'. It is indeed a very deep philosophical idea to suggest that one (or oneself) does not, literally speaking, 'own a body' (or a *body proper*), but owns *its actions*, and 'attributes' them to a body or an individual which they 'suppose' – for which, as a consequence, consciousness has a special 'concern'. As I suggested earlier, this idea can be considered a refined foundation of 'possessive individualism': it bears obvious

---

22   A very good discussion of the relation *individuality/self-knowledge* (therefore identity) is provided by Lia Levy, *L'automate spirituel. La naissance de la subjectivité moderne d'après l'Ethique de Spinoza*, Assen, Pays-Bas: Van Gorcum, 2000, who also, in an independent manner, has examined all the occurrences of *conscientia* and *conscius* in Spinoza, and the consequences to be drawn from their distribution in the book. The interested reader should also consult Vasiliki Grigoropoulou's 'Du développement de la conscience chez Spinoza' (*Coscienza nella filosofia della prima modernità*, a cura di Roberto Palaia, Lessico Intellettuale Europeo CXIX, Leo S. Olschki Editore, Firenze 2013, 115–34), which discusses many of the issues that I touch on here, albeit from a slightly different pont of view.

relations to an understanding of the person as the 'owner' of juridical responsibilities (who can be held 'answerable' for the individual with a proper name
whose actions she was conscious of doing: hence the reference to 'person' as a
forensic term), and also to a justification of private property in terms of an
incorporation of human labour into things that preserves the individual 'property in one's person'.

Although a comparison with Spinoza is not ruled out here, it seems more
adequate to remain at the theoretical level.[23] Spinoza's theory proposes an
ascending way from individuality to a 'self-conscious' identification which
requires the detour of 'reason' or 'common notions' (therefore also *communication*, at least intellectually) and it remains always *partial* (as there is no such
thing as a mind fully cognizant of the powers of its own body), but it has no
pre-established limit. Locke's theory proposes a 'descending' way or a retroac-
tive *capture* of the individual's actions (be they works of his labour or crimes
arising from his desires) within the realm of self-consciousness, whereby the
individual becomes an agent who *for himself* and, potentially, *for others*, is the
sole author of his acts (again, within the limits of 'normality'). This is not the
'open' individual of Spinoza's *conatus*, always suspended between a greater
autonomy arising from an increased power to act and 'be affected', and a lesser
autonomy arising from a more passive interaction with the world and with
others. But it is also not the 'positivistic' individual *à la Hobbes*, whose personality is purely defined as an institutional product, resting on the 'fiction' of representation (alienating all his power to the sovereign to receive every legal property in return). As I argued earlier, by comparing the doctrine of
self-consciousness in the *Essay* with the doctrine of the 'property in one's person'
in the *Second Treatise on Government*, appropriation in Locke is the mediation
for the development of the understanding just as consciousness is the mediation for the process of the (legitimate) acquisition of things. But self-consciousness remains the foundation of the 'internal' care of the self, which precedes
every external appropriation – for want, perhaps, of a symmetrical inquiry into
the 'powers' of the labouring body/organism to elaborate products which could
also be meanings, or 'ideas'. This, I submit again, is what we may call *the subject*
in Locke, or his contribution to a specifically modern concept of subjectivity.

5. Finally, we can try to derive from this virtual 'dialogue' a more accurate
understanding of the 'point of heresy' which, right from the beginning, affects
an 'understanding of the understanding' in classical philosophy – hence also, at

---

23 Spinoza's considerations on property are scarce, and his positions on the foundations of
private appropriation – limited to the two *Political Treatises*, therefore always relative to historical
circumstances and differences of social regime – are not unambiguous. See Alexandre Matheron,
'Spinoza et la propriété', in *Études sur Spinoza et les philosophies de l'âge classique*, Lyon: ENS
Éditions, 2011, 253–66.

least virtually, its anthropology or 'science of man' in the making.²⁴ I believe that the 'topography' of Locke's construction of consciousness which I suggested earlier could help us again in formulating the dilemma that is at stake here. As we may recall, it described how Locke isolated the 'mental operations' from their external conditions of possibility, but also how he would problematize the uncertain boundaries where the internal and the external overlap and appear as inverted images of the same processes: I mentioned the dependency of consciousness on a given of 'pure sensation', the transformation of mental propositions into verbal propositions (more generally consciousness into communication) and the 'uneasy' reciprocity of understanding and affectivity. Interestingly, around the same time as I was applying it to Locke, a prominent Spinoza scholar of the last period, Pierre Macherey, used the same category of 'topography' in an independent manner, in his comprehensive commentary on Spinoza's *Ethics*: 'it is striking to see here the sketch of a "topography" which allows it to dissociate, within the mental regime of the human being, regions or instances where ideas which are not of the same nature, are nevertheless associated in separated modalities, while simultaneously expressing the same events in different languages . . . this concept or idea of the mind has therefore more affinities with an unconscious than a consciousness', he writes apropos of Proposition IIP21 of the *Ethics* ('*this idea of the mind is united with the mind in the same manner as the mind itself is united with the body*'), which he interprets as evidence of the fact that Spinoza's concept of the human being consists of a 'superposition' of heterogeneous (perhaps incompatible) expressions of the same actions and affections of the body.²⁵ As a consequence, in Spinoza, the mind would be 'the object' of consciousness, and not its 'subject'. This is not incompatible, I believe, with what I tried to show in my 'note' reproduced above. Of course, we both borrow the category of the topography from Freud's theory of the unconscious, where it serves to indicate an internal 'split' of the mental activity, which is referred both to an internal conflict and a dependency with respect to external 'authorities' and 'models' (and perhaps we were also influenced by Althusser, who famously proposed extending the validity of the Freudian category to a more general critique of the 'subject'). What I have attempted, however, is to show that there is already a complexity which is

---

24   As is well known, the full programme of an 'anthropological science' (and later a 'philosophical anthropology') was elaborated only later, on the threshold of a 'second modernity' (before and after Kant). But the correlation of epistemological and ethical problems that it covers, and its conflictual relationship to 'moral theology', were already being elaborated in the classical age. As I mentioned earlier, it was Malebranche who, in the Preface to his *Recherche de la vérité* (*In The Search After Truth*) from 1674 coined the formula: 'of all human sciences, the most appropriate to man is the science of Man' ('*de toutes les sciences humaines, la science de l'homme est la plus digne de l'homme*').

25   Pierre Macherey, *Introduction à l'Éthique de Spinoza. La seconde partie: la réalité mentale*, Paris: Presses Universitaires de France, 1997, 201–3.

virtually conflictual in a theory of 'pure consciousness' like the Lockean theory of personal identity, because in fact this theory is not so 'pure', or it faces a return of its own 'externalities' as soon as it needs to problematize the *limits of interiority*. This does not preclude the fact that, within the constitutive limits which appropriate the self to (it)self, the Lockean subject is isolated, or it is supposed to be immune to the interferences of others (whose 'ideas' are in him like the ideas of any objects), because they are not able to 'invade' his self-consciousness, or claim his thoughts to be also theirs (this would be thinkable only if they were the same 'person').

The perspectives opened by a Spinozistic 'topography' as indicated by Macherey are widely different, because there is no such thing as an *immunity* of thought and affects with respect to external interactions – and especially not (as explained in the theory of the 'imitation of affects' in Part III of the *Ethics*) with respect to interactions with *other human subjects' actions and expressions*, therefore thoughts communicated through these actions and expressions (e.g. discourses, but more generally signs). The 'heterogeneity' which characterizes the structure of the mind (its division into opposite forms of consciousness, its transitions from inadequate ideas of the body and itself to adequate notions of activity and passivity) is never an endogenous phenomenon: it reflects *regimes of communication* (both verbal and non-verbal) with other humans, governed by imagination and the passions or leading to effective cooperation, of which the 'common notions' of reason which make society possible are also a part. This Spinozistic topography therefore does not reestablish (or continue) a pre-classical theory of the 'parts of the soul' with its hierarchical distribution of faculties. Rather, it opens a third possibility, neither hierarchical and cosmo-logical, nor unitary and self-reflexive, but conflictual and transindividual.[26] Such an opposition of two 'topographies' of the mind's structure, relying on inverted patterns of interiority and exteriority, or inverted vectors of the passage from one to the other, and highlighted by their different concepts and uses of 'consciousness', clearly illustrates the epistemological choice that, from the beginning, was confronting any 'philosophy of mind'. It led either towards a theory of the 'empirical-transcendental' subject, where all the complexity of the mental operations is interpreted in terms of its internal, reflective 'folding', and the heterogeneous elements or the splits of consciousness are dealt with in terms of a distinction of the normal and the pathological; or towards a transin-dividual theory of the 'association of ideas', as a process where different modes of 'social' communication are always involved, and the notion of 'self' does not represent a 'natural' superposition of identity and property, but only a generic

---

26 On the possibility of reading Spinoza's philosophy as a generalized problematic of the 'transindividual', see my essay 'Spinoza: From Individuality to Transindividuality', *Mededelingen vanwege het Spinozahuis* 71, Delft: Eburon, 1996 (also available at www.ciepfc.fr).

form of representation for the individual powers, which may correspond in practice to many different degrees of autonomy.

Thus, in the seventeenth century already, 'psychology' was at a crossroads (and elaborated its discourse on this alternative) – and it is not impossible that it remains located there, in spite of many 'technical' transformations. It is also widely believed that this dichotomy corresponds to a political choice between a 'bourgeois' individualistic anthropology and a 'subversive' anthropology of the 'multitude' or the 'community': but this is a rather quick conclusion to which I believe we should devote still another examination.

Select Bibliography

Aarsleff, Hans, 'Locke's Reputation in Nineteenth-century England', in Richard Ashcraft, ed., *John Locke: Critical Assessments*, Vol. I, London and New York: Routledge, 1991.

Allison, H.E. 'Locke's Theory of Personal Identity: A Re-Examination', in I.C. Tipton, ed., *Locke on Human Understanding*, Oxford: Oxford University Press, 1977.

Ashcraft, Richard, ed., *John Locke: Critical Assessments*, Vol. I, London and New York: Routledge, 1991.

Ashcraft, Robert, *Revolutionary Politics and Locke's Two Treatises of Government*, Princeton, NJ: Princeton University Press, 1986.

Atkins, Kim, *Narrative Identity and Moral Identity: A Practical Perspective*, London and New York: Routledge, 2008.

Ayers, Michael, *Locke: Epistemology and Ontology*, London and New York: Routledge, 1991.

Baillie, J., 'Recent Work on Personal Identity', *Philosophical Books* 34, 1993.

Balibar, Étienne, 'Citizen Subject' in Eduardo Cadava, Peter Connor, Jean-Luc Nancy, eds, *Who Comes After the Subject?*, London and New York: Routledge, 1991.

Balibar, Etienne, *Citoyen sujet et autres essais d'anthroplogie philosophique*, Paris: PUF, 2001.

Balibar, Etienne, 'Conscience', in Barbara Cassin, ed., *Vocabulaire européen des philosophies*, Paris: Seuil/Le Robert, 2004.

Balibar, Etienne, 'The Infinite Contradiction', *Yale French Studies*, No. 88, 1995.

Balibar, Etienne, 'L'institution de la vérité. Hobbes et Spinoza', in *Lieux et noms de la vérité*, Paris: Éditions de l'Aube, 1994.

Balibar, Etienne, 'L'invention de la conscience: Descartes, Locke et les autres', in Jacques Moutaux et Olivier Bloch, eds, *Traduire les philosophes*, Paris: Publications de la Sorbonne, 2000.

Balibar, Etienne, 'My Self and My Own', in Bill Maurer and Gabrielle Schwab, eds, *Accelerating Possession: Global Futures of Property and Personhood*, New York: Columbia University Press, 2006.

Balibar, Etienne, '"Possessive Individualism" Reversed: From Locke to Derrida', *Constellations*, Vol. 9, No. 3, 2002.

Balibar, Etienne, 'Spinoza: From Individuality to Transindividuality', *Mededelingen vanwege het Spinozahuis* 71, Delft: Eburon, 1996.

Balibar, Etienne, Cassin, Barbara, and de Libera, Alain, 'Subject', trans. David Macey, *Radical Philosophy* 138, July/August 2006.

Balibar, Etienne, 'Subjection and Subjectivation', in Joan Copjec, ed., *Supposing the Subject*, London and New York: Verso, 1994.

Balibar, Renée, *Le colinguisme*, Paris: PUF, 1993.

Berkeley, George, *The Works of George Berkeley, Bishop of Cloyne*, Vol. Three, *Alciphron or The Minute Philosopher*, ed. T.E. Jessop, London, etc. Thomas Nelson, 1950.

Beyssade, Jean-Marie, ed., *Entretien de Descartes avec Burman*, Paris: PUF, 1981.

Beyssade, Jean-Marie, *La philosophie première de Descartes (Le temps et la cohérence de la métaphysique)*, Paris: Flammarion, 1979.

Brémondy, F., 'Conscience', in *Les notions philosophique : Dictionnaire*, ed. S. Auroux, Paris: PUF, 1990.

Brykman, Geneviève, 'Philosophie des ressemblances contre philosophie des universaux chez Locke', *Revue de Métaphysique et de Morale*, Oct.–Dec., 1995.

Canguilhem, Georges, 'Le cerveau et la pensée', in *Georges Canguilhem: Philosophe, historien des sciences*, Paris: Albin Michel, 1993.

Carraud, Vincent, *L'invention du moi*, Paris: PUF, 2010.

Cassin, Barbara, ed. *Vocabulaire européen des philosophies,* Paris: Éditions de Seuil, 2004.

Clarke, Samuel, *The Works of Samuel Clarke*, Vol. III, John and Paul Knapton, 1738.

Collins, Anthony, *A Reply to Mr. Clark's Defence of his Letter to Mr Dodwell*, London, 1707.

Condillac, Etienne Bonnot de, *Essay on the Origins of Human Knowledge*, trans. Hans Aarsleff, Cambridge: Cambridge University Press, 2001.

Cousin, Victor, *Elements of Psychology, Included in a Critical Examination of Locke's Essay on the Human Understanding*, trans. C.S. Henry, London: Thomas Delf, 1851.

Curley, Edwin, *Spinoza's Metaphysics: An Essay in Interpretation*, Cambridge, MA: Harvard University Press, 1969.

Damasio, Antonio, *Descartes' Error: Looking for Spinoza. Joy, Sorrow, and the Feeling Brain*, New York: Vintage, 2003.

Deleuze, Gilles, *Spinoza, philosophie pratique*, Paris: Les Éditions de Minuit, 1981.

Deprun, Jean, *La philosophie de l'inquiétude en France au XVIIIe siècle*, Paris: Vrin, 1979.

Descartes, René, *Meditations on First Philosophy*, trans. John Cottingham, Cambridge: Cambridge University Press, 1996.

Descartes, René, *L'œuvre de Descartes*, ed. G. Rodis-Lewis, Paris: Vrin 1971.

Descartes, René, *Œuvres philosophiques de Descartes*, ed. Ferdinand Alquié, Paris: Garnier, 1967

Descombes, Vincent, *La denrée mentale*, Paris: Éditions de Minuit, 1995.

Ellrodt, R., *Genèse de la conscience moderne: Études sur le développement de la conscience de soi dans les littératures du monde occidental*, Paris: PUF, 1983.

Flew, Anthony, 'Locke and the Problem of Personal Identity', in C.B. Martin and D.M Armstrong eds, *Locke and Berkeley: A Collection of Critical Essays*, London: Macmillan, 1968.

Forstrom, K. Joanna S., *John Locke and Personal Identity: Immortality and Bodily Ressurection in 17th-Century Philosophy*, London and New York: Continuum, 2010.

Fox, Christopher, *Locke and the Scriblerians: Identity and Consciousness in Early Eighteenth-Century Britain*, Berkeley, LA and London: University of California Press, 1988.

Gaudemar, Martine de, *Leibniz: De la puissance au sujet*, Paris: Vrin, 1994.

Glyn Davies, Catherine, *Conscience as Consciousness: The Idea of Self-Awareness in French Philosophical Writing from Descartes to Diderot*, Oxford: The Voltaire Foundation, 1990.

Gueroult, Martial, *Descartes selon l'ordre des raisons*, Paris: Aubier, 1953.

Harris, Ian, *The Mind of John Locke: A Study of Political Theory in its Intellectual Setting*, Cambridge: Cambridge University Press, 1998.

Henry, Michel, *Généalogie de la psychanalyse*, Paris: PUF, 1985.

Hobbes, Thomas, *Leviathan*, ed. C.B. Macpherson, London: Penguin Books, 1968.

Hume, David, *A Treatise of Human Nature* (1739), Second Edition with text revised and notes by P. H. Nidditch, Oxford: Oxford University Press, 1978.

Hutton, Sarah, 'Damaris Cudworth, Lady Masham: Between Platonism and Enlightenment', in *The British Journal for the History of Philosophy*, Vol.1 No. 1, 1993.

Irigaray, Luce, *Speculum of the Other Woman*, trans. Gillian C. Gill, Ithaca, NY: Cornell University Press, 1985.

Johnson, Charlotte, 'Locke's Examination of Malebranche and Norris', *Journal of the History of Ideas*, 1958.

Jolley, Nicholas, *Liebniz and Locke: A Study of the New Essays on Human Understanding*, Oxford: Clarendon Press, 1984.

Jolley, Nicholas, *Locke: His Philosophical Thought*, Oxford and New York: Oxford University Press, 1999.

Kambouchner, D., *L'homme des passions. Commentaires sur Descartes*, Paris: Albin Michel, 1995.

Kant, Immanuel, *Critique of Pure Reason,* trans. Paul Guyer and Allen W. Wood, Cambridge: Cambridge University Press, 1998.

Libera, Alain de, *Archéologie du sujet*, Vol. I: *Naissance du sujet*, Paris: Vrin, 2010.

La Forge, Louis de, *Treatise on the Human Mind* (1664), trans. Desmond M. Clark, Dordrecht: Kluwer, 1997.

Lapoujade, David, *William James. Empirisme et pragmatisme*, Paris: PUF, 1997.

Lee, Henry, *Anti-Scepticism, Or, Notes Upon Each Chapter of Mr Lock's Essay Concerning Human Understanding*, London: Clavel and Harper, 1702.

Leibniz, G.W., *New Essays on Human Understanding*, eds. P. Remnant and J. Bennett, Cambridge: Cambridge University Press, 1996.

Levy, Lia, *L'automate spirituel. La naissance de la subjectivité moderne d'après l'Éthique de Spinoza*, Assen, Pays-Bas: Van Gorcum, 2000.

Lewis, Geneviève, *Le problème de l'inconscient et le cartésianisme*, Paris: PUF, 1950.

Locke, John, *An Essay Concerning Human Understanding*, ed. Peter H. Nidditch, Oxford: Clarendon Press, 1975.

Locke, John, *An Essay Concerning Human Understanding*, abridged and edited by A.S. Pringle-Pattison, Oxford: Clarendon Press, 1967.

Locke, John, *The Correspondence of John Locke*, ed. E.S. de Beer, Eight Volumes, Oxford: Clarendon, 1978.

Locke, John, *A Second Vindication of the Reasonableness of Christianity*, in *The Works of John Locke*, Vol. VII, London: Thomas Tegg, 1823.

Locke, John, *Essai philosophique concernant l'Entendement humain*, traduit de l'Anglois par M. Coste, ed. E. Naert, Paris: Vrin, 1972.

Locke, John, *An Examination of P. Malebranche's Opinion of 'Seeing all Things in God'*, *Locke's Philosophical Works*, Vol. II, London: George Belt and Sons, 1894.

Locke, John, 'Mr. Locke's Letter to the Bishop of Worcester' and 'Mr. Locke's Second Reply to the Bishop of Worcester', in *The Works of John Locke*, Vol. IV, London: Thomas Tegg, 1823.

Locke, John, *Two Treatises of Government*, ed. Peter Lazlett, Cambridge: Cambridge University Press, 1960.

Lowe, E.J., *Locke on Human Understanding*, Abingdon, Oxon.: Routledge, 1995.

Lowe, E.J., *Subjects of Experience*, Cambridge: Cambridge University Press, 1996.

Macherey, Pierre, *Avec Spinoza. Études sur la doctrine et l'histoire du spinozisme*, Paris: Presses Universitaires de France, 1992.

Macherey, Pierre, *Introduction à l'Éthique de Spinoza. La seconde partie: la réalité mentale*, Paris: Presses Universitaires de France, 1997.

Mackie, J.L., *Problems From Locke*, Oxford: Clarendon Press, 1976.

Macpherson, C.B., *The Political Theory of Possessive Individualism: Hobbes to Locke*, Oxford: Oxford University Press, 1962.

Malebranche, Nicolas, *Œuvres complètes de Malebranche*, ed. A. Robinet, Paris: CNRS/Librarie Vrin, 1958–78.

Malebranche, Nicolas, *The Search After Truth*, trans. Thomas M. Lennon and Paul J. Olscamp, Cambridge : Cambridge University Press, 1997.

Malebranche, Nicolas, *Traité de Morale* (1684), Paris: Garnier-Flammarion, 1995.

Marion J.L., *Questions Cartésiennes. Méthode et métaphysique*, Paris: PUF, 1991.

Marshall, John, *John Locke: Resistance, Religion and Responsibility*, Cambridge: Cambridge University Press, 1994.

Martin, Raymond, 'Locke's Psychology of Personal Identity', 2006 in Peter Anstey, ed., *John Locke: Critical Assessments*, Vol. III, Metaphysics, London and New York: Routledge, 2006.

Meiksins Wood, Ellen, *Mind and Politics: An Approach to the Meaning of Liberal and Socialist Individualism*, Berkeley and LA: University of California Press, 1972.

Michaud, Yves, *Locke*, Paris: Bordas, 1986.

Mintz, Samuel S., *The Hunting of the Leviathan: Seventeenth Century Reactions to the Materialism and Moral Philosophy of Thomas Hobbes*, Cambridge: Cambridge University Press, 1969.

Montag, Warren, 'On the Function of the Concept of Origin: Althusser's Reading of Locke', in Stephen Daniels, ed., *Current Continental Theory and Early Modern Philosophy*, Evanston, IL: Northwestern University Press, 2006.

Palaia, Roberto, ed., *Coscienza nella filosofia della prima modernità*, Lessico Intellettuale Europeo CXIX, Leo S. Olschki Editore, Firenze 2013.

Passmore, J.A., *Ralph Cudworth*, Cambridge: Cambridge University Press, 1953.

Patrides, C.A., *The Cambridge Platonists*, Cambridge: Cambridge University Press, 1969.

Perry, John, ed., *Personal Identity*, Berkeley: University of California Press, 1975.

Popkin, R., 'Cudworth', in *The Third Force in Seventeenth Century Thought*, Leiden: Brill, 1992.

Régis, Pierre-Sylvain, *Système de philosophie, contenant la Logique, la Metaphysique et la Morale*, Paris: 1690.

Ricoeur, Paul, *La mémoire, l'histoire, l'oubli*, Paris: Éditions du Seuil, 2000.

Ricoeur, Paul, *Oneself as Another*, trans. Kathleen Blamey, Chicago: University of Chicago Press, 1992.

Jacques Roger, *Les sciences de la vie dans la pensée française au XVIIIe siècle*, 1963, rééd., Paris: Albin Michel, 1993.

Ryle, Gilbert, *The Concept of Mind*, London: Penguin, 1963.

Sargeant, John, *Solid Philosophy Asserted Against the Fancies of the Ideists: Or, The Method to Science. Farther Illustrated with Reflexions on Mr Locke's Essay concerning Human Understanding*, London: Roger Clavil, 1697.

Schechtman, Marya, *The Constitution of Selves*, Ithaca and London: Cornell University Press, 1996.

Sherlock, William, *A Vindication of the Doctrine of the Holy and Ever Blessed Trinity and the Incarnation of the Son of God*, London: W. Rogers, 1690.

Solomon, Robert C., *Continental Philosophy Since 1970: The Rise and Fall of the Self*, Oxford: Oxford University Press, 1998.

Spinoza, Baruch, *Éthique, Texte original et traduction nouvelle par Bernard Pautrat*, Paris: Éditions du Seuil, 1988.

Strawson, Galen, *Locke on Personal Identity: Consciousness and Concernment*, Princeton, NJ: Princeton University Press, 2011.

Swinburne, Richard, 'Personal Identity: The Dualist Theory', in Sydney Shoemaker and Richard Swinburne, eds, *Personal Identity*, Oxford: Blackwell, 1984.

Tennant, R. C., 'The Anglican Response to Locke's Theory of Personal Identity', *Journal of the History of Ideas*, Vol. 43, 1982.

Thiel, Udo, 'Locke's Concept of Person', in Reinhard Brandt, ed., *John Locke* (Symposium Wolfenbuttel), Berlin and New York: Walter de Gruyter, 1981.

Thiel, Udo, 'Cudworth and Seventeenth-Century Theories of Consciousness', in Stephen Gaukroger, ed., *The Uses of Antiquity: The Scientific Revolution and the Classical Tradition*, Dordrecht: Kluwer Academic, 1991.

Thiel, Udo, 'Personal Identity', in Daniel Garber and Michael Ayers, eds, *The Cambridge History of Seventeenth-Century Philosophy*, Vol. 1, Cambridge: Cambridge University Press, 1998.

Thiel, Udo, 'Personal Identity', in Savonius-Wroth, Schuurman and Walmsley, eds, *The Continuum Companion to Locke*, London and New York: Continuum, 2010.

Thiel, Udo, *The Early Modern Subject: Self-Consciousness and Personal Identity from Descartes to Hume*, Oxford: Oxford University Press, 2011.

Tully, James, *An Approach to Political Philosophy: Locke in Contexts*, Cambridge: Cambridge University Press, 1993.

Tully, James, *A Discourse on Property: John Locke and His Adversaries*, Cambridge: Cambridge University Press, 1980.

Vienne, Jean-Michel, *Expérience et raison. Les fondements de morale selon Locke*, Paris: Vrin, 1991.

Wiggins, David, *Sameness and Substance*, Oxford: Blackwell, 1980.

Wood, Neal, *The Politics of Locke's Philosophy: A Social Study of An Essay Concerning Human Understanding*, Berkeley: University of California Press, 1983.

Yolton, John, *Locke: An Introduction*, Oxford: Blackwell, 1985.

Yolton, John, *Locke and the Way of Ideas*, Oxford: Oxford University Press, 1968.

Yolton, John, *The Two Intellectual Worlds of John Locke: Man, Person, and Spirits in the 'Essay'*, Ithaca: Cornell University Press, 2004.

Index

On the Typeface

This book is set in Minion, a typeface designed by Robert Slimbach for Adobe Systems in 1990, which has become one of the few contemporary book faces to rival the classic types of Caslon, Bembo, and Garamond. Though it has no obvious precursor, it retains a calligraphic sentiment that Robert Bringhurst dubs 'neohumanist' in his *Elements of Typographic Style*.

Telltale features of Minion include the subtle cant in the bar of the 'e', the angular bowl of the 'a', and the tapered bulbs that terminate the head of the 'a' and the tails of the 'y' and 'j'.

Minion's restrained personality and even colour have made it a popular workhorse type, the narrow set width of which provides economy yet does not detract from its suitability for book settings.